CAVENDISH
PLANT 🌱 GUIDES
GARDEN
HERBS

CAVENDISH PLANT GUIDES
GARDEN HERBS

DENI BOWN

CAVENDISH BOOKS
VANCOUVER

A DK PUBLISHING BOOK

Produced for Dorling Kindersley by PAGE*One*
Cairn House, Elgiva Lane, Chesham,
Buckinghamshire HP5 2JD

PROJECT DIRECTORS Bob Gordon and Helen Parker
EDITOR Charlotte Stock
DESIGNER Chris Clark and Thomas Keenes

MANAGING EDITOR Louise Abbott
MANAGING ART EDITOR Lee Griffiths
PRODUCTION Silvia La Greca
PICTURE RESEARCH Martin Copeland
and Christine Rista

First Canadian Edition 1998
2 4 6 8 10 9 7 5 3 1

Published in Canada by
Cavendish Books Inc., Unit 5, 801 West 1st Street,
North Vancouver, B.C. V7P 1A4

Copyright © 1998 Dorling Kindersley Limited, London
Text copyright © 1998 Deni Bown

All rights reserved. No part of this publication may be
reproduced, stored in a retrieval system, or transmitted
in any form or by any means, electronic, mechanical,
photocopying, recording or otherwise, without the
prior permission of the copyright owners.

Canadian Cataloguing in Publication Data for this book
is available from the National Library, Ottawa.

Main entry under title:

Garden herbs
  (Cavendish plant guides)
  Includes index.
  ISBN 0-929050-92-4

  1. Garden herbs. 2. Garden herbs -- Pictorial works. I. Series.

Color reproduction by Colourscan, Singapore
Printed and bound by Star Standard Industries, Singapore

CONTENTS

HOW TO USE THIS BOOK 8

HERBS IN
THE GARDEN 10

CATALOG OF GARDEN HERBS 17

CLIMBING 18

CREEPING 24

THYMUS 28

LARGE 38

ROSMARINUS 48

SMALL 115

OCIMUM 126

ORIGANUM 137

MEDIUM 65

MENTHA 74

MONARDA 77

PELARGONIUM 80

CAPSICUM 84

LAVANDULA 90

SALVIA 94

ARTEMISIA 97

TANACETUM 100

GUIDE TO HERB CARE 140

GLOSSARY OF TERMS 158

INDEX 160

ACKNOWLEDGMENTS 176

CONTRIBUTORS

DENI BOWN
*Consultant;
Writer, Introduction and Practical*

LINDEN HAWTHORNE
Writer, Plant Catalog

How to Use This Book

THIS BOOK PROVIDES the ideal quick reference guide to selecting and identifying herbs for the garden.

The HERBS IN THE GARDEN section is a helpful introduction to herbs and gives advice on choosing a suitable plant for a specific site or purpose, such as for a border, container, or simply as a specimen.

To choose or identify a particular herb, turn to the CATALOG OF GARDEN HERBS, where photographs are accompanied by concise plant descriptions and useful tips on cultivation and propagation. The plant entries are grouped by size as well as by color (see the color wheel below) to make your selection easier.

For additional information on herb cultivation, routine care, and propagation, turn to the GUIDE TO HERB CARE, where general advice on all aspects of caring for your herbs can be found.

At the end of the book is a useful two-page glossary, which explains key terms. An index of every herb, with synonyms and common names, together with a brief genus description, allows quick and easy access to the catalog by plant name.

The color wheel
All the herbs in the book are grouped according to the color of their main feature of interest. They are always arranged in the same order, indicated by the color wheel below. Variegated plants are categorized by the color of their variegation.

THE SYMBOLS
The symbols below indicate a plant's preferred growing conditions and hardiness. However, the climate and soil conditions of your particular site should also be taken into account, as they may affect a plant's growth.

☼ Prefers full sun
☼ Prefers partial shade
☼ Tolerates full shade
pH Needs acidic soil
◌ Prefers well-drained soil
◐ Prefers moist soil
● Prefers wet soil

HARDINESS
The range of winter temperatures that each plant is able to withstand is shown by the USDA plant hardiness zone numbers that are given in each entry. The temperature ranges for each zone are shown on the endpaper map in this book.

USES
The symbols below indicate the main uses for a plant.
⚱ Aromatic
⌂ Culinary
⚕ Medicinal
⊕ Warning (refer to plant entry for details)

Herb size categories
The herbs featured in the CATALOG OF GARDEN HERBS are divided according to the average height of a mature plant for the greater part of the year. The specific height measurement given in each individual entry reflects the plant's maximum height, where applicable in flower. Please note that heights may vary from the ones given, according to site, growing conditions, climate, and age.

LARGE   More than 4ft (1.2m)
MEDIUM   2–4ft (60cm–1.2m)
SMALL   Up to 2ft (60cm)

HOW TO USE THIS BOOK • 9

HOW TO USE THE CATALOG OF GARDEN HERBS

HEADINGS
The CATALOG OF GARDEN HERBS is divided into sections, according to the habit or average size of the plants.

The plant's *family name* appears here.

The plant's *botanical name* appear here.

The plant's *common name(s)* appears here.

PLANT PORTRAITS
The color photographs show each plant's main features and color (see the color wheel on previous page).

ENTRIES
A brief plant description giving details of growing habit, flowers, fruits, and leaves, followed by information on native habitat, tips on cultivation and propagation, and a list of other botanical names.

FEATURE PAGES
Plant groups or genera of special interest to the gardener are presented on separate feature pages. A brief introduction giving general information on appearance, use, cultivation, and propagation is followed by concise plant entries.

136 • SMALL

Ranunculaceae

RANUNCULUS FICARIA var. FLORE PLENO
Habit Tuberous perennial. *Flowers* Solitary, double, shallow-cupped, borne in spring. Bright yellow. *Leaves* Heart-shaped, glossy. Dark green.
• NATIVE HABITAT Grassy places in Europe, northwest Africa, and southwest Asia.
• CULTIVATION Grow in moist soil that is neutral to alkaline, in a sunny or shady site. Likely to be less invasive than the species.
• PROPAGATION By division in autumn or spring.
• WARNING Contact with sap may irritate skin.

Z4–9
HEIGHT 2–6in (5–15cm)
SPREAD 12in (30cm)

Asteraceae   FRENCH MARIGOLD

TAGETES PATULA
Habit Bushy annual. *Flowers* Single, daisylike, borne throughout summer. Yellow, orange, or red-brown. *Leaves* Aromatic, deeply divided into toothed segments. Bright green.
• NATIVE HABITAT Dry slopes and valley beds in Mexico.
• CULTIVATION Grow in fertile, well-drained soil in sun. Deadhead regularly to prolong flowering. May be used as a slug repellant in organic gardens.
• PROPAGATION Sow seed in spring at 64°F (18°C).
• WARNING Contact with foliage may irritate skin.

ANNUAL
HEIGHT 12in (30cm)
SPREAD 12in (30cm)

Asteraceae   ARNICA, MOUNTAIN TOBACCO

ARNICA MONTANA
Habit Clump-forming, aromatic, rhizomatous perennial. *Flowers* Solitary, daisylike, borne in summer. Deep yellow to orange-yellow. *Leaves* Oval to lance-shaped, mostly basal. Mid-green.
• NATIVE HABITAT From Europe to western Asia.
• CULTIVATION Grow in moist but well-drained soil enriched with organic matter, in a sunny site.
• PROPAGATION By seed sown in autumn or by division in spring.
• WARNING Contact with may irritate skin. All parts may cause severe discomfort if eaten.

Z4–9
HEIGHT to 20in (50cm)
SPREAD 12in (30cm)

Asteraceae   POT MARIGOLD

CALENDULA OFFICINALIS
Habit Upright, aromatic annual. *Flowers* Daisy-like, borne throughout summer. Bright yellow to orange. *Leaves* Lance-shaped. Bright green.
• NATIVE HABITAT Origin uncertain. Naturalized in rocky places and on cultivated and waste land, especially around the Mediterranean.
• CULTIVATION Grow in any well-drained soil in a sunny site. Deadhead regularly to prolong flowering and to prevent excessive self-seeding. Self-sows freely.
• PROPAGATION Sow seed in autumn or spring.

ANNUAL
HEIGHT 20–28in (50–70cm)
SPREAD 20–28in (50–70cm)

90 • LAVANDULA

LAVANDULA

The genus *Lavandula* consists of about 24 species of aromatic evergreen shrubs and subshrubs, which are native to dry, rocky, open habitats in the Mediterranean, the Canary Islands, and from North Africa to southwest Asia and India.

Commonly known as lavender, these plants are grown for their strongly scented foliage and spikes of fragrant flowers, which are an important source of nectar for bees and other beneficial insects. The flowers may be air dried for use in winter arrangements and potpourri. Those of *L. angustifolia* have long been used medicinally for their calming effect, along with *L. x intermedia*, is also widely used in cosmetics and perfumery.

Lavenders are invaluable in mixed or herbaceous borders. The lower-growing types are ideal for rock gardens, containers, and as low edging, while taller species and cultivars may be used in informal hedging.

Grow in well-drained, moderately fertile soil in full sun. Species and cultivars that are less than fully hardy need a warm site with shelter from harsh winter winds. In cold-winter climates, tender types can be grown in pots and overwintered under glass in frost-free conditions. *L. lanata* needs sharp drainage and prefers a top-dressing of grit or gravel. Deadhead and lightly trim plants after flowering; trim hedges and specimen plants in spring. Lavenders tolerate fairly close clipping, but this must be performed annually to maintain a dense habit, since they will not re-grow from old wood (see p. 148). Harvest flowers for drying before they are fully open, and hang them upside down in a cool, airy place (see p. 156).

Sow seed in containers in a cold frame or cool greenhouse in early autumn or spring. Stratify for more reliable germination. Root semi-ripe cuttings during summer.

SYMBOLS
The symbols indicate the sun, soil, and temperature requirements (see THE SYMBOLS on previous page). Minimum temperatures are given for plants that cannot survive below 32°F (0°C).

FEATURE PLANT DESCRIPTIONS
As with the main Catalog entries, a brief plant description is followed by useful tips on cultivation and propagation where these are not already given in the general introduction.

SIZES
The average height and spread of the plants are given, although these may vary according to site, growing conditions, climate, and age.

Herbs in the Garden

Herbs add much to the enjoyment of a garden, offering soft, subtle colors, inviting aromas, and a catalog of associations in history and folklore. A welcome bonus of herbs is that many of them have a practical use – from making herbal teas or simple home remedies, to ingredients for potpourri or cooking. The term "herb" is difficult to define accurately, since it embraces any plant that has beneficial effects on the body when used in the right quantity. This definition allows plants from all groups – annuals, biennials, bulbs, perennials (both herbaceous and evergreen), trees, shrubs, and climbers – to be described as herbs.

As herbs vary greatly in appearance, size, and cultivation requirements, they are extremely versatile as garden plants. Some, such as foxgloves and French marigolds (*Tagetes patula*), are popular garden plants in their own right and are more often grown for their ornamental qualities than for practical purposes. Evergreen (and hardy in favorable areas) herbs, such as thymes, rosemaries, sages, and bay (*Laurus nobilis*), provide year-round interest and value.

Highly bred garden plants produce flowers that have little to offer to visiting insects. In contrast, most herbs are wild species and are rich sources of nectar and pollen for beneficial insects. The presence of herbs in vegetable plots and orchards increases the numbers of pollinating and otherwise useful insects, such as hoverflies which prey on aphids.

Formal designs
Traditionally, herb gardens are laid out in geometrical patterns of small beds that are defined by narrow paths or dwarf hedges of aromatic shrubs.

Classic formal herb garden
A simple symmetrical pattern is outlined by clipped boxwood hedges and infilled with low-growing lavender and purple sage. The strong, upright shapes of boxwood topiary and the hedge contrast with the more complex forms of statuary and the trellis.

Herbs suitable for dwarf hedges include boxwood, lavender cotton (*Santolina chamaecyparissus*), hyssop, and lavender, evenly spaced at about 9–12in (22–30cm) apart. Unless there is a large amount of dwarf hedging to trim, this style of garden is not difficult to maintain and provides an eye-catching focal point, particularly when viewed from an upper window or high vantage point within the garden. Classic formal effects are achieved by planting low-growing herbs in blocks of different colors, placing greater emphasis on the design than on individual plants. Although it is labor-intensive and can prove quite expensive, landscaping and planting a formal design is rewarding and soon looks established.

Informal designs

Avid herb gardeners often choose a semi-formal or informal effect, using a formal framework to provide structure and a more relaxed style of planting. This plan gives scope for designing

Structured informality
A formal outline of boxwood hedges and low-growing herbs is softened by the casual plantings of fennel, sage, and lady's mantle.

beds according to a theme, such as medicinal or aromatic uses, or in ways that emphasize the colors and textures of the plants. Semi-formal herb gardens are most effective when the overall design is kept simple. They are best outlined by pathways rather than by dwarf hedges, which may suffer damage from tall or invasive herbs.

An informal design, such as a mixed border, depends more for its success upon the complementary habits and colors of the herbs grown. It allows trees, shrubs, and large herbs such as mullein, angelica, or Chinese rhubarb (*Rheum palmatum*) to be used to full effect, and provides greater freedom and scope for the inclusion of bold, colorful associations and plants of contrasting heights and habits. For example, golden forms of herbs, such as marjoram, lemon balm (*Melissa officinalis*), feverfew (*Tanacetum parthenium*), and elder, could be planted against a backdrop of dark hedging or a fence, punctuated by yellow-flowered greater celandine (*Chelidonium majus*) and the contrasting blue of Jacob's ladder and borage (*Borago officinalis*). Equally, a Mediterranean-style planting consisting of silver-leaved herbs and the vibrant flower colors of sages, hyssops, poppies, and pinks looks effective against a sun-baked wall.

Herbs in containers

Containers are ideal for growing herbs, since they can be positioned in or around the kitchen, where they are convenient for picking, or placed near doorways and garden seats to release a welcoming fragrance. Topiary bay trees are traditional centerpieces for herb gardens or ornaments for restaurant entrances. Some tender herbs, such as myrtle, scented geraniums, and lemon verbena (*Aloysia triphylla*), make attractive container plants inside homes, and in conservatories and patios. Basils, which are sensitive to cold and frost, often grow more successfully in pots, since the plants can be brought indoors during inclement weather. Containers make gardening possible for those with little or no garden, and can be displayed on steps, balconies, walls, and windowsills.

Many species have neat, colorful variants that are better suited to small pots or mixed plantings. These include several compact marjorams, *Salvia officinalis* 'Tricolor', *Hyssopus officinalis* subsp. *aristatus*, *Lavandula angustifolia* 'Nana Alba', and prostrate rosemaries (*Rosmarinus officinalis* Prostratus Group). Large or invasive herbs, such as fennels or mints, are best grown alone as they soon overrun a community planting. For planting up summer-flowering containers, purple-leaved basils and *Perilla* species are indispensable, while in winter there is an attractive choice of evergreen golden thymes and sages with purple or golden foliage.

Container gardening
Container-grown herbs make an interesting feature when arranged on steps or among other plants. Golden hops (Humulus lupulus 'Aureus') trained on a frame is the center of attention in this arrangement.

Herbs in the flower border

When chosen for their color and texture, herbs need not look out of place among other garden plants. Popular garden plants, such as cornflowers (*Centaurea cyanus*), bergamots, marigolds, and nasturtiums (*Tropaeolum majus*) are easily accommodated in a mixed border, but it is also worth experimenting with other species. Corianders, fennels, and dills have lacy foliage and flowers that complement bolder shapes, while well-established specimens of Chinese chives (*Allium tuberosum*) and *Allium schoenoprasum* 'Forescate' are both handsome and floriferous. Creeping savory (*Satureja spicigera*) is just as suitable as thyme for use as an edging plant and produces flowers much later in the season.

Herbs among the vegetables

Planting herbs with vegetables in the garden works well, adding color and interest as well as keeping them at hand for harvesting. Salad herbs such as arugula (*Eruca vesicaria*), purslane,

Planting with contrasting colors
(Above) This color scheme of green, silver, and purple consists of barberry and willow infilled with herbs including Thymus vulgaris *'Silver Posie' and lavender.*

Color in the herb garden
Delicate cilantro makes an ideal foil for purple anise hyssop (Agastache foeniculum), *orange pot marigolds, and mallow and bergamot in shades of pink.*

A vegetable potager
Herbs are good companions for vegetables, being both ornamental and adding variety to home-grown produce. Here, a bed of leeks is edged with colorful nasturtiums, which have edible leaves, flowers, and seeds. In turn, the foliage of nasturtiums may help to shade and blanch the bases of the leeks.

and sorrel can be raised among lettuce and radishes, while parsley, chervil (*Anthriscus cerefolium*), cilantro, and other frequently used herbs can be sown in rows at intervals between vegetables or along the edges of a plot. Where space is at a premium, flowers, vegetables, fruits, and herbs may be combined in a potager; a kitchen garden with a formal framework of small beds which are designed to be both practical and ornamental. Some herbs act as "companion plants," helping to keep the vegetable plot healthy and even improving yields. Various herbs, perhaps through aromas and root secretions, seem to help protect neighboring plants: French marigolds deter whitefly and soil pests; chives (*Allium schoenoprasum*) and garlic (*Allium sativum*) act as deterrents against various diseases and pests; and chamomile is reputed to benefit the health and vigor of surrounding plants.

Size, habit, and color

The habit and eventual dimensions of a plant should be considered when choosing herbs. Though they may be sold in similar-sized pots, the plants of creeping thyme and angelica, for example, soon differ hugely in height and spread. Extremes such as these are often better suited to planting in garden niches: creeping and compact forms are good for containers and for edging borders or paths, while large, vigorous herbs are best positioned at the back of a border. Architectural plants such as angelica, mullein, and Chinese rhubarb can be used to give height to plantings or to draw the eye from a distance.

Many herbs have natural variants that differ in appearance from the species. This adds to their versatility as garden plants for certain situations or planting designs, while their uses and properties remain the same. Some varieties of rosemary, lavender, and hyssop produce pink flowers; thyme is available in golden or silver forms; marigolds and feverfew may have single or double flowers, and there are purple-leaved cultivars of basil, orache (*Atriplex hortensis*), sage, and elder. White-flowered herbs stand out against dark backgrounds or where they are backlit by shafts of sunlight, and combine well with silver-leaved herbs for an ethereal effect. Some herbs have dwarf, prostrate, and upright variants that are much neater for confined spaces. Specialty herb nurseries often stock a wide range of variants, but it is also worth looking for herbs among other plant groups in a garden center. For example, a good selection of thymes can often be found among alpine plants.

Growing conditions

Although most common culinary herbs are from dry, sunny Mediterranean regions, many others tolerate and often thrive in moist soil, shade, and other garden microclimates. Herbs that enjoy damp, even wet, soil and a shady site might include a colorful elder, bugles, meadowsweet (*Filipendula ulmaria*), and mints, which can be combined in an attractive planting. Many herbs are unreliably hardy in many areas or dislike winter moisture. These plants are more likely to thrive in the shelter of a warm, sunny wall, especially where a "rainshadow" forms. When grown in containers, less hardy varieties can be moved closer to a wall or taken under cover for protection during the winter. Some herbs originate from coastal regions and tolerate salt-laden winds and rocky or sandy conditions. Fennel is a good choice for such sites and, despite its height, the plant seldom needs to be supported with stakes.

The key to success is understanding an herb's natural habitat and finding the nearest equivalent in terms of moisture, soil, light levels, temperature, and shelter. Armed with this knowledge, the imaginative gardener can grow herbs in areas as diverse as rock gardens, ponds, and paving crevices, as well as in borders, vegetable plots, or under glass.

Companion planting
Some plant associations have a practical purpose as well as being colorful. French marigolds are used in companion plantings to form a protective barrier around cabbage and asparagus, as they seem to deter or distract pests.

Planters' Guide to Garden Herbs

For containers
Hyssopus officinalis
  subsp. aristatus
Lavandula angustifolia
  'Nana Alba'
Mentha pulegium
  'Cunningham Mint'
Mentha requienii
Ocimum basilicum
  var. minimum
Origanum 'Norton Gold'
Origanum vulgare
  'Compactum'
Pelargonium crispum
  'Variegatum'
Pelargonium 'Galway Star'
Rosmarinus officinalis
  Prostratus Group
Satureja spicigera
Tanacetum parthenium
  'Golden Moss'
Thymus most

For dry shade
Aegopodium podagraria
  'Variegata'
Buxus sempervirens and cvs.
Chelidonium majus and cvs.
Fragaria vesca
Hedera helix and cvs.
Vinca major and cvs.
Vinca minor and cvs.

For moist shade
Aegopodium podagraria
  'Variegata'
Ajuga reptans and cvs.
Asarum canadense
Convallaria majalis and cvs.
Galium odoratum
Glechoma hederacea
  'Variegata'
Hamamelis virginiana
Melissa officinalis 'Aurea'
Mentha species
Myrrhis odorata
Primula vulgaris

Pulmonaria officinalis
Sambucus nigra and cvs.
Valeriana officinalis
Viola odorata and cvs.

For hot sunny sites
Aloe vera
Artemisia species
Capparis spinosa
Crocus sativus
Ecballium elaterium
Eryngium maritimum
Eucalyptus globulus
Ficus carica
Helichrysum italicum
Iris germanica 'Florentina'
Lavandula species
Olea europaea
Rosmarinus most
Ruta graveolens and cvs.
Salvia most
Thymus most
Satureja most
Sempervivum tectorum

Architectural herbs
Angelica archangelica
Artemisia 'Powis Castle'
Digitalis species
Ruta graveolens
Inula helenium
Iris germanica 'Florentina'
Laurus nobilis
Papaver somniferum and cvs.
Rheum palmatum
Ricinus communis and cvs.
Rosmarinus officinalis
  'Miss Jessopp's Upright'
Verbascum thapsus

For flower borders
Achillea millefolium f. rosea
Alcea rosea
Allium tuberosum
Borago officinalis
Cichorium intybus
Cimicifuga racemosa

Cynara cardunculus
  Scolymus Group
Dictamnus albus and cvs.
Echinacea purpurea
Eruca vescaria subsp. sativa
Foeniculum vulgare
  'Purpureum'
Galega officinalis and cvs.
Gillenia trifoliata
Hyssopus officinalis and cvs.
Inula helenium
Iris germanica 'Florentina'
Isatis tinctoria
Lavandula most
Mentha suaveolens
  'Variegata'
Mentha longifolia
  Buddleia Mint Group
Monarda most
Paeonia officinalis
Papaver most
Pelargonium most
Polemonium caeruleum
Rosa species
Salvia most
Sambucus nigra
  'Guincho Purple'
Saponaria officinalis
Symphytum × uplandicum
  'Variegatum'
Tanacetum most
Tropaeolum majus and cvs.
Verbascum thapsus
Verbena officinalis
Veronicastrum virginicum

CATALOG OF
GARDEN
HERBS

Oleaceae	COMMON JASMINE

JASMINUM OFFICINALE

Habit Woody-stemmed, twining, deciduous climber. **Flowers** Very fragrant, saucer-shaped, borne in clusters from summer to early autumn. White. **Leaves** Pinnate. Mid- to dark green.
• NATIVE HABITAT Woodlands from the Caucasus to the Himalayas and western China.
• CULTIVATION Grow in fertile, well-drained soil, in a sunny or partially shaded site. Thin crowded and flowered shoots after flowering, if necessary.
• PROPAGATION By semi-ripe cuttings taken in summer, or by layering in autumn.

Z9–11

Height to 40ft (12m)

Oleaceae	ARABIAN JASMINE

JASMINUM SAMBAC

Habit Vigorous, twining or scrambling, evergreen climber. **Flowers** Very fragrant, saucer-shaped, borne mainly in summer. White, fading to pink. **Leaves** Oval and lustrous. Dark green.
• NATIVE HABITAT Probably tropical Asia.
• CULTIVATION Grow in fertile, well-drained soil. Under glass, use soil-based mix, kept just moist in winter. Needs shade from hot sun and humidity. Thin old shoots after flowering.
• PROPAGATION By seed in spring at 68°F (21°C), or by semi-ripe cuttings taken in summer.

Z9–10

Height 6–10ft (2–3m)

Oleaceae	

JASMINUM SAMBAC 'Grand Duke of Tuscany'

Habit Vigorous, twining or scrambling, evergreen climber. **Flowers** Very fragrant, double, gardenia-like, borne mainly in summer. White, fading to pink. **Leaves** Oval and lustrous. Dark green.
• NATIVE HABITAT Garden origin.
• CULTIVATION Grow in fertile, well-drained soil. Under glass, use soil-based mix, kept just moist in winter. Needs shade from hot sun and humidity. Thin old shoots after flowering.
• PROPAGATION By semi-ripe cuttings in summer.

Z9–10

HEIGHT 6–10ft (2–3m)

Oleaceae	

JASMINUM OFFICINALE 'Fiona Sunrise'

Habit Woody-stemmed, twining, deciduous climber. **Flowers** Very fragrant, saucer-shaped, borne in clusters from summer to early autumn. White. **Leaves** Pinnate. Bright yellow-green.
• NATIVE HABITAT Garden origin. Species occurs in woodlands in the Caucasus and western China.
• CULTIVATION Grow in fertile, well-drained soil, in a sunny or partially shaded site. Thin crowded and flowered shoots after flowering, if necessary.
• PROPAGATION By semi-ripe cuttings taken in summer, or by layering in autumn.

Z9–11

HEIGHT to 40ft (12m)

CLIMBING • 19

| Liliaceae | GLORY LILY, MOZAMBIQUE LILY |

GLORIOSA SUPERBA

Habit Tuberous, climbing, herbaceous perennial.
Flowers Nodding, axillary, with 6 strongly reflexed petals with wavy margins and long, conspicuous stamens, borne from summer through to autumn. Red, purple, or occasionally yellow, with yellow margins. **Leaves** Oval to oblong, glossy, with terminal tendrils. Dark green.
• NATIVE HABITAT Forests and woods, often along watersides, in Africa and India.
• CULTIVATION Plant tubers at a depth of 3–4in (7–10cm) in fertile, well-drained soil, in spring.

In frost-prone areas, grow under glass, in soil-based potting mix with added grit. Provide support for the plant. Water freely when in growth and apply a balanced liquid fertilizer every two weeks. Keep dry tubers in their pots over winter. *Gloriosa superba* flowers best when pot-bound.
• PROPAGATION By seed at 66–75°F (19–24°C), or by division of the tubers, both in spring.
• OTHER NAMES *G. carsonii, G. minor, G. simplex.*
• WARNING The tubers are extremely toxic if eaten, and handling them may irritate the skin.

Z11

HEIGHT
6ft (2m)

Vitaceae	BURGUNDY GRAPE

VITIS VINIFERA 'Pinot Noir'
Habit Woody-stemmed, deciduous climber.
Flowers Tiny, borne in clusters in summer. Green. **Leaves** Rounded, 5-lobed. Yellow-green. **Fruits** Almost spherical. Black-purple.
• NATIVE HABITAT Cultivated origin.
• CULTIVATION Grow in full sun, in a sheltered site, in well-drained soil that is neutral to alkaline. Needs a long, warm, dry season for fruits to ripen.
• PROPAGATION By hardwood cuttings in late autumn, or by vine-eye cuttings in late winter.
• OTHER NAME *V. vinifera* 'Spätburgunder'.

Z6–10

HEIGHT
to 20ft (6m)

Piperaceae	BLACK PEPPER, WHITE PEPPER

PIPER NIGRUM
Habit Woody-stemmed, climbing, evergreen perennial. **Flowers** Tiny, borne in spikes in summer. White. **Leaves** Heart-shaped, leathery. Dark green. **Fruits** Round. Green, ripening to red.
• NATIVE HABITAT India and Sri Lanka.
• CULTIVATION Grow in fertile, well-drained soil in dappled shade. Under glass, use soil-based mix. Water moderately and feed monthly when in growth; water sparingly in winter.
• PROPAGATION By seed sown at 61°F (16°C), or by semi-ripe cuttings taken in summer.

Min. 61°F (16°C)

HEIGHT
12ft (4m)
or more

Passifloraceae	MAYPOPS

PASSIFLORA INCARNATA
Habit Tendril, herbaceous climber.
Flowers Fragrant, bowl-shaped, borne in summer. Pale purple to white, with white and purple crown.
Leaves Deeply lobed, toothed. Dark green.
Fruits Edible, egg-shaped. Yellow.
• NATIVE HABITAT Woodlands in eastern US.
• CULTIVATION Grow in poor, sandy, slightly acidic soil, in a sunny site. Shelter from winter moisture.
• PROPAGATION By semi-ripe cuttings taken in summer, or by layering in spring or autumn. Sow seed at 64–70°F (18–21°C) in spring.

Z7–10

HEIGHT
6ft (2m)

Vitaceae	GRAPE

VITIS VINIFERA
Habit Woody-stemmed, deciduous climber.
Flowers Tiny, borne in clusters in summer. Pale green. **Leaves** Rounded, 5-lobed. Mid-green.
Fruits Oval to rounded. Green to purple-black.
• NATIVE HABITAT Probably northwest Asia.
• CULTIVATION Grow in full sun, in a sheltered site in deep, moist but well-drained soil that is neutral to alkaline. Train to a framework, then spur-prune annually in winter or early spring.
• PROPAGATION By hardwood cuttings in late autumn, or by vine-eye cuttings in late winter.

Z6–10

HEIGHT
to 20ft (6m)

CLIMBING • 21

| Araliaceae | ENGLISH IVY |

HEDERA HELIX

Habit Vigorous, evergreen climber. Self-clings by means of adhesive pads, or trails as groundcover. *Flowers* Tiny, star-shaped. At adult stage, borne in clusters in late summer to autumn. Yellow-green. *Leaves* Broadly oval when juvenile; triangular, 3- to 5-lobed, glossy, and leathery at adult stage. Dark green. *Fruits* Round berries appear at adult stage. Black.
• NATIVE HABITAT Light woodland in Europe.
• CULTIVATION Tolerant of a wide range of soils and situations, including full sun and deep shade.

Grows best in moderately fertile to fertile, moist but well-drained soil, preferably alkaline, in dappled or part-shade. Ivies have two distinct stages of growth. Creeping or climbing growth is known as the juvenile stage; aerial "bushy" growth is known as the adult stage.
• PROPAGATION By semi-ripe cuttings of juvenile growth to obtain trailing plants, or by grafts or cuttings of adult growth for bushy habit.
• WARNING All parts are toxic if eaten. Contact with sap may irritate skin.

☼ ◊

Z6–9

HEIGHT
30ft (10m)

Cannabidaceae	HOPS

HUMULUS LUPULUS

Habit Deciduous, rhizomatous perennial. Vigorous, twining climber with bristly stems.
Flowers Aromatic, broadly oval, drooping spikes of female flowers borne in summer. Male flowers, borne on separate plant, are insignificant. Pale green, ripening to straw yellow. ***Leaves*** Divided, 3–5 coarsely toothed lobes. Mid-green.
• NATIVE HABITAT Woodlands and hedgerows in Europe, western Asia, and N. America.
• CULTIVATION Grow in fertile, moist but well-drained soil enriched with organic matter, in sun or in dappled or part shade. Support the plant with stake or trellis to clothe fences and arbors, or train to scramble through host shrubs and trees. Remove any growth from the previous season before the emergence of new growth in spring. Swags of branches are suitable for cutting and drying for use in winter arrangements.
• PROPAGATION By softwood cuttings taken in late spring or early summer, or by greenwood or leaf-bud cuttings taken in summer. Sow seed in spring at 59°F (15°C).

Z3–8

HEIGHT
20ft (6m)

CLIMBING • 23

| Cannabidaceae | GOLDEN HOPS |

HUMULUS LUPULUS 'Aureus'
Habit Vigorous, twining, deciduous perennial.
Flowers Aromatic, borne in oval spikes in summer. Pale green, ripening to straw yellow.
Leaves Divided into 3–5 coarsely toothed lobes. Bright yellow-green.
• NATIVE HABITAT Garden origin.
• CULTIVATION Grow in fertile, moist but well-drained soil in sun or in dappled or part shade.
• PROPAGATION By softwood cuttings in late spring, or by greenwood or leaf-bud cuttings in summer. May come partially true from seed.

| Tropaeoleaceae | INDIAN CRESS, GARDEN NASTURTIUM |

TROPAEOLUM MAJUS
Habit Vigorous, scrambling or climbing annual.
Flowers Funnel-shaped, long-spurred, borne from summer to autumn. Red, yellow, or orange.
Leaves Kidney-shaped, wavy-edged. Light green.
• NATIVE HABITAT From Bolivia to Colombia.
• CULTIVATION Grow in any poor but well-drained soil in a sunny site. Rich soils are likely to encourage foliage at the expense of flowers.
• PROPAGATION Sow seed in mid-spring, or at 55–61°F (13–16°C) in early spring; set out seedlings when danger of frost has passed.

☼ ◊

Z5–8

HEIGHT
20ft (6m)

☼ ◊

ANNUAL

HEIGHT
3–10ft
(0.9–3m)

| Cucurbitaceae | SQUIRTING CUCUMBER |

ECBALLIUM ELATERIUM
Habit Trailing perennial, grown as an annual.
Flowers Female: solitary; male: in spikes. Funnel-shaped, borne in summer. Pale yellow.
Leaves Oval, lobed, hairy. Mid-green. **Fruits** Cylindrical, eject seeds if touched. Blue-green.
• NATIVE HABITAT Dry, stony sites, Mediterranean.
• CULTIVATION Grow in poor, well-drained soil.
• PROPAGATION By seed at 64°F (18°C) in early spring; set out after danger of frost has passed.
• WARNING Fruits are toxic if eaten and may cause injury if seeds are ejected into the eyes.

| Tropaeoleaceae | |

TROPAEOLUM MAJUS 'Jewel of Africa'
Habit Vigorous, climbing annual.
Flowers Funnel-shaped, borne from summer to autumn. Cream, red, mahogany, pink, yellow, or orange. **Leaves** Rounded to kidney-shaped, with wavy margins. Light green, with cream variegation.
• NATIVE HABITAT Garden origin.
• CULTIVATION Grow in any poor, well-drained soil in sun. Good in containers and for groundcover.
• PROPAGATION Sow seed in mid-spring, or at 55–61°F (13–16°C) in early spring; set out seedlings when all danger of frost has passed.

☼ ◊

Z10

HEIGHT
20in (50cm)

SPREAD
3ft (0.9m)
or more

☼ ◊

ANNUAL

HEIGHT
3–10ft
(0.9–3m)

Lamiaceae	CREEPING SAVORY

SATUREJA SPICIGERA

Habit Creeping, prostrate subshrub.
Flowers Tubular, 2-lipped, borne in loose, whorled sprays during late summer. White.
Leaves Linear to lance-shaped. Mid-green.
• NATIVE HABITAT Dry, sunny places in Turkey, Iran, and the Caucasus.
• CULTIVATION For best results, grow in soil that is neutral to alkaline.
• PROPAGATION By seed in early spring at 55–61°F (13–16°C), or by greenwood cuttings in summer.
• OTHER NAMES *S. repanda, S. reptans.*

☼ ◊
Z7–8

Height
6in (15cm)

Spread
12in (30cm)
or more

Violaceae	WHITE SWEET VIOLET

VIOLA ODORATA 'Alba'

Habit Rhizomatous perennial. **Flowers** Sweetly fragrant, with short spurs, borne from late winter to late spring. Pure white. **Leaves** Aromatic, semi-evergreen, and heart-shaped. Bright green.
• NATIVE HABITAT Woods and hedgerows in western and southern Europe; widely naturalized.
• CULTIVATION Excellent as groundcover or for naturalizing. Tolerant of sun or shade.
• PROPAGATION By seed sown in autumn or spring, or by division in autumn or after flowering. Often self-seeds, but may not come true.

☼ ◊
Z6–9

Height
8in (20cm)

Spread
12in (30cm)
or more

Rubiaceae	SWEET WOODRUFF

GALIUM ODORATUM

Habit Spreading, rhizomatous perennial.
Flowers Small, star-shaped, borne in terminal clusters in spring and early summer. Pure white.
Leaves Lance-shaped, in whorls. Light green.
• NATIVE HABITAT Woods and hedgerows in Europe and from N. Africa to Siberia.
• CULTIVATION Grow in fertile, moist soil, in sun or part shade. Suitable for use as groundcover. Leaves are strongly fragrant when dried.
• PROPAGATION By division in spring.
• OTHER NAME *Asperula odorata.*

☼ ◊
Z3–9

Height
to 18in
(45cm)

Spread
indefinite

Apocynaceae	

VINCA MINOR 'Gertrude Jekyll'

Habit Mat-forming shrub. **Flowers** Propeller-shaped, borne freely from mid-spring to autumn. Pure white. **Leaves** Evergreen, oval to lance-shaped, glossy, leathery. Dark green.
• NATIVE HABITAT Garden origin.
• CULTIVATION For best results, grow in moist soil, either in a sunny or partially shaded site. Suitable for use as groundcover.
• PROPAGATION By semi-ripe cuttings in summer, or by division during the dormant season.
• WARNING All parts of the plant are toxic if eaten.

☼ ◊
Z4–9

Height
4–8in
(10–20cm)

Spread
indefinite

CREEPING • 25

Asteraceae	DOUBLE CHAMOMILE

CHAMAEMELUM NOBILE 'Flore Pleno'
Habit Compact, mat-forming perennial.
Flowers Double, buttonlike, borne in summer.
White, with yellow disk. **Leaves** Aromatic, finely
divided into threadlike segments. Bright green.
• NATIVE HABITAT Garden origin.
• CULTIVATION Suitable for growing as border
edging. When used in chamomile lawns, set out
plants 4in (10cm) apart.
• PROPAGATION By division in spring.
• WARNING Contact with foliage may irritate skin.
• OTHER NAME *Anthemis nobilis* 'Flore Pleno'.

Z4–8

HEIGHT
6in (15cm)

SPREAD
18in (45cm)

Asteraceae	LAWN CHAMOMILE, ROMAN CHAMOMILE

CHAMAEMELUM NOBILE
Habit Mat-forming perennial. **Flowers** Single,
daisylike, borne in summer. White, with yellow
disk. **Leaves** Apple-scented, feathery, finely
divided into threadlike segments. Bright green.
• NATIVE HABITAT Pasture in western Europe.
• CULTIVATION Grow in light, well-drained soil.
Suitable for growing in an herb garden and for
use in chamomile lawns, spaced 4in (10cm) apart.
• PROPAGATION Sow *in situ*, or divide in spring.
• OTHER NAME *Anthemis nobilis*.
• WARNING Contact with foliage may irritate skin.

Z4–8

HEIGHT
12in (30cm)

SPREAD
18in (45cm)

Menyanthaceae	BOG BEAN

MENYANTHES TRIFOLIATA
Habit Aquatic, rhizomatous perennial.
Flowers Star-shaped, with fringed and bearded
petals, borne in spikes in summer. White.
Leaves Divided into 3 oval leaflets. Mid-green.
• NATIVE HABITAT Ponds, lakes, and water margins
in Europe, northern Asia, and N. America.
• CULTIVATION Grow in aquatic containers
or in pond margins, in water up to 9in (23cm)
deep, in a sunny site.
• PROPAGATION By division or by stem cuttings
in early summer, or by seed sown in spring.

Z4–9

HEIGHT
8–10in
(20–30cm)

SPREAD
indefinite

Asteraceae	PELLITORY, PELLITORY OF SPAIN

ANACYCLUS PYRETHRUM
Habit Compact, rosette-forming perennial.
Flowers Single, daisylike, borne in summer.
White and red, with white-striped reverse.
Leaves Finely divided. Gray-green.
• NATIVE HABITAT Stony mountain slopes in the
Atlas mountains, Morocco, Tunisia, and Algeria.
• CULTIVATION Grow in moderately fertile,
sharply drained soil, in a sunny site. Suitable
for growing in an herb or rock garden.
• PROPAGATION By seed sown in autumn
or by softwood cuttings taken in early summer.

Z6–10

HEIGHT
12in (30cm)

SPREAD
10–12in
(25–30cm)

| Liliaceae | LILY OF THE VALLEY |

CONVALLARIA MAJALIS

Habit Creeping, rhizomatous perennial.
Flowers Very fragrant, drooping, bell-shaped, borne in late spring and early summer. White.
Leaves Broadly oval. Bright green.
• NATIVE HABITAT Woodlands in northern temperate zones.
• CULTIVATION Grow in moist, leaf-rich soil in deep, partial, or dappled shade. Flowers best in light, dappled shade. Good for use as groundcover.
• PROPAGATION Sow ripe seed or divide in autumn.
• WARNING All parts of the plant are toxic if eaten.

Z4–8

HEIGHT
9in (23cm)

SPREAD
12in (30cm)
or more

| Liliaceae | PINK LILY OF THE VALLEY |

CONVALLARIA MAJALIS var. ROSEA

Habit Creeping, rhizomatous perennial.
Flowers Very fragrant, drooping, bell-shaped, borne in late spring and early summer. Pale mauve-pink. **Leaves** Broadly oval. Bright green.
• NATIVE HABITAT Woodlands in northern temperate zones.
• CULTIVATION Grow in moist, leaf-rich soil in deep, partial, or dappled shade. Flowers best in light dappled shade. Suitable for groundcover.
• PROPAGATION By division in autumn.
• WARNING All parts of the plant are toxic if eaten.

Z4–8

HEIGHT
9in (23cm)

SPREAD
12in (30cm)
or more

| Lamiaceae | |

AJUGA REPTANS 'Burgundy Glow'

Habit Creeping, rhizomatous perennial.
Flowers Tubular, 2-lipped, borne in upright spikes during late spring. Deep blue.
Leaves Evergreen, oval to spoon-shaped. Gray-green, variegated cream and suffused pink-red.
• NATIVE HABITAT Garden origin.
• CULTIVATION Grow in moist but well-drained soil that is rich in leaf mold in partial or dappled shade or part-day sun. Ideal as groundcover.
• PROPAGATION Divide or separate rooted stems in early summer, after flowering.

Z3–9

HEIGHT
6in (15cm)

SPREAD
24–36in
(60–90cm)
or more

CREEPING • 27

| Ericaceae | WINTERGREEN, CHECKERBERRY |

GAULTHERIA PROCUMBENS
Habit Creeping, rhizomatous shrub.
Flowers Tiny, urn-shaped, borne during summer. White or pale pink. ***Leaves*** Aromatic, evergreen, oval, glossy. Dark green.
Fruits Aromatic, round. Bright red.
• NATIVE HABITAT Woods in eastern N. America.
• CULTIVATION Grow in moist, fertile, acidic soil in partial or dappled shade. Suitable for growing as groundcover.
• PROPAGATION Surface-sow seed in autumn in a cold frame, using an acid, seed soil mix.

| Crassulaceae | COMMON HOUSELEEK, HEN AND CHICKS |

SEMPERVIVUM TECTORUM
Habit Succulent, evergreen, mat-forming perennial. ***Flowers*** Small, star-shaped, borne in sprays on erect stems during summer. Pink-purple. ***Leaves*** Fleshy, oval to oblong, rosetted. Blue-green, often flushed red-purple.
• NATIVE HABITAT Mountains in southern Europe.
• CULTIVATION Grow in poor, gritty soil. Suitable for growing in a trough or scree bed, or for planting in drystone retaining walls.
• PROPAGATION Separate offsets in spring or early summer. Sow seed in spring in a cold frame.

Z3–7

HEIGHT
6in (15cm)

SPREAD
36in (90cm)
or more

Z5–10

HEIGHT
6in (15cm)

SPREAD
20in (50cm)

| Ericaceae | KINNIKINNICK |

ARCTOSTAPHYLOS UVA-URSI
Habit Creeping, mat-forming shrub.
Flowers Tiny, urn-shaped, borne in summer. White, tinted pink. ***Leaves*** Evergreen, oval, leathery. Dark green. ***Fruits*** Rounded. Scarlet.
• NATIVE HABITAT Moorland, Eurasia, N. America.
• CULTIVATION Grow in moist, fertile, acidic soil in partial or dappled shade. Suitable for growing as groundcover.
• PROPAGATION By seed in autumn in acidic seed soil mix, in a cold frame. Layer in spring or take semi-ripe cuttings in summer.

Z2–6

HEIGHT
4in (10cm)

SPREAD
20in (50cm)

THYMUS

The genus *Thymus* consists of about 350 species of evergreen, aromatic, woody-based perennials, shrubs, and subshrubs, which occur naturally in rocky places and on dry grassland, usually on chalky or limy soils, in Eurasia.

Commonly known as thyme, the plants are valued for their aromatic foliage and small, 2-lipped tubular flowers, which attract bees and other beneficial insects. They are ideally suited to rock gardens, troughs, sinks, and walls, and may be used as underplantings or companion plantings in a herbaceous or mixed border.

Most thymes have a culinary use. All of them are rich in aromatic oils, particularly thymol, which has antiseptic properties. The oils may vary in aroma between species and from plant to plant. The classic culinary thyme is *T. vulgaris*; the hybrid *T.* × *citriodorus* has a lemon scent; and *T. herba-barona* is caraway scented.

Grow in well-drained, neutral to alkaline soil in a warm site in full sun. Top-dress the plant with a layer of grit or fine-grade gravel, to protect the neck from excessive winter moisture and to prevent soil from splashing on the foliage. Trim back the plant annually after flowering to keep it bushy and compact, but avoid cutting into old wood. Remove any reverted (all-green) shoots from variegated cultivars as soon as visible. Harvest the leaves in summer when flowering begins. Pick sprigs throughout the growing season for culinary use, and use them either fresh or air-dried.

Propagate species by sowing seed in containers in a greenhouse or cold frame during spring. Take softwood cuttings in early summer, or root semi-ripe cuttings in mid- to late summer. Rooted stem sections may be lifted during spring or summer, and are best potted up until they become well established.

T. SERPYLLUM var. *ALBUS*
Habit Creeping, mat-forming subshrub.
Flowers Small, tubular, 2-lipped, borne in dense whorls during summer. Pure white.
Leaves Aromatic, linear, oval. Mid-green.
• HEIGHT ½–3in (1–7cm).
• SPREAD 36in (90cm).

T. serpyllum var. *albus*
☼ ◊ Z4–8

T. CITRIODORUS 'Silver Queen'
Habit Dense, rounded subshrub.
Flowers Small, tubular, 2-lipped, borne in heads, in summer. Pale lilac.
Leaves Lemon-scented, narrowly oval to lance-shaped. Mid-green, marbled silver-green, with pink tips in winter.
• HEIGHT 9in (23cm).
• SPREAD 12–16in (30–40cm).

T. × *citriodorus* 'Silver Queen'
☼ ◊ Z5–9

T. × *CITRIODORUS* 'Fragrantissimus'
Habit Clump-forming subshrub.
Flowers Tubular, 2-lipped, borne in rounded heads in early to mid-summer. Pale mauve-pink.
Leaves Fresh orange-scented, oval to lance-shaped. Grayish green.
• HEIGHT 4–6in (10–15cm).
• SPREAD 20in (50cm).

T. × *citriodorus* 'Fragrantissimus'
☼ ◊ Z5–9

T. VULGARIS
Habit Mound-forming subshrub.
Flowers Small, tubular, 2-lipped, borne in whorled spikes throughout summer. White to bright purple.
Leaves Linear to oval and finely hairy. Gray-green.
• HEIGHT 12–18in (30–45cm).
• SPREAD 24in (60cm).

T. vulgaris
Common thyme, Garden thyme
☼ ◊ Z4–8

THYMUS • 29

T. SERPYLLUM
'Annie Hall'
Habit Creeping, mat-forming subshrub.
Flowers Small, tubular, 2-lipped, borne in tight heads, in summer. Pale purple-pink.
Leaves Linear to oval. Pale green.
• HEIGHT to 3in (7cm).
• SPREAD to 36in (90cm).

T. serpyllum
'Annie Hall'
☼ ◊ Z4–8

T. CAESPITITIUS
Habit Mat- or mound-forming subshrub.
Flowers Tubular, borne in whorled heads from late spring to summer. White, pink, or lilac.
Leaves Citrus-pine scented, narrowly spoon-shaped. Dark green.
• OTHER NAMES *T. azoricus*, *T. micans*.
• HEIGHT 2–6in (5–15cm).
• SPREAD 18in (45cm).

T. caespititius
Azores thyme
☼ ◊ Z4–9

T. SERPYLLUM
'Minor'
Habit Compact, mat-forming subshrub.
Flowers Small, tubular, 2-lipped, borne in dense whorls, in summer. Pink.
Leaves Tiny, lance-shaped. Mid-green.
• HEIGHT ½in (1cm).
• SPREAD 24in (60cm).

T. serpyllum **'Minor'**
☼ ◊ Z4–8

T. SERPYLLUM
Habit Creeping, mat-forming subshrub.
Flowers Small, tubular, 2-lipped, borne in dense whorls during summer. Pink to purple.
Leaves Narrowly oval. Mid-green.
• HEIGHT to 4in (10cm).
• SPREAD 36in (90cm).

T. serpyllum
Wild thyme, Creeping thyme, Mother-of-thyme
☼ ◊ Z4–8

T. SERPYLLUM
'Pink Chintz'
Habit Vigorous, mat-forming subshrub.
Flowers Small, tubular, 2-lipped, borne in dense whorls, in summer. Salmon-pink.
Leaves Hairy, linear to oval. Gray-green.
• HEIGHT ½–3in (1–7cm).
• SPREAD 24in (60cm).

T. serpyllum
'Pink Chintz'
☼ ◊ Z4–8

T. × CITRIODORUS
'Bertram Anderson'
Habit Dense, rounded subshrub.
Flowers Borne in summer. Lavender-pink.
Leaves Lemon-scented, narrowly oval. Gray-green, suffused yellow.
• OTHER NAME *T. × c.* 'Anderson's Gold'.
• HEIGHT 6–9in (15–23cm).
• SPREAD 12–24in (30–60cm).

T. × citriodorus
'Bertram Anderson'
☼ ◊ Z5–9

T. MASTICHINA
Habit Robust, hairy-stemmed, upright subshrub.
Flowers Small, tubular, borne in rounded heads in summer. White to off-white.
Leaves Camphor-scented, oval, with shallowly scalloped margins, and downy. Mid-green.
• HEIGHT 12in (30cm).
• SPREAD 18in (45cm).

T. mastichina
Mastic thyme, Spanish wood marjoram
☼ ◊ Z7–9

T. × CITRIODORUS
'Golden King'
Habit Dense subshrub with upright stems.
Flowers Small, tubular, 2-lipped, borne in irregular, cylindrical heads, in summer. Pink-lavender to pale lilac.
Leaves Lemon-scented, narrowly oval to lance-shaped. Mid-green, margined golden-yellow.
• HEIGHT 10in (25cm).
• SPREAD 18in (45cm).

T. × citriodorus
'Golden King'
☼ ◊ Z5–9

30 • THYMUS

T. SERPYLLUM
'Minimus'
Habit Very compact, mat-forming subshrub.
Flowers Small, tubular, 2-lipped, borne in dense whorls, in summer. Pink.
Leaves Tiny, lance-shaped. Mid-green.
• HEIGHT ½in (1cm).
• SPREAD 8in (20cm).

T. serpyllum 'Minimus'
☼ ◊ Z4–8

T. CILICICUS
Habit Compact, cushion- or tussock-forming subshrub, with hairy, upright stems.
Flowers Small, tubular, 2-lipped, borne in dense, semi-rounded heads from early to mid-summer. Lilac-pink to mauve.
Leaves Scented, linear, fine-haired. Dark green.
• HEIGHT 4–6in (10–15cm).
• SPREAD 18in (45cm).

T. cilicicus
Cilician thyme
☼ ◊ Z6–8

T. PULEGIOIDES
Habit Spreading subshrub with sprawling, semi-erect stems.
Flowers Borne in whorled spikes with leaf-like bracts from late spring to early summer. Pink to purple.
Leaves Aromatic, lance-shaped. Mid-green.
• HEIGHT 2–10in (5–25cm).
• SPREAD 16–18in (40–45cm).

T. pulegioides
Broad-leaved thyme, Large thyme
☼ ◊ Z4–8

T. POLYTRICHUS
subsp. BRITANNICUS
Habit Creeping, mat-forming subshrub with softly hairy stems.
Flowers Small, tubular, borne in rounded heads in summer. Pale to deep purple.
Leaves Narrowly oval, hairy-edged. Dark green.
• OTHER NAME *T. praecox* subsp. *arcticus*.
• HEIGHT to 2in (5cm).
• SPREAD 24in (60cm).

T. polytrichus subsp. *britannicus*
☼ ◊ Z5–9

T. VULGARIS
'Silver Posie'
Habit Bushy, mound-forming subshrub.
Flowers Small, tubular, 2-lipped, borne throughout summer. Pale mauve-pink.
Leaves Linear to oval. Gray-green with white margins.
• HEIGHT 10in (25cm).
• SPREAD 18in (45cm).

T. vulgaris
'Silver Posie'
☼ ◊ Z5–8

T. HERBA-BARONA
Habit Wiry-stemmed, loosely mat-forming subshrub.
Flowers Tubular, borne in loose, oblong to semi-rounded heads in mid-summer. Pink to mauve.
Leaves Caraway-, nutmeg-, or lemon-scented, lance-shaped. Dark green.
• HEIGHT 2–4in (5–10cm).
• SPREAD 24in (60cm).

T. herba-barona
Caraway thyme
☼ ◊ Z6–8

T. SERPYLLUM
COCCINEUS
Habit Creeping, mat-forming subshrub.
Flowers Small, tubular, 2-lipped, borne in dense heads throughout summer. Crimson-magenta.
Leaves Oval. Dark green.
• OTHER NAME *T.* 'Coccineus'.
• HEIGHT to 2¾in (7cm).
• SPREAD 36in (90cm).

T. serpyllum coccineus
☼ ◊ Z4–8

T. SERPYLLUM 'Elfin'
Habit Compact, mound-forming subshrub.
Flowers Small, tubular, 2-lipped, usually sparsely borne during summer. Magenta.
Leaves Tiny, linear to oval. Gray-green.
• HEIGHT 2in (5cm).
• SPREAD to 8in (20cm).

T. serpyllum 'Elfin'
☼ ◊ Z4–8

THYMUS • 31

T. POLYTRICHUS
Habit Creeping, mat-forming subshrub.
Flowers Small, tubular, borne in terminal clusters in summer. Mauve to deep purple, with purple leaflike bracts.
Leaves Narrowly oval, fringed with fine hairs. Dark green.
• OTHER NAME
T. praecox.
• HEIGHT 2in (5cm).
• SPREAD 18in (45cm).

T. polytrichus
Creeping thyme,
Wild thyme
☼ ◊ Z5–9
ᔕ ᔖ

T. 'Doone Valley'
Habit Mat-forming subshrub.
Flowers Small, tubular, 2-lipped, borne in rounded heads throughout summer. Lavender-pink, maturing from crimson buds.
Leaves Lemon-scented, lance-shaped. Dark olive-green, spotted yellow.
• HEIGHT to 5in (12cm).
• SPREAD 14in (35cm) or more.

T. 'Doone Valley'
☼ ◊ Z6–9

ᔕ ᔖ ᔗ

**T. × CITRIODORUS
'Archer's Gold'**
Habit Dense, compact, rounded subshrub.
Flowers Tubular, borne in irregular, oblong heads in summer. Pale purple.
Leaves Lemon-scented, narrowly oval to lance-shaped. Bright yellow or mid-green with yellow margins.
• HEIGHT 6–9in (15–23cm).
• SPREAD 18in (45cm).

T. × citriodorus
'Archer's Gold'
☼ ◊ Z5–9
ᔕ ᔖ

**T. SERPYLLUM
'Goldstream'**
Habit Vigorous, mound-forming subshrub.
Flowers Small, tubular, 2-lipped, borne during summer. Pale lilac.
Leaves Linear to oval. Light green with golden-yellow variegation.
• HEIGHT to 2¼in (7cm).
• SPREAD to 36in (90cm).

T. serpyllum
'Goldstream'
☼ ◊ Z4–8

ᔕ ᔖ

T. pseudolanuginosus
Habit Creeping, mat-forming subshrub with hairy stems.
Flowers Small, tubular, 2-lipped, borne in few-flowered clusters in the leaf axils in mid-summer. Pale pink.
Leaves Tiny, oval, densely woolly-downy. Gray-green.
• HEIGHT 1–3in (2.5–7cm).
• SPREAD to 3ft (0.9m).

T. pseudolanuginosus
Woolly thyme
☼ ◊ Z6–8
ᔕ ᔖ

**T. × CITRIODORUS
'Aureus'**
Habit Dense, upright to spreading subshrub.
Flowers Small, tubular, 2-lipped, borne in summer. Pale lilac to lavender-pink.
Leaves Lemon-scented, narrowly oval to lance-shaped. Pale green, dappled golden-yellow.
• HEIGHT 4–6in (10–15cm).
• SPREAD 24in (60cm).

T. × CITRIODORUS
Habit Dense, rounded sub-shrub.
Flowers Small, tubular, borne in irregular heads in summer. Pink-lavender to pale lilac.
Leaves Lemon-scented, narrowly oval to lance-shaped. Mid-green.
• HEIGHT 10–12in (25–30cm).
• SPREAD 24in (60cm).

T. × citriodorus
Lemon thyme, Lemon-scented thyme
☼ ◊ Z5–9
ᔕ ᔖ ᔗ

T. × citriodorus
'Aureus'
Golden lemon thyme
☼ ◊ Z5–9
ᔕ ᔖ ᔗ

| Lamiaceae | BRONZE BUGLE |

AJUGA REPTANS 'Atropurpurea'

Habit Low, creeping, evergreen, rhizomatous perennial, spreading rapidly by stolons.
Flowers Tubular, 2-lipped with leaflike bracts, borne in upright, spikelike whorls, in late spring and early summer. Deep blue.
Leaves Evergreen, oval to spoon-shaped, shiny, wrinkled. Dark brownish purple.
• NATIVE HABITAT Garden origin.
• CULTIVATION Grow in moist soil in partial, dappled, or deep shade, or in part-day sun. Also tolerant of low-fertility soils and deep shade.

Shade is essential, since the leaves of this and other cultivars are prone to scorch in hot sun. Bugles are excellent for use as groundcover in damp, shady borders. They are also suitable for growing in a woodland garden.
• PROPAGATION By division or separation of rooted sections in early summer, after flowering. Sow seed in a cold frame in autumn or spring. The resulting seedlings must be selected for good color forms, since they may not come reliably true from seed. Germination can be erratic.

Z3–9

Height
6in (15cm)

Spread
24–36in
(60–90cm)
or more

| Lamiaceae | VARIEGATED GROUND IVY |

GLECHOMA HEDERACEA 'Variegata'

Habit Stoloniferous perennial. **Flowers** Tiny, tubular, 2-lipped, borne in summer. Pale mauve. **Leaves** Kidney-shaped, with scalloped margins. Pale green, with white edging and marbling.
- NATIVE HABITAT Garden origin.
- CULTIVATION Grow in moist but well-drained soil in a sunny or partially shaded site.
- PROPAGATION By softwood cuttings taken in late spring, or by division in autumn or spring.
- OTHER NAMES *Nepeta glechoma* 'Variegata', *N. hederacea* 'Variegata'.

Z5–9

HEIGHT
6in (15cm)

SPREAD
6ft (2m)
or more

| Lamiaceae | GROUND IVY |

GLECHOMA HEDERACEA

Habit Stoloniferous perennial. **Flowers** Tiny, tubular, 2-lipped, borne in summer. Pale to deep blue-mauve. **Leaves** Kidney-shaped, with scalloped margins. Dark green.
- NATIVE HABITAT Woodlands, hedgerows, and grassland from Europe to the Caucasus.
- CULTIVATION Grow in moist but well-drained soil in sun or partial shade. Tends to be invasive.
- PROPAGATION By seed or softwood cuttings in late spring, or by division in autumn or spring.
- OTHER NAMES *Nepeta glechoma*, *N. hederacea*.

Z4–9

HEIGHT
6in (15cm)

SPREAD
6ft (2m)
or more

| Lamiaceae | BASIL THYME, MOTHER OF THYME |

ACINOS ARVENSIS

Habit Spreading annual or short-lived perennial. **Flowers** Tubular, 2-lipped, borne in whorls from mid-summer. Violet. **Leaves** Oval. Mid-green.
- NATIVE HABITAT Dry, sunny places on chalky soils in northern Europe, Mediterranean, and western Asia.
- CULTIVATION Grow in well-drained alkaline soils that are moderately fertile, in full sun.
- PROPAGATION Sow seed in a cold frame in autumn or spring. Will self-seed.
- OTHER NAME *Clinopodium arvensis*.

Z7–8

HEIGHT
8in (20cm)

SPREAD
12in (30cm)

Lamiaceae	SELFHEAL

Prunella vulgaris

Habit Creeping perennial. **Flowers** Tubular, 2-lipped, borne in dense, upright spikes, from summer to autumn. Deep purple. **Leaves** Toothed, oval, wrinkled. Mid-green.
• NATIVE HABITAT Woods and grassland, Europe.
• CULTIVATION Grow in moist but well-drained soil in sun or dappled shade. Suitable for a wild or herb garden, sited where it will not swamp other plants, and for naturalizing in grass.
• PROPAGATION By seed in a cold frame or by division, both in autumn or spring.

Z4–9

Height to 20in (50cm)

Spread indefinite

Apocynaceae	

Vinca major 'Variegata'

Habit Vigorous, prostrate shrub. **Flowers** Propeller-shaped, from mid-spring to autumn. Blue-violet to deep violet. **Leaves** Evergreen, oval to lance-shaped. Mid-green, variegated cream.
• NATIVE HABITAT Garden origin.
• CULTIVATION Grow in moist soil in sun or part-shade. Flowers best in sun. Ideal for growing as groundcover, and less invasive than the species.
• PROPAGATION By semi-ripe cuttings in summer, or by division during the dormant season.
• WARNING All parts of the plant are toxic if eaten.

Z7–9

Height 18in (45cm)

Spread indefinite

Apocynaceae	GREATER PERIWINKLE

Vinca major

Habit Vigorous, prostrate shrub. **Flowers** Propeller-shaped, borne from mid-spring to autumn. Blue-violet to deep violet. **Leaves** Evergreen, oval to lance-shaped. Dark green.
• NATIVE HABITAT Woods, western Mediterranean.
• CULTIVATION Grow in moist soil. Tolerates sun or part shade but flowers best in sun. Ideal as groundcover but tends to be invasive.
• PROPAGATION By semi-ripe cuttings taken in summer, or by division when dormant.
• WARNING All parts of the plant are toxic if eaten.

Z7–9

Height 18in (45cm)

Spread indefinite

Violaceae	SWEET VIOLET

Viola odorata

Habit Rhizomatous perennial. **Flowers** Fragrant, short-spurred, borne from late winter through to late spring. Blue, violet, or white. **Leaves** Semi-evergreen, heart-shaped. Bright green.
• NATIVE HABITAT Woods and hedges in western and southern Europe; widely naturalized.
• CULTIVATION Grow in moist but well-drained, fertile soil, in a sunny or shaded site. Suitable for use as groundcover or for naturalizing.
• PROPAGATION By seed in autumn, or by division in autumn or after flowering. Self-seeds freely.

Z6–9

Height to 8in (20cm)

Spread 12in (30cm) or more

CREEPING • 35

| Apocynaceae | LESSER PERIWINKLE |

Vinca minor

Habit Prostrate, mat-forming shrub, with trailing shoots. **Flowers** Solitary, axillary, propeller-shaped, borne freely over long periods from mid-spring to autumn. Blue-violet, sometimes red-purple, pale blue, or pure white. **Leaves** Evergreen, oval to lance-shaped, glossy, leathery. Dark green.
• NATIVE HABITAT Woodlands in Europe, southern Russia, and the northern Caucasus.
• CULTIVATION Grow in moist but well-drained soil for best results, although it is tolerant of any but very dry soils. Site in sun or part shade, but flowers most freely in full sun. Cut back hard in spring where necessary to keep the plant in bounds. Trim overlong shoots in summer, preferably before they take root at the nodes. Ideal as groundcover in a shrub or mixed border, or for planting beneath trees in a woodland garden. It is also suitable for clothing steep, shady banks.
• PROPAGATION By semi-ripe cuttings in summer, or by division during the dormant season.
• WARNING All parts of the plant are toxic if eaten.

Z4–9

Height
4–8in
(10–20cm)

Spread
indefinite

Lamiaceae	BUGLE

AJUGA REPTANS

Habit Creeping, rhizomatous, carpet-forming perennial, spreading widely by stolons.
Flowers Tubular, 2-lipped, borne in upright, spike-like whorls, in late spring and early summer. Deep blue, sometimes pink or white.
Leaves Evergreen, oval to spoon-shaped, glossy, mostly in basal rosettes. Dark green.
• NATIVE HABITAT Woodland and grassland from Europe to the Caucasus and Iran.
• CULTIVATION Grow in moist soil, either in partial or dappled shade, or part-day sun. The leaves are prone to scorch in hot sun. Bugle is excellent for growing at the front of damp, partially shaded borders and is suitable for underplanting in wild and woodland gardens, since it is low enough to form an attractive carpet beneath other sturdy and vigorous perennials. Although it makes good groundcover, especially under shrubs and trees, it is often invasive when sited near smaller plants.
• PROPAGATION Divide or separate rooted stems in early summer, after flowering. Sow seed in spring or as soon as ripe, in containers in a cold frame.

Z3–9

HEIGHT
6in (15cm)

SPREAD
24–36in (60–90cm) or more

CREEPING • 37

Aristolochiaceae	WILD GINGER

ASARUM CANADENSE
Habit Creeping, rhizomatous perennial.
Flowers Tubular, urn-shaped, with spreading petal lobes, borne near ground level, in late spring. Purple-brown. **Leaves** Broadly kidney-shaped, glossy. Dark green.
• NATIVE HABITAT Woods from Manitoba to N. Carolina in eastern N. America.
• CULTIVATION Grow in neutral to slightly acidic, moist, well-drained soil enriched by organic matter.
• PROPAGATION By seed sown as soon as ripe in a cold frame. Divide in early spring.

Z3–8

HEIGHT
3in (8cm)

SPREAD
24in (60cm)

Rosaceae	PARSLEY PIERT, BREAKSTONE PARSLEY

APHANES ARVENSIS
Habit Low-growing, spreading annual with stems radiating from a central rootstock.
Flowers Minute, borne in clusters between spring and autumn. Pale green. **Leaves** Hairy, fan-shaped. Pale green.
• NATIVE HABITAT Bare ground in Europe, N. Africa, and N. America.
• CULTIVATION Grow in sharply drained, neutral or alkaline, stony soil in sun or part shade. May be used for edging, although not highly ornamental.
• PROPAGATION By seed *in situ*, in early summer.

ANNUAL

HEIGHT
1in (2.5cm)

SPREAD
8in (20cm)

Asteraceae	

CHAMAEMELUM NOBILE 'Treneague'
Habit Low, tufted, stem-rooting perennial.
Flowers None. **Leaves** Strongly aromatic, finely divided into threadlike segments. Bright emerald.
• NATIVE HABITAT Garden origin.
• CULTIVATION Grow in light, well-drained soil in sun. When used in chamomile lawns, set out plants 4in (10cm) apart.
• PROPAGATION By division in spring.
• OTHER NAME *Anthemis nobilis* 'Treneague'.
• WARNING Contact with foliage may irritate skin.

Z4–8

HEIGHT
4in (10cm)

SPREAD
18in (45cm)

38 • LARGE

Liliaceae	MADONNA LILY

LILIUM CANDIDUM
Habit Bulbous perennial. **Flowers** Fragrant, broadly trumpet-shaped, borne in spikes of 5–20 in mid-summer. Pure white, with yellow base. **Leaves** Lance-shaped, scattered on stem, with overwintering, broader basal leaves. Bright green.
- NATIVE HABITAT Eastern Mediterranean.
- CULTIVATION Grow in neutral to alkaline, well-drained soil enriched with organic matter, in full sun. Place bulb nose at or just below soil level.
- PROPAGATION By seed when ripe in a cold frame, and by scales or offsets in mid- to late summer.

Z4–9

HEIGHT
3–6ft
(0.9–1.8m)

Myrtaceae	MYRTLE

MYRTUS COMMUNIS
Habit Bushy, upright shrub. **Flowers** Fragrant, solitary, 5-petaled, with conspicuous stamens, borne from mid-summer to autumn. White. **Leaves** Aromatic, evergreen, oval. Dark green.
- NATIVE HABITAT Mediterranean scrub.
- CULTIVATION Grow in moist but well-drained, neutral to alkaline soil in a sunny, sheltered site. May be grown in containers outdoors, but should be overwintered under glass in cooler areas.
- PROPAGATION By seed in autumn in a cold frame, or by semi-ripe cuttings taken in summer.

Z9–10

HEIGHT
to 10ft (3m)

SPREAD
to 10ft (3m)

Ranunculaceae	BLACK COHOSH, BLACK SNAKE ROOT

CIMICIFUGA RACEMOSA
Habit Erect, clump-forming perennial. **Flowers** Malodorous, tiny, borne in spikes during summer. White. **Leaves** Broadly oval, with 3 toothed lobes. Dark green.
- NATIVE HABITAT Woods in eastern N. America.
- CULTIVATION Grow in moist, leaf-rich, fertile soil in partial or dappled shade. Suitable for growing in an herb or woodland garden.
- PROPAGATION By seed as soon as ripe in a cold frame, or by division in spring.
- WARNING Leaves and rhizomes harmful if eaten.

Z3–9

HEIGHT
4–6ft
(1.2–2m)

SPREAD
24in (60cm)

| Caprifoliaceae | GUELDER ROSE |

VIBURNUM OPULUS

Habit Vigorous, bushy shrub. **Flowers** Lace-capped, borne in late spring to early summer. White. **Leaves** Maplelike, 3-lobed. Dark green, turning red in autumn. **Fruits** Round. Bright red.
- NATIVE HABITAT Woods in Europe and N. Africa.
- CULTIVATION Grow in moist but well-drained soil in sun or dappled shade. Suitable for a wildlife or woodland garden, and in mixed borders.
- PROPAGATION By seed as soon as ripe, or by greenwood cuttings taken in early summer.
- WARNING Berries are harmful if eaten.

☼ ◊

Z3–9

HEIGHT
to 15ft (5m)

SPREAD
to 12ft (4m)

| Apiaceae | SWEET CICELY |

MYRRHIS ODORATA

Habit Vigorous, clumping perennial. **Flowers** Tiny, star-shaped, borne in flat clusters in early to mid-summer. White. **Leaves** Anise-scented, fern-like, finely divided into toothed segments. Fresh green. **Fruits** Large, ridged, shiny seeds. Black.
- NATIVE HABITAT Mountains in southern Europe.
- CULTIVATION Grow in moist but well-drained soil in sun or dappled shade. Suitable for a herbaceous or mixed border, and an herb or woodland garden.
- PROPAGATION By seed in spring in a cold frame (may self-seed), or by division in autumn or spring.

☼ ◊

Z3–7

HEIGHT
3–6ft
(0.9–2m)

SPREAD
2–4ft
(0.6–1.2m)

| Caprifoliaceae | BOURTREE, ELDER |

SAMBUCUS NIGRA

Habit Vigorous, bushy shrub. **Flowers** Scented, small, borne in flat sprays in early summer. Creamy white. **Leaves** Divided, toothed, oval. Mid-green. **Fruits** Round berries. Black-purple.
- NATIVE HABITAT Woodlands and thickets in Europe, N. Africa, and southwest Asia.
- CULTIVATION Prefers moist but well-drained soil, but tolerates almost any soil in sun or part shade.
- PROPAGATION By seed as soon as ripe in a cold frame, or by hardwood cuttings taken in winter.
- WARNING Leaves or raw berries harmful if eaten.

☼ ◊

Z5–9

HEIGHT
to 20ft (6m)

SPREAD
to 20ft (6m)

Apiaceae	BULLWORT

AMMI MAJUS

Habit Slender, branching annual. ***Flowers*** Small, borne in flat-topped clusters in summer. White. ***Leaves*** Finely divided into oval to lance-shaped leaflets. Bright green.
- NATIVE HABITAT Scrub in Turkey and N. Africa.
- CULTIVATION Grow in any moist but well-drained soil in full sun. Provide light support with peasticks. Deadhead to prolong flowering.
- PROPAGATION By seed *in situ* in spring or autumn.

ANNUAL

HEIGHT 3ft (0.9m) or more

SPREAD 18in (45cm)

Verbenaceae	MEXICAN OREGANO

LIPPIA GRAVEOLENS

Habit Open, branching shrub. ***Flowers*** Small, tubular, borne in slender spikes from spring to winter. Yellow-white. ***Leaves*** Aromatic, narrowly oval. Grayish green.
- NATIVE HABITAT Dry habitats from Texas to S. America.
- CULTIVATION Grow in light, sandy soil in full sun. In cooler areas, grow under glass. Use soil-based potting mix with sharp sand.
- PROPAGATION By seed in spring at 64°F (18°C), or by softwood cuttings taken in early summer.

Min 41°F (5°C)

HEIGHT 6ft (2m)

SPREAD to 5ft (1.5m)

Valerianaceae	ALL HEAL, COMMON VALERIAN

VALERIANA OFFICINALIS

Habit Clump-forming, rhizomatous perennial. ***Flowers*** Small, borne in rounded heads in summer. White or pink. ***Leaves*** Divided, with toothed, lance-shaped leaflets. Rich green.
- NATIVE HABITAT Damp grass and woodland in western Europe.
- CULTIVATION Grow in moist soil in a sunny or partially shaded site. Suitable for growing in a woodland or wild garden.
- PROPAGATION By seed in an open frame in spring, or by division in spring or autumn.

Z5–9

HEIGHT 4–6ft (1.2–2m)

SPREAD 16–32in (40–80cm)

Lythraceae	HENNA

LAWSONIA INERMIS

Habit Open, usually spiny shrub or small tree. ***Flowers*** Tiny, fragrant, borne in pyramidal clusters in summer. White, red, or pink. ***Leaves*** Narrowly oval. Mid- to dark green.
- NATIVE HABITAT Tropical forests in N. Africa, southwest Asia, and northern Australia.
- CULTIVATION Grow in fertile, well-drained soil in full sun. In cooler areas, grow under glass.
- PROPAGATION By seed in spring at 64–70°F (18–21°C), or by hardwood cuttings in autumn.
- OTHER NAME *L. alba*.

Min. 55°F (13°C)

HEIGHT 10–20ft (3–6m)

SPREAD to 12ft (4m)

LARGE • 41

| Verbenaceae | LEMON VERBENA |

ALOYSIA TRIPHYLLA

Habit Bushy, upright, deciduous shrub. **Flowers** Tiny, borne in slender sprays in late summer. White or pale lilac. **Leaves** Lemon-scented, lance-shaped, borne in whorls. Bright green.
• NATIVE HABITAT Rocks in Chile and Argentina.
• CULTIVATION Grow in light, well-drained soil in a warm, sunny, sheltered site. Good for containers outdoors, but overwinter under glass in cool areas.
• PROPAGATION By heeled softwood or greenwood cuttings taken in summer.
• OTHER NAMES *A. citriodora*, *Lippia citriodora*.

Z9

HEIGHT
to 10ft (3m)

SPREAD
10ft (3m)

| Fabaceae | GOAT'S RUE |

GALEGA OFFICINALIS

Habit Vigorous, clump-forming perennial. **Flowers** Pealike, borne in long, slender spikes during summer. Lilac-pink. **Leaves** Divided, with lance-shaped, oblong or oval leaflets. Soft green.
• NATIVE HABITAT Damp meadows, from Europe to Turkey and Pakistan.
• CULTIVATION Grow in moist, fertile soil, in sun or partial shade. Provide light support with pea sticks.
• PROPAGATION By pre-soaked seed sown in a cold frame in spring, or by division between autumn and spring.

Z3–9

HEIGHT
1–5ft
(0.3–1.5m)

SPREAD
36in (90cm)

| Malvaceae | MARSH MALLOW |

ALTHAEA OFFICINALIS

Habit Upright, strong-stemmed perennial. **Flowers** Solitary or in small clusters, 5-petaled, borne from summer to autumn. Pale pink. **Leaves** Velvet-haired, shallowly lobed. Mid-green.
• NATIVE HABITAT Damp coastal sites in Europe.
• CULTIVATION Prefers fertile, moist but well-drained soil in full sun, but tolerates a wide range of soils and conditions. Suitable for growing in borders or at pond margins.
• PROPAGATION Sow seed in drills in mid-summer, or divide in autumn. Self-sows freely.

Z3–9

HEIGHT
to 6ft (2m)

SPREAD
to 5ft
(1.5m)

| Caprifoliaceae | BRONZE ELDER |

SAMBUCUS NIGRA 'Guincho Purple'

Habit Vigorous, bushy shrub. **Flowers** Small, borne in flat sprays in early summer. Creamy white with pink stamens. **Leaves** Divided, with toothed, oval leaflets. Purple-bronze. **Fruits** Round berries. Black-purple.
• NATIVE HABITAT Garden origin.
• CULTIVATION Prefers moist but well-drained soil in dappled shade, but tolerant of most soil types.
• PROPAGATION By softwood cuttings taken in summer, or hardwood cuttings taken in winter.
• WARNING Leaves or raw berries harmful if eaten.

Z5–9

HEIGHT
to 20ft (6m)

SPREAD
to 20ft (6m)

| Boraginaceae | COMFREY, KNITBONE |

SYMPHYTUM OFFICINALE
Habit Vigorous, rhizomatous perennial. **Flowers** Drooping, borne in forked heads from late spring to summer. Pink, violet, or pale yellow. **Leaves** Bristly, oval to lance-shaped. Mid- to dark green.
- NATIVE HABITAT Europe and western Asia.
- CULTIVATION Grow in any moist soil in a sunny or partially shaded site.
- PROPAGATION Sow seed in autumn or spring, divide in spring, or take root cuttings in winter.
- WARNING Leaves and roots are harmful if eaten. Contact with foliage may irritate skin.

Z4–9

Height 5ft (1.5m)

Spread 6ft (2m)

| Rosaceae | EGLANTINE, SWEET BRIAR |

ROSA EGLANTERIA
Habit Sturdy, arching, prickly shrub. **Flowers** Single, cupped, borne in mid-summer. Rose-pink. **Leaves** Apple-scented, with 5–9 leaflets. Dark green. **Fruits** Egg-shaped to rounded hips. Red.
- NATIVE HABITAT Hedgerows and woodland margins in Europe, N. Africa, and Asia.
- CULTIVATION Grow in fertile, moist but well-drained, neutral to alkaline soil in sun.
- PROPAGATION By seed in autumn in an open frame, or by hardwood cuttings in late autumn.
- OTHER NAME *R. rubiginosa*.

Z5–8

Height 8ft (2.5m)

Spread 8ft (2.5m)

| Malvaceae | HOLLYHOCK |

ALCEA ROSEA
Habit Upright perennial, usually treated as a biennial. **Flowers** Funnel-shaped, borne in early to mid-summer. Purple, pink, white, or yellow. **Leaves** Coarse-haired, shallow-lobed. Light green.
- NATIVE HABITAT Possibly western Asia.
- CULTIVATION Grow in well-drained soil in full sun. Support the plant with stakes in exposed sites. Good for growing in a mixed or herbaceous border.
- PROPAGATION By seed *in situ* in mid-summer, or in containers at 55°F (13°C) in early spring.
- OTHER NAME *Althaea rosea*.

Z2–9

Height to 8ft (2.5m)

Spread 24in (60cm)

| Asteraceae | JOE PYE WEED |

EUPATORIUM PURPUREUM
Habit Clump-forming perennial.
Flowers Tiny, borne in domed sprays, in summer and early autumn. Creamy white, pink, or pink-purple. **Leaves** Lance-shaped to oval, coarse. Dark green, tinted purple.
• NATIVE HABITAT Damp thickets and grassland in eastern US.
• CULTIVATION Grow in any moist soil in a sunny or partially shaded site.
• PROPAGATION By seed sown in spring in a cold frame, or by division in autumn or spring.

☼ ◊

Z3–10

HEIGHT
7ft (2.2m)

SPREAD
36in (90cm)

| Rosaceae | RAMANAS ROSE, JAPANESE ROSE |

ROSA RUGOSA
Habit Dense, vigorous shrub. **Flowers** Single, fragrant, cupped, borne from summer to autumn. Magenta-red. **Leaves** Divided into wrinkled leaflets. Bright green. **Fruits** Large hips. Scarlet.
• NATIVE HABITAT Scrubland and woodland edges in Russia, N. China, Korea, and Japan.
• CULTIVATION Grow in fertile, moist but well-drained soil that is neutral to slightly acidic and enriched with organic matter. Ideal for hedging.
• PROPAGATION By seed in autumn in an open frame, or by hardwood cuttings in late autumn.

☼ ◊

Z2–8

HEIGHT
3–8ft
(0.9–2.5m)

SPREAD
8ft (2.5m)

| Phytolaccaceae | POKEWEED, POKEROOT |

PHYTOLACCA AMERICANA
Habit Fleshy-stemmed perennial.
Flowers Small, star-shaped, borne in long spikes in summer. White or pink. **Leaves** Oval. Mid-green. **Fruits** Rounded, glossy. Black-maroon.
• NATIVE HABITAT Woods in eastern N. America.
• CULTIVATION Grow in moist soil in a sunny or partially shaded site.
• PROPAGATION By seed in early spring at 55–64°F (13–18°C).
• OTHER NAME *P. decandra*.
• WARNING All parts of the plant are toxic if eaten.

☼ ◊

Z3–9

HEIGHT
to 12ft (4m)

SPREAD
4–8ft
(1.2–2.5m)

| Punicaceae | POMEGRANATE |

PUNICA GRANATUM

Habit Upright, often spiny shrub or small, round-headed tree. **Flowers** Funnel-shaped, borne solitary or in clusters of up to 5, in summer. Bright orange-red. **Leaves** Narrowly oblong, glossy. Bright green, with coppery-red veins when young. **Fruits** Edible, round, leathery. Golden-yellow to yellow-brown, with pink-red pulp.
• NATIVE HABITAT Scrubland from southeast Europe to the Himalayas.
• CULTIVATION Grow in fertile, well-drained soil in full sun. Pomegranates need long hot summers to ripen fruit. In areas where the growing season is short and winters are cold, grow under glass. Use a soil-based potting mix. Admit full light, water freely, and apply a balanced liquid fertilizer monthly when in full growth. In autumn, provide a minimum temperature of 55–64°F (13–18°C) to ripen fruit. Water sparingly in winter.
• PROPAGATION By semi-ripe cuttings taken in summer, by hardwood cuttings taken in autumn, or by root suckers removed in autumn. Sow seed in spring at 72°F (22°C).

☼ ◊

Z7–10

HEIGHT
20ft (6m)

SPREAD
15ft (5m)

LARGE • 45

| Scrophulariaceae | CULVER'S ROOT, BLACKROOT |

VERONICASTRUM VIRGINICUM
Habit Clump-forming perennial. **Flowers** Tiny, borne in slender spikes from mid-summer to early autumn. White, pink, or blue. **Leaves** Lance-shaped, toothed, pointed, in whorls. Dark green.
• NATIVE HABITAT Meadows in N. America.
• CULTIVATION Grow in moderately fertile, moist but well-drained soil rich in organic matter, in sun or part shade. Suits mixed or herbaceous borders.
• PROPAGATION Sow seed in autumn in a cold frame, or divide in spring.
• OTHER NAME *Veronica virginica*.

Z3–9

HEIGHT
to 6ft (2m)

SPREAD
18in (45cm)

| Fabaceae | LICORICE, SWEETWOOD |

GLYCYRRHIZA GLABRA
Habit Taprooted perennial. **Flowers** Small, pealike, borne in spikes in summer. Blue, pale violet, or white. **Leaves** Divided. Mid-green.
• NATIVE HABITAT From the Mediterranean to southwest Asia.
• CULTIVATION Grow in deep, fertile, moist but well-drained soil that is neutral to alkaline, in full sun.
• PROPAGATION Divide in early spring, or sow seed in an open frame in autumn or spring.
• OTHER NAME *G. glandulifera*.

Z7–9

HEIGHT
4ft (1.2m)

SPREAD
36in (90cm)

| Verbenaceae | CHASTE TREE, AGNUS CASTUS |

VITEX AGNUS-CASTUS
Habit Spreading, slender-stemmed shrub. **Flowers** Scented, tubular, borne in slender spikes during early autumn. Lilac- to dark blue. **Leaves** Aromatic, narrowly oval, pointed. Dark green.
• NATIVE HABITAT Scrub and woodland from the Mediterranean to central Asia.
• CULTIVATION Grow in well-drained soil in full sun in a warm site. Shelter from cold, dry winds.
• PROPAGATION By seed in autumn or spring, or by semi-ripe cuttings taken in summer.

Z7–10

HEIGHT
6–25ft
(2–8m)

SPREAD
6–25ft
(2–8m)

Lamiaceae	ROUND-LEAVED MINT BUSH

PROSTANTHERA ROTUNDIFOLIA

Habit Spreading, hoary-stemmed shrub.
Flowers Small, bell-shaped, borne in short spikes from late spring to early summer. Lilac-purple.
Leaves Small, evergreen, rounded to oval. Dark green.
- NATIVE HABITAT Heathland, southeast Australia.
- CULTIVATION Grow in very well-drained, moderately fertile soil, in a warm sheltered site in full sun. Dried leaves may be used in potpourri.
- PROPAGATION By seed in spring at 13–18°C (55–64°F), or by semi-ripe cuttings in summer.

Z9–10

HEIGHT
6–12ft
(2–4m)

SPREAD
3–10ft
(0.9–3m)

Asteraceae	BURDOCK, LAPPA, BEGGAR'S BUTTONS

ARCTIUM LAPPA

Habit Vigorous, taprooted biennial.
Flowers Thistlelike, borne in summer. Purple. *Leaves* Coarse, oval. Mid-green.
Fruits Rounded, with hooked spines. Pale brown.
- NATIVE HABITAT Rough ground in Europe and western Asia.
- CULTIVATION Grow in moist, neutral to alkaline soil in sun or part shade. Tends to be invasive, but suitable for growing in wild gardens.
- PROPAGATION Sow seed *in situ* in spring. Self-seeds freely.

Z2–10

HEIGHT
5ft (1.5m)

SPREAD
36in (90cm)

Boraginaceae	RUSSIAN COMFREY

SYMPHYTUM × UPLANDICUM

Habit Bristly perennial. *Flowers* Tubular, borne in heads from late spring to summer. Blue-purple.
Leaves Coarse, oblong to oval. Mid-green.
- NATIVE HABITAT Garden origin.
- CULTIVATION Grow in any moist soil in sun or part shade. Slightly less invasive than *S. officinale*.
- PROPAGATION Divide in spring, or take root cuttings in winter.
- OTHER NAME *S. peregrinum* of gardens.
- WARNING Leaves and roots harmful if eaten. Contact with foliage may irritate skin.

Z4–9

HEIGHT
to 6ft (2m)

SPREAD
4ft (1.2m)

Asteraceae	GLOBE ARTICHOKE

CYNARA CARDUNCULUS
Scolymus Group

Habit Robust, clump-forming perennial.
Flowers Thistlelike, with fleshy, edible bracts, borne in late summer and early autumn. Purple.
Leaves Deeply lobed. Gray-green.
- NATIVE HABITAT Origin unknown.
- CULTIVATION Grow in fertile, well-drained soil in a warm, sheltered site in sun.
- PROPAGATION Sow seed in a cold frame, divide suckers in spring, or take root cuttings in winter.
- OTHER NAME *C. scolymus*.

Z9

HEIGHT
6ft (2m)

SPREAD
6ft (2m)

Euphorbiaceae

RICINUS COMMUNIS 'Carmencita'

Habit Upright, well-branched shrub, usually grown as an annual in most areas.
Flowers Female are small, cup-shaped, and borne in spikes in summer. Bright red. Male are borne in clusters. Greenish yellow.
Leaves Very broadly oval, deeply lobed, glossy. Dark red-bronze. *Fruits* Egg-shaped, prickly capsules, with shiny, cream-mottled seeds.
• NATIVE HABITAT Garden origin.
• CULTIVATION Grow in fertile, moist but well-drained soil in a warm, sheltered site, in full sun.
Provide support. Suitable for growing as a statuesque specimen in tropical bedding designs.
• PROPAGATION Sow presoaked seed in spring at 70°F (21°C). Sow seeds individually in 3½in (9cm) pots. Transplant the seedlings just before roots spread and fill the pots, since they may flower prematurely if pot-bound. Plant out when all danger of frost has passed.
• WARNING All parts of the plant, especially the seeds, are extremely toxic if eaten. Contact with foliage or seeds may irritate skin.

Z9–10

Height
6–10ft
(2–3m)

Spread
36in (90cm)

ROSMARINUS

The genus *Rosmarinus* consists of two species of evergreen shrubs, which are native to dry scrub, rocky places, and open woodlands around the Mediterranean. They have strongly aromatic, leathery, linear leaves, which are usually dark green above and white-felted beneath. Short heads of tubular, 2-lipped flowers are borne in the leaf axils from mid-spring through to early summer.

Commonly known as rosemary, this plant is grown as an ornamental in borders or containers; upright types are also used for hedging in mild areas. Use prostrate cultivars on dry, sunny banks, the tops of retaining walls, and in containers.

In the herb garden, rosemary is grown for culinary use with meat (especially lamb) and is also used in oil or vinegar to flavor sauces and dressings. Extracts of rosemary have medicinal uses and are used in hair, skin, and bath preparations.

Grow in well-drained, neutral to alkaline soil that is not too rich in nitrogen. Site plants in full sun, with shelter from cold winds. Trim annually after flowering, but avoid cutting into old wood. All rosemaries dislike the combination of cold with winter moisture, but many survive temperatures to 14°F (-10°C) given good drainage. Cultivars such as *R. officinalis* 'Majorca Pink', Prostratus Group, and 'Tuscan Blue' are more tender. In cold areas, they may be grown in a container and overwintered in a frost-free greenhouse.

Harvest sprigs for culinary use, fresh or air-dried, in the growing season. Gather leaves and flowers in spring and early summer, and use fresh for oil extraction or dried for infusions and tinctures.

Sow seed of species in a cold frame or greenhouse in spring; cultivars do not come true. Semi-ripe cuttings may be taken during summer.

R. OFFICINALIS var. ALBIFLORUS
Habit Dense, bushy, erect or rounded shrub.
Flowers Tubular, 2-lipped, borne in spring and early summer. White.
Leaves Linear, leathery. Dark green.
• TIPS Suitable for floral arrangements or white-themed borders.
• HEIGHT to 6ft (2m).
• SPREAD 5–6ft (1.5–2m).

R. officinalis var. *albiflorus*
☼ ◊ Z8–10

R. OFFICINALIS 'Roseus'
Habit Dense, bushy, erect or rounded shrub.
Flowers Tubular, 2-lipped, borne in spring and early summer. Pink.
Leaves Linear, leathery. Rich green.
• TIPS Good for growing in herb and mixed borders, or for hedging.
• HEIGHT to 6ft (2m).
• SPREAD 5–6ft (1.5–2m).

R. officinalis 'Roseus'
☼ ◊ Z8–10

R. OFFICINALIS 'Majorca Pink'
Habit Columnar, arching shrub.
Flowers Tubular, 2-lipped, borne in spring and early summer. Soft mauve-pink.
Leaves Linear, leathery. Rich green.
• TIPS Ideal as a focal point, especially in pots.
• HEIGHT 4ft (1.2m).
• SPREAD 12–24in (30–60cm).

R. officinalis 'Majorca Pink'
☼ ◊ Z8–10

R. OFFICINALIS Prostratus Group
Habit Dense, spreading, prostrate shrub.
Flowers Tubular, 2-lipped, borne in spring and summer. Pale blue.
Leaves Broadly linear, leathery. Dark green.
• TIPS Ideal for clothing a dry, sunny bank.
• HEIGHT 6–12in (15–30cm).
• SPREAD to 36in (90cm).

R. officinalis Prostratus Group
Creeping rosemary
☼ ◊ Z8–10

R. OFFICINALIS 'McConnell's Blue'
Habit Dense, spreading, prostrate shrub.
Flowers Tubular, 2-lipped, borne in spring and early summer. Clear blue.
Leaves Broadly linear, leathery. Dark green.
• TIPS Ideal for clothing a dry, sunny bank.
• HEIGHT 12–16in (30–40cm).
• SPREAD 36in (90cm).

R. officinalis 'McConnell's Blue'
☼ ◊ Z8–10

R. OFFICINALIS 'Sissinghurst Blue'
Habit Dense, bushy, upright shrub.
Flowers Tubular, 2-lipped, borne freely in spring and early summer. Clear blue.
Leaves Linear, leathery. Dark green.
• TIPS Good for use as low hedging and in mixed borders.
• HEIGHT to 4ft (1.2m).
• SPREAD 36in (90cm).

R. officinalis 'Sissinghurst Blue'
☼ ◊ Z8–10

R. OFFICINALIS 'Tuscan Blue'
Habit Vigorous, upright shrub, with reddish brown stems.
Flowers Tubular, borne in spring and early summer. Dark blue.
Leaves Linear, leathery, glossy. Bright green.
• TIPS Ideal for large tubs or pots, especially if used as a focal point.
• HEIGHT 3–6ft (0.9–2m).
• SPREAD 3–6ft (0.9–2m).

R. officinalis 'Tuscan Blue'
☼ ◊ Z8–10

R. OFFICINALIS 'Miss Jessopp's Upright'
Habit Dense, bushy, strongly upright shrub.
Flowers Tubular, 2-lipped, borne in spring and early summer. Pale blue.
Leaves Linear, leathery. Dark green.
• OTHER NAME *R. o.* 'Fastigiatus'.
• HEIGHT to 6ft (2m).
• SPREAD 5–6ft (1.5–2m).

R. officinalis 'Miss Jessopp's Upright'
☼ ◊ Z8–10

R. OFFICINALIS 'Severn Sea'
Habit Dense, spreading, arching shrub.
Flowers Tubular, 2-lipped, borne in spring and early summer. Violet-blue.
Leaves Linear, leathery. Dark green.
• TIPS Good for growing in containers or on the top of a retaining wall.
• HEIGHT 36in (90cm).
• SPREAD 36in (90cm).

R. officinalis 'Severn Sea'
☼ ◊ Z8–10

R. OFFICINALIS
Habit Dense, bushy, erect or rounded shrub.
Flowers Tubular, 2-lipped, borne in spring and early summer. Pale to deep purple-blue to white.
Leaves Linear, leathery. Dark green.
• TIPS Good for hedging or in mixed borders.
• HEIGHT to 6ft (2m).
• SPREAD 5–6ft (1.5–2m).

R. officinalis
Rosemary
☼ ◊ Z8–10

R. OFFICINALIS 'Primley Blue'
Habit Dense, bushy, upright shrub.
Flowers Tubular, 2-lipped, borne in spring and early summer. Clear blue.
Leaves Linear, leathery. Dark green.
• TIPS Good for low hedging, and adds color to a mixed border.
• HEIGHT 36in (90cm).
• SPREAD 24in (60cm).

R. officinalis 'Primley Blue'
☼ ◊ Z8–10

R. OFFICINALIS 'Benenden Blue'
Habit Bushy, compact, trailing shrub.
Flowers Tubular, borne in dense whorls in spring and early summer. Deep blue.
Leaves Narrowly linear, leathery, and glossy. Dark green.
• OTHER NAME *R. o.* 'Collingwood Ingram'.
• HEIGHT 36in (90cm).
• SPREAD 36in (90cm).

R. officinalis 'Benenden Blue'
☼ ◊ Z8–10

R. OFFICINALIS 'Aureus'
Habit Bushy shrub.
Flowers Tubular, borne in spring and early summer. Purple-blue.
Leaves Linear, leathery. Dark green, with yellow variegation.
• OTHER NAMES *R. o.* 'Gilded', *R. o.* 'Aureovariegatus'.
• HEIGHT to 6ft (2m).
• SPREAD 5–6ft (1.5–2m).

R. officinalis 'Aureus'
☼ ◊ Z8–10

| Myrtaceae | TASMANIAN BLUE GUM, BLUE GUM |

Eucalyptus globulus

Habit Spreading tree. **Flowers** Small, solitary, borne in summer. White to cream. **Leaves** Evergreen, oval to sickle-shaped. Pale blue-white, maturing to deep green.
• NATIVE HABITAT Australia and Tasmania.
• CULTIVATION Grow in moisture-retentive soil that is neutral to slightly acidic, in a sunny site. Provide shelter from cold, dry winds. Young plants are suitable for use as summer bedding.
• PROPAGATION By seed sown at 70°F (21°C) in spring.

Z9–10

Height
50–160ft
(15–50m)

Spread
30–80ft
(10–25m)

| Rutaceae | CURRY LEAF |

Murraya koenigii

Habit Bushy shrub. **Flowers** Fragrant, borne in clusters in summer. White. **Leaves** Evergreen, pinnate. Mid-green. **Fruits** Small, pepper-flavored berries. Black.
• NATIVE HABITAT India, Pakistan, and Sri Lanka.
• CULTIVATION Grow in sun or part shade with high humidity. In cold areas, grow under glass in soil-based potting mix. Water freely and feed monthly. Water sparingly during winter.
• PROPAGATION Sow seed in spring at 70°F (21°C), or take semi-ripe cuttings in summer.

Min.
59–64°F
(15–18°C)

Height
20ft (6m)

Spread
to 15ft (5m)

| Myrtaceae | VARIEGATED MYRTLE |

Myrtus communis 'Variegata'

Habit Bushy, upright shrub. **Flowers** Fragrant, solitary, 5-petaled, with conspicuous stamens, borne from mid-summer to autumn. White. **Leaves** Aromatic, evergreen, oval, glossy. Dark green, with creamy white margins.
• NATIVE HABITAT Garden origin.
• CULTIVATION Grow in moist but well-drained, neutral to alkaline soil in a warm, sunny, sheltered site. Suitable for growing in containers outdoors, but overwinter under glass in cold areas.
• PROPAGATION By semi-ripe cuttings in summer.

Z9–10

Height
to 10ft (3m)

Spread
to 10ft (3m)

52 • LARGE

| Ginkgoaceae | MAIDENHAIR TREE |

Ginkgo biloba

Habit Upright, tall and narrow to spreading tree.
Flowers Borne in summer. Male: catkinlike, drooping, in clusters. Yellow. Female: tiny, rounded, solitary. Yellow. ***Leaves*** Deciduous, fan-shaped, produced alternately on long shoots, clustered on spur shoots. Rich bright green, aging to yellow. ***Fruits*** Borne on female plant, fetid-smelling upon decay, plumlike, with edible nuts within. Yellow-green.
• NATIVE HABITAT Originally from southern China, it is now rare in the wild but widely cultivated as a specimen tree in parks and gardens in China and other parts of the world.
• CULTIVATION Grow in fertile, moist but well-drained soil in full sun. Tolerant of atmospheric pollution. Male and female trees must be grown in proximity for fruits to be produced. The fruits only set and ripen well in regions that enjoy long, hot summers. Avoid pruning causes the tree to die back.
• PROPAGATION By seed in an open frame when ripe, or by semi-ripe cuttings taken in summer.

Z3–9

Height
to 130ft
(40m)

Spread
to 25ft (8m)

LARGE • 53

Rhamnaceae	ALDER BUCKTHORN

Rhamnus frangula
Habit Spreading, bushy shrub. *Flowers* Tiny, cup-shaped, borne in late spring and early summer. Green. *Leaves* Oval, glossy. Dark green. *Fruits* Round, fleshy. Red, ripening to black.
- NATIVE HABITAT Damp woods in Europe, N. Africa, Russia, and Altai mountains.
- CULTIVATION Grow in moist, moderately fertile soil that is neutral to acidic, in a sunny site.
- PROPAGATION Sow seed in autumn, or take greenwood cuttings in early summer.
- WARNING All parts of the plant harmful if eaten.

Z2–9

HEIGHT
15ft (5m)

SPREAD
15ft (5m)

Apiaceae	LOVAGE

Levisticum officinale
Habit Vigorous perennial. *Flowers* Tiny, star-shaped, borne in flat-topped clusters in mid-summer. Yellow-green. *Leaves* Divided, triangular to diamond-shaped segments. Dark green.
- NATIVE HABITAT Mountains in the eastern Mediterranean.
- CULTIVATION Prefers fertile, moist, well-drained soil in sun, but tolerates a range of conditions.
- PROPAGATION Sow seed in a seed bed when ripe, or divide in spring.
- WARNING Contact with foliage may irritate skin.

Z5–8

HEIGHT
6ft (2m)

SPREAD
36in (90cm)

Monimiaceae	BOLDO

Peumus boldus
Habit Bushy, shrubby tree. *Flowers* Scented, small, male and female borne on separate plants in late summer. Pale green. *Leaves* Lemon-camphor-scented, evergreen, oval, leathery, glossy. Dark green. *Fruits* Fleshy drupes. Yellow.
- NATIVE HABITAT Mountain foothills in Chile.
- CULTIVATION Grow in moist but well-drained, sandy, acidic soil in sun. Provide shelter from cold, dry winds.
- PROPAGATION By seed in spring at 55°F (13°C), or by semi-ripe cuttings taken in summer.

Z9–10

HEIGHT
22ft (7m)

SPREAD
15ft (5m)

54 • LARGE

Euphorbiaceae	CASTOR BEAN

RICINUS COMMUNIS
Habit Upright shrub, usually grown as an annual.
Flowers Small, petalless, borne in summer. Male: greenish yellow. Female: beardlike globes. Red.
Leaves Lobed. Green, often tinted red or bronze.
• NATIVE HABITAT Stony slopes in N. Africa and western Asia.
• CULTIVATION Grow in fertile, moist but well-drained soil in full sun, in a warm, sheltered site.
• PROPAGATION Sow pre-soaked seed in spring at 70°F (21°C).
• WARNING All parts of the plant are toxic if eaten.

Z9–10

HEIGHT
6ft (1.8m)

SPREAD
36in (90cm)

Polygonaceae	CHINESE RHUBARB

RHEUM PALMATUM
Habit Rhizomatous perennial. ***Flowers*** Tiny, star-shaped, borne in massive clusters in early summer. Pale green to deep red. ***Leaves*** Divided into 3 to 9 lobes, toothed. Dark green.
• NATIVE HABITAT Northwest China and northeastern Tibet.
• CULTIVATION Grow in deep, moist but well-drained, fertile soil in sun or light, dappled shade.
• PROPAGATION Divide in early spring, or sow seed in a cold frame in autumn.
• WARNING Leaves are harmful if eaten.

Z5–8

HEIGHT
to 8ft (2.5m)

SPREAD
to 6ft (1.8m)

Lamiaceae	MOTHERWORT

LEONURUS CARDIACA
Habit Strong-smelling, downy perennial.
Flowers Tubular, 2-lipped, borne in whorls in late summer. Pink to off-white. ***Leaves*** Divided into 3 to 7 lobes. Mid-green, white-downy beneath.
• NATIVE HABITAT Wasteland from Europe to Russia.
• CULTIVATION Grow in moist but well-drained soil in sun or part shade. Suitable for growing as a foliage plant in a mixed border or herb garden.
• PROPAGATION Sow seed in a cold frame in spring, or divide in spring or autumn.

Z4–8

HEIGHT
4ft (1.2m)

SPREAD
24in (60cm)

| Zingiberaceae | CARDAMOM |

ELETTARIA CARDAMOMUM

Habit Erect, rhizomatous perennial. ***Flowers*** Tri-petaled, borne in summer. White, with violet veins and yellow- or lilac-marked lips. ***Leaves*** Linear to lance-shaped, evergreen. Dark green. ***Fruits*** Papery, with aromatic seeds. Pale green.
• NATIVE HABITAT Tropical rainforest in India.
• CULTIVATION Grow in fertile, moist but well-drained soil in part shade. Under glass, use soil-based potting mix with leafmold.
• PROPAGATION Divide in spring, or sow seed at 66–75°F (19–24°C) as soon as ripe.

Min. 50°F (10°C)

HEIGHT to 10ft (3m)

SPREAD to 10ft (3m)

| Zingiberaceae | GALANGAL, SIAMESE GINGER |

ALPINIA GALANGA

Habit Rhizomatous perennial. ***Flowers*** Tri-petaled, borne all year. Pale green, with white lips. ***Leaves*** Evergreen, lance-shaped. Dark green.
• NATIVE HABITAT Tropical rainforest in Asia.
• CULTIVATION Grow in fertile, moist but well-drained soil in part shade. Under glass, grow in soil-based potting mix with leafmold and ground bark in a greenhouse bed. Water freely and maintain high humidity during growth, but water moderately in winter.
• PROPAGATION By division in spring.

Min. 61°F (16°C)

HEIGHT to 6ft (2m)

SPREAD indefinite

| Zingiberaceae | GINGER |

ZINGIBER OFFICINALE

Habit Rhizomatous perennial. ***Flowers*** Tri-petaled, borne in summer. Yellow-green, with deep purple, yellow-marked lips. ***Leaves*** Lance-shaped, on erect stems. Fresh green. ***Fruits*** Fleshy, 3-valved capsules. Rarely produced.
• NATIVE HABITAT Tropical rainforest in Asia.
• CULTIVATION Grow in fertile, moist but well-drained soil that is neutral to alkaline, in sun or part shade. Needs a ten-month growing season. Grow under glass in cooler areas.
• PROPAGATION Divide in late spring.

Min. 30°F (-1°C)

HEIGHT 5ft (1.5m)

SPREAD indefinite

| Poaceae | LEMON GRASS |

CYMBOPOGON CITRATUS

Habit Clump-forming perennial grass with cane-like stems. ***Flowers*** Tiny spikelets, borne in loose clusters in summer. ***Leaves*** Lemon-scented, evergreen, linear. Dark green.
• NATIVE HABITAT Grassland, Sri Lanka and India.
• CULTIVATION Grow in fertile, moist but well-drained soil in sun. Under glass, use soil-based potting mix and admit full light. Water freely in growth. Flowers rarely borne under glass.
• PROPAGATION Divide in late spring, or sow seed at 64°F (18°C) in early spring.

Min. 45°F (7°C)

HEIGHT to 5ft (1.5m)

SPREAD 36in (90cm)

| Apiaceae | BRONZE FENNEL |

FOENICULUM VULGARE 'Purpureum'

Habit Robust, deep-rooted perennial. **Flowers** Tiny, borne in flattened clusters in mid-summer. Yellow. **Leaves** Aromatic, finely cut into hairlike segments. Bronze-purple, maturing to glaucous dark green. **Fruits** Aromatic seeds. Gray-brown.
- NATIVE HABITAT Garden origin.
- CULTIVATION Grow in fertile, moist but well-drained soil in sun. Suitable for using as foliage contrast in a mixed or herbaceous border.
- PROPAGATION Sow seed *in situ* in spring, or transplant self-sown seedlings. Self-sows freely.

Z4–9

HEIGHT
to 2m (6ft)

SPREAD
45cm (18in)

| Apiaceae | ANGELICA |

ANGELICA ARCHANGELICA

Habit Perennial, usually grown as a biennial; dies after flowering. **Flowers** Tiny, borne in rounded clusters in early and mid-summer. Yellow-green. **Leaves** Diamond-shaped, divided. Mid-green.
- NATIVE HABITAT Damp, grassy sites in northern Europe.
- CULTIVATION Grow in deep, fertile, moist soil in sun or part shade. Removing flowerheads before the seed develops may prolong life of the plant.
- PROPAGATION Surface-sow seed *in situ* as soon as ripe or in spring.

Z4–9

HEIGHT
3–8ft
(0.9–2.5m)

SPREAD
4ft (1.2m)

| Apiaceae | ASAFOETIDA, DEVIL'S DUNG |

FERULA ASSA-FOETIDA

Habit Robust, malodorous perennial; dies after flowering. **Flowers** Tiny, borne in clusters in summer. Yellow. **Leaves** Ill-smelling, divided. Dark green. **Fruits** Small seeds. Pale brown.
- NATIVE HABITAT Rocky and coastal sites in Iran.
- CULTIVATION Grow in fertile, well-drained soil in sun. Flowers after several years and then usually dies. Removing flowerheads before the seed is set may prolong life of the plant.
- PROPAGATION Sow seed *in situ* when ripe in late summer.

Z7–9

HEIGHT
6ft (2m)

SPREAD
5ft (1.5m)

Apiaceae	FENNEL

FOENICULUM VULGARE

Habit Robust, deep-rooted perennial.
Flowers Tiny, borne in flattened clusters in mid-summer. Yellow. ***Leaves*** Aromatic, feathery, with hairlike leaflets. Mid-green.
Fruits Aromatic seeds. Gray-brown.
• NATIVE HABITAT Waste ground, often in coastal sites, in southern Europe and Asia.
• CULTIVATION Grow in fertile, moist but well-drained soil in sun.
• PROPAGATION Sow seed *in situ* in spring, or transplant self-sown seedlings. Self-sows freely.

Z4–10

HEIGHT
to 6ft (2m)

SPREAD
18in (45cm)

Rutaceae	HOP TREE, WATER ASH

PTELEA TRIFOLIATA

Habit Bushy, upright shrub, with aromatic bark.
Flowers Star-shaped, borne in heads in summer. Greenish white. ***Leaves*** Deciduous, 3-lobed. Dark green. ***Fruits*** Winged, rounded. Pale green.
• NATIVE HABITAT Thickets and rocky sites in N. America.
• CULTIVATION Grow in moist but well-drained soil in sun or light, dappled shade.
• PROPAGATION Sow seed in an open frame in autumn or spring, or take greenwood cuttings in early summer.

Z4–10

HEIGHT
25ft (8m)

SPREAD
12ft (4m)

Anacardiaceae	LENTISC, MASTIC TREE

PISTACIA LENTISCUS

Habit Aromatic shrub or small, bushy tree.
Flowers Small, borne in clusters in spring or early summer. Green, with red stamens on male. ***Leaves*** Divided, glossy. Dark green.
Fruits Small, round. Red, ripening to black.
• NATIVE HABITAT Dry sites in southern Europe.
• CULTIVATION Grow in well-drained, even stony, alkaline soil in sun. Under glass, use soil-based potting mix with added sharp sand.
• PROPAGATION By seed sown in spring, or by semi-ripe cuttings taken in summer.

Z9–10

HEIGHT
3–10ft
(0.9–3m)

SPREAD
3–10ft
(0.9–3m)

| Cupressaceae | COMMON JUNIPER |

JUNIPERUS COMMUNIS
Habit Spreading shrub or small, narrow tree.
Flowers Insignificant. **Leaves** Scented, evergreen, needlelike, borne in threes. Dark to blue-green.
Fruits Egg-shaped to round. Green, ripening through glaucous blue to black in the third year.
• NATIVE HABITAT Moors, heathland, scrubland, and conifer woods in the northern hemisphere.
• CULTIVATION Grow in almost any but water-logged soil, in a sunny or partially shaded site.
• PROPAGATION By ripewood cuttings in autumn.
• WARNING Contact with foliage may irritate skin.

Z2–8

HEIGHT
6–12ft
(2–4m)

SPREAD
to 12ft (4m)

| Caricaceae | PAPAYA |

CARICA PAPAYA
Habit Short-lived, round-headed tree. **Flowers** Saucer-shaped, borne in leaf axils or on trunk all year round. White, yellow, or green. **Leaves** Divided, 7-lobed. Dark green. **Fruits** Large, pear-shaped. Yellow-green, with apricot-coloured flesh.
• NATIVE HABITAT Tropical forest in S. America.
• CULTIVATION Grow in moist, fertile soil, in sun. In cold areas, grow under glass in soil-based potting mix. Water freely in growth.
• PROPAGATION By seed in spring at 75–86°F (24–30°C).

Min. 55°F
(13°C)

HEIGHT
to 20ft (6m)

SPREAD
10ft (3m)

| Moraceae | COMMON FIG |

FICUS CARICA
Habit Shrub or small tree with a spreading crown.
Flowers Insignificant. **Leaves** Rounded, 3- to 5-lobed. Mid-green. **Fruits** Pear-shaped. Pale green, ripening to dark green, purple, or brown.
• NATIVE HABITAT Eastern Mediterranean and western Asia.
• CULTIVATION Grow in fertile well-drained soil that is neutral to alkaline, in sun.
• PROPAGATION By hardwood cuttings in autumn, or by semi-ripe cuttings or layering in summer.
• WARNING Contact with foliage may irritate skin.

Z7–10

HEIGHT
10ft (3m)
or more

SPREAD
12ft (4m)

Oleaceae	OLIVE

OLEA EUROPAEA

Habit Slow-growing, round-headed tree.
Flowers Tiny, fragrant, borne in axillary sprays in summer. Creamy white. **Leaves** Evergreen, leathery, oval to lance-shaped. Gray-green, silver-gray beneath. **Fruits** Edible, round to egg-shaped. Green, ripening to black.
• NATIVE HABITAT Dry, rocky hillsides in the Mediterranean.
• CULTIVATION Grow in deep, fertile, sharply drained soil in a warm, sheltered site in full sun. In colder areas, provide the shelter of a warm, sunny wall. Alternatively, grow under glass in a soil-based potting mix with added sharp sand. Admit full light and apply a balanced liquid fertilizer every month. Water moderately when in growth, but sparingly during winter. Cut back in spring to keep growth in bounds. Fruit is borne mainly on one-year-old wood. It is produced freely only in areas with a Mediterranean-type climate.
• PROPAGATION By semi-ripe cuttings taken in summer. Sow seed at 55–59°F (13–15°C) in spring.

Z9–10

Height
30ft (10m)

Spread
30ft (10m)

Malvaceae	ROSELLE, JAMAICA SORREL

HIBISCUS SABDARIFFA

Habit Woody-based, prickly-stemmed perennial that may be grown as an annual. ***Flowers*** Funnel-shaped, borne all year. Pale yellow, sometimes pink, maturing to red. ***Leaves*** Divided, with 3 to 5 oval lobes. Bright green.
• NATIVE HABITAT Disturbed land in Africa and Eurasia.
• CULTIVATION Grow in well-drained soil in full sun. In cooler areas, grow under glass.
• PROPAGATION Sow seed in spring at 64–70°F (18–21°C). Set out when any frosts have passed.

Z9–11

HEIGHT
8ft (2.5m)

SPREAD
6ft (2m)

Gentianaceae	GREAT YELLOW GENTIAN, BITTERWORT

GENTIANA LUTEA

Habit Clump-forming, fleshy-rooted perennial. ***Flowers*** Star-shaped, borne in terminal and axillary clusters in mid-summer. Yellow. ***Leaves*** Oval, pleated at base, smaller and paired on stem. Bluish green.
• NATIVE HABITAT Mountain meadows in the Alps, Pyrenees, Apennines, and Carpathians.
• CULTIVATION Grow in moist but well-drained, alkaline soil in sun or light, dappled shade.
• PROPAGATION By seed in autumn in a cold frame, or by basal cuttings or division, both in spring.

Z6–9

HEIGHT
to 5ft
(1.5m)

SPREAD
24in (60cm)

Scrophulariaceae	GREAT MULLEIN, AARON'S ROD

VERBASCUM THAPSUS

Habit Vigorous, woolly, rosette-forming biennial. ***Flowers*** Saucer-shaped, borne in long spikes in summer of the second year. Yellow. ***Leaves*** Oval to oblong, woolly. Gray-green.
• NATIVE HABITAT Dry grassland and bare sites in Eurasia.
• CULTIVATION Prefers alkaline conditions, but grows in most well-drained soils in sun and tolerates poor and dry soils. Good for a wild garden.
• PROPAGATION Sow seed in a cold frame in late spring or early summer. Self-sows freely.

Z5–9

HEIGHT
4–6ft
(1.2–2m)

SPREAD
18in (45cm)

| Lauraceae | BAY, LAUREL, SWEET BAY |

LAURUS NOBILIS

Habit Large, bushy, aromatic shrub or conical tree. **Flowers** Small, male and female borne on separate plants, in clusters in spring. Greenish yellow. **Leaves** Strongly aromatic when crushed, evergreen, narrowly oval, glossy. Bright green. **Fruits** Broadly egg-shaped berries. Black.
• NATIVE HABITAT Scrub and rocky places in the Mediterranean.
• CULTIVATION Grow in fertile, well-drained soil, in a warm, sunny site. Provide shelter from cold, dry winter winds. Suitable for growing outdoors in containers, which must be moved under cover during winter and early spring in cold areas. Tolerates hard pruning and may be clipped during summer to form topiary shapes. May be used as hedging and windbreaks in warmer, Mediterranean-type climates. The leaves dry particularly well, although they lose much of their flavor after a year. Harvest whole twigs and air-dry them upside down in a warm, airy place.
• PROPAGATION Take semi-ripe cuttings in summer, or sow seed in a cold frame in autumn.

Z8–10

Height
to 40ft
(12m)

Spread
30ft (10m)

Buxaceae	COMMON BOXWOOD

BUXUS SEMPERVIRENS

Habit Bushy shrub or small tree. **Flowers** Small, fragrant, star-shaped, male and female borne on the same plant in spring. Yellow-green. **Leaves** Oval to oblong, glossy. Dark green.
- NATIVE HABITAT Dry hills, Europe and N. Africa.
- CULTIVATION Grow in well-drained, neutral to alkaline soil in sun or part shade. Tolerates hard pruning; may be shaped for topiary.
- PROPAGATION By semi-ripe cuttings in summer.
- WARNING All parts of the plant are toxic if eaten. Contact with foliage may irritate skin.

Z5–8

HEIGHT
15ft (5m)

SPREAD
15ft (5m)
or more

Tiliaceae	LITTLELEAF LINDEN

TILIA CORDATA

Habit Broadly columnar tree. **Flowers** Small, fragrant, with oblong bracts, borne in drooping heads in mid-summer. Pale yellow. **Leaves** Rounded. Dark green, with blue green underside.
- NATIVE HABITAT Woodlands in Europe and the Caucasus.
- CULTIVATION Grow in fertile, moist but well-drained soil that is neutral to alkaline. Remove suckers in winter.
- PROPAGATION Stratify seed for 3–5 months and sow in a seed bed outdoors in spring.

Z4–8

HEIGHT
90ft (25m)

SPREAD
50ft (15m)

Brassicaceae	BLACK MUSTARD

BRASSICA NIGRA

Habit Well-branched annual. **Flowers** Cross-shaped, borne in terminal spikes during summer. Yellow. **Leaves** Lyre-shaped, lobed. Bluish green, slightly glaucous. **Fruits** Erect, 4-angled pods, with shiny, brown-black seeds.
- NATIVE HABITAT Bare ground in Eurasia.
- CULTIVATION Grow in fertile, well-drained soil in sun. Seed pods may be harvested when they start to color, and then air-dried.
- PROPAGATION Sow seed *in situ* in spring.
- OTHER NAME *Sinapis nigra*.

ANNUAL

HEIGHT
3–10ft
(0.9–3m)

SPREAD
to 4ft
(1.2m)

LARGE • 63

| Onagraceae | EVENING PRIMROSE |

OENOTHERA BIENNIS

Habit Upright annual or biennial. **Flowers** Fragrant, bowl-shaped, borne in spikes, opening on summer evenings. Yellow. **Leaves** Oblong to lance-shaped, sticky, in basal rosettes. Mid-green.
• NATIVE HABITAT Dry, sunny, well-drained places in eastern N. America; widely naturalized.
• CULTIVATION Grow in light, well-drained, poor to moderately fertile, or even stony, soil in full sun. Suitable for use in cottage-garden plantings.
• PROPAGATION Sow seed in a cold frame in early summer, or *in situ* in late summer to autumn.

Z5–8

HEIGHT
to 5ft
(1.5m)

SPREAD
24in (60cm)

| Brassicaceae | WOAD |

ISATIS TINCTORIA

Habit Taprooted perennial or biennial. **Flowers** Small, cross-shaped, borne in branched sprays in early summer. Yellow. **Leaves** Oblong to lance-shaped, in basal rosettes. Gray-green.
• NATIVE HABITAT Chalky soil in central and southern Europe and western Asia.
• CULTIVATION Grow in fertile, well-drained soil that is neutral to alkaline, in a sunny site.
• PROPAGATION Sow seed in autumn or spring in containers in a cold frame, or *in situ*. Transplant any self-sown seedlings to a fresh site.

Z3–8

HEIGHT
24–48in
(60–120cm)

SPREAD
18in (45cm)

| Asteraceae | ELECAMPANE |

INULA HELENIUM

Habit Sturdy, rhizomatous perennial. **Flowers** Daisylike, borne in mid- to late summer. Bright yellow. **Leaves** Large, coarse, narrowly oval, in basal rosettes. Mid-green, with downy undersides.
• NATIVE HABITAT Woods and grassy places, from Europe to western Asia.
• CULTIVATION Grow in moist but well-drained soil in a sunny site.
• PROPAGATION By seed sown in a cold frame or by division, both in spring or autumn.

Z3–9

HEIGHT
3–6ft
(0.9–2m)

SPREAD
3ft (0.9m)

Rutaceae	LEMON

CITRUS LIMON

Habit Large shrub or small, well-branched tree.
Flowers Fragrant, cup-shaped, borne from spring to summer. White, from red-tinted bud. **Leaves** Evergreen, narrowly oval, glossy. Dark green.
Fruits Broadly oval, ripe after 12 months. Yellow.
• NATIVE HABITAT Thickets and scrubland in Asia.
• CULTIVATION Grow in moist but well-drained, neutral to slightly acidic soil in full sun. In cold areas, grow under glass. Use a soil-based mix and provide shade from hot sun.
• PROPAGATION By semi-ripe cuttings in summer.

Min 37–41°F (3–5°C)

HEIGHT 6–22ft (2–7m)

SPREAD to 10ft (3m)

Lauraceae	GOLDEN BAY

LAURUS NOBILIS '**Aurea**'

Habit Large, bushy, aromatic shrub or conical tree. **Flowers** Small, male and female borne on separate plants in clusters in spring. Greenish yellow. **Leaves** Strongly aromatic, evergreen, narrowly oval, glossy. Golden-yellow.
Fruits Broadly egg-shaped berries. Black.
• NATIVE HABITAT Garden origin.
• CULTIVATION Grow in fertile, well-drained soil in a warm, sunny site. Provide shelter from dry, cold winter winds. Suitable for containers.
• PROPAGATION By semi-ripe cuttings in summer.

Z8–10

HEIGHT to 40ft (12m)

SPREAD 30ft (10m)

Hamamelidaceae	COMMON WITCH HAZEL

HAMAMELIS VIRGINIANA

Habit Upright shrub. **Flowers** Small, with narrow, strap-shaped petals in autumn. Yellow.
Leaves Deciduous, broadly oval to rounded. Mid-green, turning yellow in autumn.
• NATIVE HABITAT Woodland, eastern N. America.
• CULTIVATION Grow in fertile, moist but well-drained soil that is enriched with organic matter, in sun or dappled shade. Prefers acidic soils but tolerates alkaline soils.
• PROPAGATION Sow ripe seed in a cold frame, take softwood cuttings in summer, or layer in autumn.

Z4–9

HEIGHT 12ft (4m)

SPREAD 12ft (4m)

MEDIUM • 65

Rutaceae	GAS PLANT, DITTANY

DICTAMNUS ALBUS

Habit Clumping perennial. **Flowers** Asymmetric, 5-petaled, with long stamens, borne in early summer. Pure white to pale pink, with dark marks. **Leaves** Lemon-scented, divided. Mid-green.
• NATIVE HABITAT Woods, dry grass, and rocks in central and southern Europe, N. China, and Korea.
• CULTIVATION Grow in dry to well-drained soil that is neutral to alkaline, in full sun or light shade.
• PROPAGATION By seed in a cold frame when ripe.
• OTHER NAME *D. fraxinella*.
• WARNING Contact with foliage may irritate skin.

Z2–9

HEIGHT
16–36in
(40–90cm)

SPREAD
24in (60cm)

Liliaceae	CHINESE CHIVES, GARLIC CHIVES

ALLIUM TUBEROSUM

Habit Bulbous perennial with short rhizomes. **Flowers** Small, fragrant, star-shaped, borne in clusters from late summer to autumn. White. **Leaves** Garlic-scented, keeled, linear, both basal and stem-sheathing. Mid-green.
• NATIVE HABITAT Dry and mountainous terrain in southeast Asia.
• CULTIVATION Grow in fertile, well-drained soil in full sun.
• PROPAGATION Sow seed *in situ* in spring, or divide in autumn or spring.

Z3–9

HEIGHT
10–30in
(25–75cm)

SPREAD
18in (45cm)

Polemoniaceae	

POLEMONIUM CAERULEUM var. *LACTEUM*

Habit Clumping perennial. **Flowers** Bell-shaped, borne in loose sprays, in early to mid-summer. Pure white. **Leaves** Divided. Bright green.
• NATIVE HABITAT Meadows in northern Asia, western N. America, northern and central Europe.
• CULTIVATION Grow in fertile, moist but well-drained soil in sun or light shade.
• PROPAGATION By seed sown in a cold frame in autumn or spring, or by division in spring.
• OTHER NAME *P. caeruleum* var. *album*.

Z3–9

HEIGHT
12–36in
(30–90cm)

SPREAD
12in (30cm)

Rosaceae	MEADOWSWEET

FILIPENDULA ULMARIA

Habit Clump-forming perennial. **Flowers** Tiny, borne in dense, feathery heads in mid-summer. Creamy white. **Leaves** Irregularly divided. Dark green, heavily veined, and white-downy beneath.
- NATIVE HABITAT Damp meadows in Europe and western Asia.
- CULTIVATION Grow in fertile, moist to boggy soil in a sunny or lightly shaded site.
- PROPAGATION By seed in autumn in a cold frame, by division in autumn or spring, or by root cuttings taken in late winter.

☼ ●

Z3–9

HEIGHT
24–36in
(60–90cm)

SPREAD
24in (60cm)

Apiaceae	CARAWAY

CARUM CARVI

Habit Taprooted biennial. **Flowers** Tiny, borne in clusters in mid-summer. White. **Leaves** Aromatic, finely divided. Bright green. **Fruits** Ribbed, with licorice-tasting seeds. Pale brown.
- NATIVE HABITAT Grassland and waste ground from Europe to western Asia.
- CULTIVATION Grow in deep, fertile, well-drained soil in full sun. Needs long, warm, growing season to produce seeds reliably.
- PROPAGATION Sow seed *in situ* from late spring or late summer. May self-seed.

☼ ◊

Z5–8

HEIGHT
24in (60cm)

SPREAD
12in (30cm)

Rosaceae	BOWMAN'S ROOT, INDIAN PHYSIC

GILLENIA TRIFOLIATA

Habit Upright, clump-forming perennial. **Flowers** Small, irregularly star-shaped, borne in airy sprays during mid-summer. White, tinged red. **Leaves** Three-lobed, coarsely toothed. Dark bronze-green.
- NATIVE HABITAT Woods in eastern N. America.
- CULTIVATION Grow in light, fertile, moist but well-drained soil that is neutral to slightly acidic, in dappled or partial shade.
- PROPAGATION Sow seed in a cold frame or divide, both in spring or autumn.

☼ ●

Z4–8

HEIGHT
to 36in
(90cm)

SPREAD
24in (60cm)

MEDIUM • 67

| Brassicaceae | ARUGULA, ROQUETTE, RUCOLA, SALAD ROCKET |

ERUCA VESICARIA var. *SATIVA*

Habit Robust, upright, mustardlike annual.
Flowers Cross-shaped, borne in spikes between late winter and autumn. Creamy white with purple veins. **Leaves** Pepper-flavored, asymmetric, cut into 2–5 pairs of lateral lobes and one larger terminal lobe. Dark green.
• NATIVE HABITAT Originally from eastern Asia and the Mediterranean, salad rocket has long been cultivated elsewhere. This cultivar holds varietal status as it is larger leaved and paler flowered than the wild species.
• CULTIVATION Grow in any well-drained soil in a sunny site. Plants grown in hot, dry conditions have a more pungent flavor than those in moist, fertile soils. Suitable as a catch crop, grown in between plants in the flower border. Harvest young leaves before the flowering stem appears, since the leaves produced at or after flowering are hotter in flavor. The flowers are also edible.
• PROPAGATION Sow seed *in situ* in succession between late winter and early summer, or in late summer for an autumn crop. Self-seeds readily.

ANNUAL

HEIGHT
24–36in
(60–90cm)

SPREAD
6–8in
(15–20cm)

Lamiaceae	CATNIP

NEPETA CATARIA

Habit Aromatic, clump-forming perennial.
Flowers Tubular, 2-lipped, borne in branched whorls from summer to autumn. White, spotted purple. **Leaves** Oval, toothed, hairy. Gray-green.
- NATIVE HABITAT Hot, dry scrub in southwest and central Asia.
- CULTIVATION Grow in moist but well-drained, moderately fertile soil in a sunny site.
- PROPAGATION By seed in autumn in a cold frame, or by division in autumn or spring. Take stem-tip cuttings in spring or early summer. May self-seed.

Z4–9

HEIGHT
24–48in
(60–120cm)

SPREAD
24in (60cm)

Asteraceae	MILFOIL, YARROW

ACHILLEA MILLEFOLIUM

Habit Rhizomatous, mat-forming perennial.
Flowers Tiny, borne in flat sprays in summer. White, gray-white, cream, or pale mauve-pink. **Leaves** Feathery, divided, linear. Dark green.
- NATIVE HABITAT Grassland in Europe and western Asia.
- CULTIVATION Grow in fertile, well-drained soil in sun. Tolerant of a range of soils and conditions, and may be invasive where conditions suit.
- PROPAGATION Divide in autumn or spring, or sow seed *in situ* in spring.

Z3–10

HEIGHT
12–24in
(30–60cm)

SPREAD
24in (60cm)

Apiaceae	CILANTRO, CORIANDER

CORIANDRUM SATIVUM

Habit Aromatic annual. **Flowers** Tiny, 5-petaled, borne in clusters from mid-summer to autumn. White. **Leaves** Divided, glossy. Bright green.
- NATIVE HABITAT Scrub and wasteland in the eastern Mediterranean.
- CULTIVATION Grow in well-drained soil; in light shade for succulent, edible leaves (cilantro), or in a sunny site for seed production (coriander).
- PROPAGATION By seed sown *in situ*, in succession from spring to early summer. Keep seedlings well watered, since they bolt rapidly in dry conditions.

ANNUAL

HEIGHT
20–28in
(50–70cm)

SPREAD
8in (20cm)

Iridaceae	ORRIS

IRIS GERMANICA 'Florentina'

Habit Sturdy, rhizomatous perennial.
Flowers Scented, borne on branched stems in summer. White, tinted violet, with yellow beard. **Leaves** Sword-shaped, in basal fans. Gray-green.
- NATIVE HABITAT Possibly the Mediterranean.
- CULTIVATION Grow in well-drained, fertile soil that is neutral to alkaline, in full sun.
- PROPAGATION By division after flowering in late summer. Sow seed in autumn in a cold frame.
- OTHER NAMES *I. g.* var. *florentina*, *I. florentina*.
- WARNING All parts of the plant harmful if eaten.

Z4–10

HEIGHT
24–48in
(60–120cm)

SPREAD
indefinite

MEDIUM • 69

| Capparidaceae | CAPER BUSH, COMMON CAPER |

CAPPARIS SPINOSA

Habit Prostrate, evergreen shrub, with trailing stems. **Flowers** Solitary, cupped, with a central boss of long stamens, borne in early summer to autumn. White to pink, with pink stamens. **Leaves** Oval to rounded, glossy, with 2 spines at the base. Dark green.
• NATIVE HABITAT Widely distributed in tropical and subtropical areas.
• CULTIVATION Grow in well-drained, sandy soil, in a warm, sunny site. Ideal for use as an ornamental specimen or for growing as ground-cover. It is also well suited to dry, stony, or rocky slopes and may be grown as a trailing plant in crevices. Needs shelter from cold, dry winds. Pickled capers are made from the flower buds, which are picked early in the morning.
• PROPAGATION By ripewood cuttings taken in late summer.

Z9

HEIGHT
24–36in
(60–90cm)

SPREAD
7ft (2.2m)

| Rutaceae | GAS PLANT |

DICTAMNUS ALBUS var. *PURPUREUS*
Habit Woody-based perennial. **Flowers** Scented, star-shaped, with long stamens, borne in upright spikes in early summer. Purplish pink, with dark veins. **Leaves** Aromatic, lance-shaped. Mid-green.
- NATIVE HABITAT Open woods and rocky places in southern Europe, northern China, and Korea.
- CULTIVATION Grow in any well-drained soil that is moderately fertile, in a warm, sunny site. Tolerant of light shade, but dislikes disturbance.
- PROPAGATION Sow seed as soon as ripe.
- WARNING Contact with foliage may irritate skin.

Z2–9

HEIGHT
16–36in
(40–90cm)

SPREAD
24in (60cm)

| Lamiaceae | BALM OF GILEAD |

CEDRONELLA CANARIENSIS
Habit Woody-based perennial. **Flowers** Tubular, 2-lipped, borne in whorls in mid-summer. White, pink, or lilac. **Leaves** Cedar-scented, divided into 3 lance-shaped lobes. Bright green.
- NATIVE HABITAT Rocky slopes, Canary Islands.
- CULTIVATION Grow in light, well-drained soil in a warm, sunny, sheltered site. Good for containers, but overwinter under glass in cold areas.
- PROPAGATION By seed at 64°F (18°C) in early spring, or take stem-tip cuttings in summer.
- OTHER NAME *C. triphylla*.

Min. 41°F (5°C)

HEIGHT
4ft (1.2m)

SPREAD
24in (60cm)

| Caryophyllaceae | BOUNCING BET, SOAPWORT |

SAPONARIA OFFICINALIS
Habit Straggling, rhizomatous perennial. **Flowers** Flat, 5-petaled, borne in branched heads during summer. White, red, or pinkish purple. **Leaves** Broadly oval to lance-shaped. Mid-green.
- NATIVE HABITAT Hedges and woods, especially beside streams, in Europe.
- CULTIVATION Grow in neutral to alkaline soil.
- PROPAGATION By seed or division, both in autumn or spring.
- WARNING Avoid pondside plantings, since roots and foliage are toxic to fish.

Z2–8

HEIGHT
24–36in
(60–90cm)

SPREAD
24in (60cm)

| Papaveraceae | |

PAPAVER SOMNIFERUM 'Peony-flowered'
Habit Upright annual. **Flowers** Large, double, borne in summer, in shades of white, pink, red, or purple. **Leaves** Oblong and deeply lobed. Blue-green. **Fruits** Large, rounded seed pods. Blue-green.
- NATIVE HABITAT Origin uncertain.
- CULTIVATION Grow in fertile, well-drained soil in a sunny site. Seed pods are good for drying.
- PROPAGATION Sow seed *in situ* in spring.
- WARNING All parts, except the seeds, are toxic.

ANNUAL

HEIGHT
to 4ft
(1.2m)

SPREAD
12in (30cm)

| Papaveraceae | OPIUM POPPY |

PAPAVER SOMNIFERUM

Habit Upright annual. ***Flowers*** Large, solitary, bowl-shaped, with satin-textured petals. Borne in summer, in shades of white, pink, red, and mauve-purple and red, sometimes with dark blotches at the petal base. ***Leaves*** Oblong, deeply lobed, and slightly fleshy. Blue-green. ***Fruits*** Large, rounded, seed pods. Blue-green, drying to buff and brown.
• NATIVE HABITAT Origin uncertain.
• CULTIVATION Grow in fertile, well-drained soil in full sun. Ideal as a filler in a mixed or herbaceous border. The seed pods may be air-dried for winter arrangements. The seeds are often used to flavor and decorate breads, cakes, and pastries. Note that the cultivation of *P. somniferum* is subject to legal restrictions in some countries.
• PROPAGATION Sow seed *in situ* in spring. Seedlings of *P. somniferum*, as with many other poppies, resent disturbance and can rarely be transplanted successfully. Species and cultivars often self-seed, but cultivars tend to revert.
• WARNING All parts, except the seeds, are toxic if eaten.

ANNUAL

HEIGHT
to 4ft
(1.2m)

SPREAD
12in (30cm)

| Lamiaceae | PINK HYSSOP |

HYSSOPUS OFFICINALIS f. *ROSEUS*

Habit Aromatic, semi-evergreen shrub.
Flowers Tubular, 2-lipped, borne in slim, whorled spikes, from mid-summer to autumn. Pink-purple.
Leaves Linear to narrowly lance-shaped or oblong. Mid-green.
• NATIVE HABITAT Dry, rocky sites in southern Europe.
• CULTIVATION Grow in fertile soil that is neutral to alkaline, in a sunny site.
• PROPAGATION By seed sown in autumn or spring, or by softwood cuttings in summer.

Z3–9

HEIGHT
18–24in
(45–60cm)

SPREAD
24–36in
(60–90cm)

| Paeoniaceae | COMMON PEONY |

PAEONIA OFFICINALIS

Habit Upright, clump-forming perennial.
Flowers Single, cup-shaped, satin-textured, borne in early and mid-summer. Deep red or rose-pink.
Leaves Divided, oval to oblong. Dark green.
• NATIVE HABITAT Europe.
• CULTIVATION Grow in deep, moist but well-drained soil that is enriched with organic matter, in a sunny or lightly shaded site. Resents disturbance.
• PROPAGATION By division in autumn or spring, or by seed, which germinates slowly, sown in an open frame in autumn or early winter.

Z2–8

HEIGHT
24–28in
(60–70cm)

SPREAD
24–28in
(60–70cm)

| Scrophulariaceae | COMMON FOXGLOVE |

DIGITALIS PURPUREA

Habit Rosette-forming biennial or short-lived perennial. ***Flowers*** Tubular to bell-shaped, borne in tall spikes, from early to mid-summer. White, pink, or purple, with dark, inner spots.
Leaves Oval to lance-shaped, hairy. Dark green.
• NATIVE HABITAT Woods, hedgerows in Europe.
• CULTIVATION Grow in moist but well-drained, fertile, preferably acidic soil in part shade or sun.
• PROPAGATION Sow seed in a cold frame between spring and early summer.
• WARNING All parts are highly toxic if eaten.

Z4–8

HEIGHT
36in (90cm)
or more

SPREAD
12in (30cm)

MEDIUM • 73

| Rosaceae | APOTHECARY'S ROSE, CRIMSON DAMASK |

ROSA GALLICA var. *OFFICINALIS*

Habit Neat, rounded shrub. **Flowers** Fragrant, cupped to flat, semi-double, borne in summer. Intense red-pink. **Leaves** Broadly oval. Dark green. **Fruits** Round to oval hips. Orange-red.
• NATIVE HABITAT From southern and central Europe to the Caucasus.
• CULTIVATION Grow in fertile, moist but well-drained soil in a sunny site. Suitable for hedging.
• PROPAGATION By hardwood cuttings taken in autumn.
• OTHER NAME *R. officinalis*, *R.* 'Red Damask'.

Z4–8

Height 32in (80cm)

Spread 36in (90cm)

| Papaveraceae | CORN POPPY, FIELD POPPY |

PAPAVER RHOEAS

Habit Erect, hairy annual. **Flowers** Solitary, bowl-shaped, borne in summer. Scarlet, often marked black at petal base. **Leaves** Oblong, cut or divided. Light green. **Fruits** Rounded seed capsule.
• NATIVE HABITAT Disturbed ground in Eurasia and N. Africa.
• CULTIVATION Grow in light, well-drained soil in a sunny site.
• PROPAGATION Sow seed *in situ* in autumn or spring. Self-sows freely.
• WARNING All parts, except seeds, toxic if eaten.

Annual

Height to 36in (90cm)

Spread 12in (30cm)

| Asteraceae | |

ACHILLEA MILLEFOLIUM f. *ROSEA*

Habit Rhizomatous, mat-forming perennial. **Flowers** Tiny, borne in flat heads, in summer. Pale to deep pink. **Leaves** Feathery, divided, linear. Dark green.
• NATIVE HABITAT Grassland in Europe and western Asia.
• CULTIVATION Grow in fertile, well-drained soil in sun. Tolerant of a range of soils and conditions, and may be invasive where conditions suit.
• PROPAGATION By division in autumn or spring, or by seed sown *in situ* in spring.

Z3–10

Height to 24in (60cm)

Spread 24in (60cm)

| Rosaceae | GREAT BURNET |

SANGUISORBA OFFICINALIS

Habit Rhizomatous, clump-forming perennial. **Flowers** Tiny, borne in short, dense, egg-shaped spikes throughout summer. Red-brown. **Leaves** Divided into oblong leaflets. Mid-green.
• NATIVE HABITAT Damp meadows in Europe, northern and western Asia, and N. America.
• CULTIVATION Grow in moist, moderately fertile soil enriched with organic matter, in sun or part shade. May be naturalized in wet meadows.
• PROPAGATION By seed or division; both in autumn or spring. Self-sows freely.

Z4–8

Height to 4ft (1.2m)

Spread 24in (60cm)

MENTHA

The genus *Mentha* consists of 25 species of aromatic perennials (rarely annuals), which are widely distributed throughout Europe, Africa, and Asia, in moist or even wet soils.

Commonly known as mints, these plants have square stems and tubular to bell-shaped, 2-lipped flowers, which are usually borne in spikes of whorl-like clusters from summer to early autumn.

Most mints are vigorous and likely to be invasive. They are best confined to a border of their own, or grown in deep containers plunged into the soil to restrict their spread (see p. 144). Less invasive species, such as *M. suaveolens* 'Variegata' and *M.* x *gracilis* 'Variegata', are effective in mixed or herbaceous borders.

Mints have long been grown for their culinary uses in teas, sauces, and salads. They are rich in essential oils, particularly menthol, which has antiseptic and decongestant properties. They improve digestion and are often included in indigestion remedies. *M. spicata* and *M.* x *piperita* are grown on a large scale for oils, which are used in confectionery and oral hygiene preparations.

Grow in fertile, moist soil, in full sun or in partial or dappled shade. *M. requienii* needs moist, shady conditions, while *M. pulegium* and its variants need sandy, moist but well-drained, preferably acidic soil, either in a sunny or shady site. *M. longifolia* is tolerant of drier conditions, and *M. aquatica* is suitable for growing in bog gardens or pond margins.

Sow the seed of *M. pulegium* and *M. requienii* in pots in a cold frame in spring; *M. requienii* will self-sow. Most other mints are increased easily by division in spring or autumn, or by tip cuttings taken in spring or summer. Sections of the rhizome will root at any time during the growing season.

M. SUAVEOLENS 'Variegata'
Habit Rhizomatous, spreading perennial.
Flowers Seldom appear, borne on dense spikes in summer. Pink or white.
Leaves Fruit-scented, oblong to rounded. Grayish green, variegated cream.
• TIPS May scorch in full sun, so keep shaded.
• HEIGHT to 3ft (0.9m).
• SPREAD indefinite.

M. suaveolens 'Variegata'
Pineapple mint
☼ ◐ Z7–9
⚭ ⌂

M. x *VILLOSA* f. *ALOPECUROIDES*
Habit Rhizomatous, spreading perennial.
Flowers Borne in large, leafy spikes in summer. Pale pink to lilac.
Leaves Mint-scented, softly hairy, broadly oval to rounded, toothed. Bright green.
• TIPS Good in salads or with vegetables.
• HEIGHT to 3ft (0.9m).
• SPREAD indefinite.

M. x *villosa* f. *alopecuroides*
Bowles' mint
☼ ◐ Z5–9
⚭ ⌂ ✂

M. SUAVEOLENS
Habit Vigorous, rhizomatous, spreading perennial.
Flowers Borne in whorls, in branched spikes in summer. Pink or white.
Leaves Apple-scented, softly hairy, oblong-oval wrinkled, often wavy-edged. Grayish green.
• OTHER NAME *M. rotundifolia* of gardens.
• HEIGHT to 3ft (0.9m).
• SPREAD indefinite.

M. suaveolens
Apple mint, Woolly mint
☼ ◐ Z5–9
⚭ ⌂

M. x *PIPERITA*
Habit Vigorous, spreading perennial.
Flowers Borne in dense, oblong, terminal spikes in summer. Lilac-pink.
Leaves Sharply scented, smooth, slightly shiny, and lance-shaped. Dark green.
• TIPS Good in teas, iced drinks, and salads.
• HEIGHT 12–36in (30–90cm).
• SPREAD indefinite.

M. x *piperita*
Peppermint
☼ ◐ Z4–9
⚭ ⌂ ✂

MENTHA • 75

M. PULEGIUM
Habit Spreading perennial with upright and low-lying stems.
Flowers Tiny, borne in whorls on short spikes in summer. Lilac.
Leaves Sharply scented, narrowly oval to rounded. Bright green.
• TIPS Prefers damp, sandy, acidic soil.
• HEIGHT 4–16in (10–40cm).
• SPREAD indefinite.

M. pulegium
Pennyroyal
☼ ◊ pH Z6–9

M. × *GRACILIS*
Habit Rhizomatous perennial with upright, often red-tinted stems.
Flowers Borne in widely spaced, whorled clusters in summer. Lilac.
Leaves Sweet-scented, smooth, oval to lance-shaped. Mid-green.
• TIPS Use fresh leaves in fruit salads.
• HEIGHT 12–36in (30–90cm).
• SPREAD indefinite.

M. × *gracilis*
Gingermint, Red mint
☼ ◊ Z7–9

M. × *PIPERITA* 'Citrata'
Habit Vigorous, spreading perennial.
Flowers Borne in dense, oblong, terminal spikes in summer. Pink-purple.
Leaves Lavender-scented, lance-shaped. Green, flushed red in sun, or copper in shade.
• TIPS Suitable for use in potpourri.
• HEIGHT to 3ft (0.9m).
• SPREAD indefinite.

M. × *piperita* 'Citrata'
Eau-de-Cologne, lemon, or bergamot mint
☼ ◊ Z4–9

M. × *SMITHIANA*
Habit Vigorous, rhizomatous perennial.
Flowers Borne in dense whorls, well-spaced or clustered around the stem tips, during summer. Rose-purple.
Leaves Strongly sweet-scented, oval, toothed. Dark green, tinted red.
• TIPS Good flavor for culinary use.
• HEIGHT to 3ft (0.9m).
• SPREAD indefinite.

M. × *smithiana*
Red raripila mint
☼ ◊ Z7–9

M. AQUATICA
Habit Marginal, aquatic perennial.
Flowers Borne in whorls, in dense, rounded heads in summer. Lilac.
Leaves Peppermint-scented, oval to lance-shaped. Dark green, tinted purple.
• TIPS Plant in water up to 6in (15cm) deep.
• HEIGHT 6–36in (15–90cm).
• SPREAD indefinite.

M. aquatica
Water mint
☼ ◊ Z6–11

M. SPICATA 'Crispa'
Habit Rhizomatous perennial.
Flowers Borne in dense, cylindrical spikes at the stem tips in summer. Lilac, pink, or white.
Leaves Peppermint-scented, lance-shaped to oval, with crinkled margins. Bright green.
• TIPS Less invasive than the species.
• HEIGHT 18in (45cm).
• SPREAD indefinite.

M. spicata 'Crispa'
Curly spearmint
☼ ◊ Z4–9

M. LONGIFOLIA
Habit Vigorous, rhizomatous perennial.
Flowers Whorled, borne in dense spikes in summer. Lilac or white.
Leaves Peppermint-scented, oblong-oval. Gray-green to silver-gray.
• TIPS Retains scent well when dried.
• OTHER NAMES *M. sylvestris, M. incana.*
• HEIGHT to 4ft (1.2m).
• SPREAD indefinite.

M. longifolia
Horse mint
☼ ◊ Z6–9
◊ ◊

M. LONGIFOLIA Buddleia Mint Group
Habit Vigorous, rhizomatous perennial.
Flowers Borne in long, dense, terminal spikes in summer. Lilac or white.
Leaves Peppermint-scented, oblong-oval. Gray-green to silver-gray.
• TIPS Suitable for flower arrangements.
• HEIGHT to 4ft (1.2m).
• SPREAD indefinite.

M. longifolia
Buddleia Mint Group
☼ ◊ Z6–9
◊ ◊

M. SPICATA
Habit Vigorous, rhizomatous perennial.
Flowers Borne in dense, cylindrical spikes at the stem tips in summer. Lilac, pink, or white.
Leaves Spearmint-flavored, lance-shaped to oval, toothed. Bright green.
• OTHER NAME *M. viridis.*
• HEIGHT to 3ft (0.9m).
• SPREAD indefinite.

M. spicata
Spearmint
☼ ◊ Z4–9
◊ ◊ ◊

M. SPICATA 'Moroccan'
Habit Rhizomatous perennial.
Flowers Borne in dense spikes at the stem tips during summer. Lilac, pink, or white.
Leaves Spearmint-flavored, lance-shaped to oval, toothed, close-set. Lime-green.
• TIPS Ideal for mint tea.
• HEIGHT to 3ft (0.9m).
• SPREAD indefinite.

M. spicata 'Moroccan'
Moroccan spearmint
☼ ◊ Z4–9
◊ ◊ ◊

M. REQUIENII
Habit Mat-forming, stem-rooting perennial.
Flowers Minute, borne in whorls on short spikes, in summer. Lilac.
Leaves Peppermint-scented, broadly oval to rounded. Fresh green.
• TIPS Prefers shade or dappled shade.
• OTHER NAME *M. corsica.*
• HEIGHT ½in (1cm).
• SPREAD indefinite.

M. requienii
Corsican mint
☼ ◊ Z7–9
◊

M. × GRACILIS 'Variegata'
Habit Rhizomatous perennial.
Flowers Borne in clusters in summer. Lilac.
Leaves Ginger-flavored, smooth, oval to lance-shaped. Dark green, variegated gold.
• TIPS Use fresh leaves in fruit salad.
• HEIGHT 12–18in (30–45cm).
• SPREAD indefinite.

M. × *gracilis*
'Variegata'
☼ ◊ Z7–9
◊ ◊

M. PULEGIUM 'Cunningham Mint'
Habit Spreading, stem-rooting perennial.
Flowers Tiny, borne in widely spaced whorls in short spikes during summer. Lilac.
Leaves Sharply scented, oval. Light green.
• TIPS Prefers damp, sandy, acidic soil.
• HEIGHT 4–6in (10–15cm).
• SPREAD indefinite.

M. pulegium
'Cunningham Mint'
Creeping pennyroyal
☼ ◊ Z6–9
◊ ◊ ◊

MONARDA

The genus *Monarda* consists of about 15 species of annuals and rhizomatous, herbaceous perennials, which occur in dry scrub and prairies or moist, fertile woodlands in North America. Monardas are sometimes known as bergamot, since their aroma resembles that of the bergamot orange (*Citrus bergamia*), which yields an oil that is used to flavor Earl Grey tea. Monardas have lance-shaped to oval, usually dark green leaves and bear sage-like, tubular, irregularly 2-lipped, hooded flowers arranged in dense terminal whorls, often with contrasting bracts.

There are many named variants of *Monarda*, especially selections of *M. didyma* or hybrids between *M. didyma* and *M. fistulosa*, that are highly ornamental and valued for their form, color, and long flowering period from mid-summer to autumn. They are ideal for growing in a mixed or herbaceous border, and seldom need staking. The nectar-rich flowers of monardas are very attractive to bees and other beneficial insects. All are more or less aromatic, and the leaves and flowers make a colorful and well-scented addition to potpourris. Notably, the flowers of *M. didyma* make an unusual and attractive decoration in green salads.

Grow in fertile, moist but well-drained soil in sun or light, dappled shade. Protect the crowns from excessive winter moisture and do not allow them to dry out entirely in summer. Where conditions are too dry, *M. didyma* and several of its variants are likely to become infected with powdery mildew; however, some of the newer cultivars are mildew resistant. *M. punctata* and *M. fistulosa* prefer to grow in drier, slightly alkaline soils, in a sunny site.

Sow seed in pots in a cold frame in spring or autumn. Divide in spring, or take basal cuttings in early summer.

M. 'Fishes'
Habit Clump-forming, rhizomatous, herbaceous perennial.
Flowers Tubular, 2-lipped, borne in terminal whorls during summer. Pale pink, with green sepals.
Leaves Oval, toothed. Dark green.
- OTHER NAME *M.* 'Pisces'.
- HEIGHT 36in (90cm).
- SPREAD indefinite.

M. 'Fishes'
☀ ◐ Z4–8

M. 'Croftway Pink'
Habit Clump-forming, rhizomatous, herbaceous perennial.
Flowers Tubular, 2-lipped, borne in terminal whorls over long periods during summer. Clear rose-pink, with pink-tinted bracts.
Leaves Oval, toothed. Dark green.
• HEIGHT 36in (90cm).
• SPREAD indefinite.

M. 'Croftway Pink'
☼ ◊ Z4–8

M. FISTULOSA
Habit Bushy, well-branched, rhizomatous, herbaceous perennial.
Flowers Tubular, 2-lipped, borne in terminal whorls throughout summer. Lilac-purple to pale pink, with purple-tinted bracts.
Leaves Oval to lance-shaped, softly hairy. Dull mid-green.
• HEIGHT 48in (120cm).
• SPREAD indefinite.

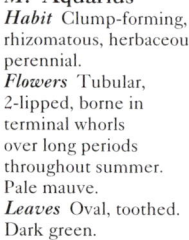
M. fistulosa
Wild bergamot
☼ ◊ Z3–7

M. 'Aquarius'
Habit Clump-forming, rhizomatous, herbaceous perennial.
Flowers Tubular, 2-lipped, borne in terminal whorls over long periods throughout summer. Pale mauve.
Leaves Oval, toothed. Dark green.
• HEIGHT 36–48in (90–120cm).
• SPREAD indefinite.

M. 'Aquarius'
☼ ◊ Z4–8

M. 'Mohawk'
Habit Clump-forming, rhizomatous, herbaceous perennial.
Flowers Tubular, 2-lipped, borne in terminal whorls over long periods during summer. Deep pink.
Leaves Oval, toothed. Dark green.
• HEIGHT 36–48in (90–120cm).
• SPREAD indefinite.

M. 'Mohawk'
☼ ◊ Z4–8

M. 'Scorpion'
Habit Clump-forming, rhizomatous, herbaceous perennial.
Flowers Tubular, 2-lipped, borne in terminal whorls over long periods in summer. Magenta-pink.
Leaves Oval, toothed. Dark green.
• OTHER NAME *M.* 'Scorpio'.
• HEIGHT 36in (90cm).
• SPREAD indefinite.

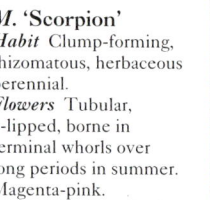
M. 'Scorpion'
☼ ◊ Z4–8

M. 'Balance'
Habit Clump-forming, rhizomatous, herbaceous perennial.
Flowers Tubular, 2-lipped, borne in terminal whorls during summer. Cerise-pink.
Leaves Oval, toothed. Dark green.
• OTHER NAME *M.* 'Libra'.
• HEIGHT 36–48in (90–120cm).
• SPREAD indefinite.

M. 'Balance'
☼ ◊ Z4–8

M. 'Cambridge Scarlet'
Habit Clump-forming, rhizomatous, herbaceous perennial.
Flowers Tubular, 2-lipped, borne in terminal whorls over long periods in summer. Rich scarlet, with red-brown bracts.
Leaves Oval, toothed. Dark green.
• HEIGHT 90cm (36in).
• SPREAD 45cm (18in).

M. 'Cambridge Scarlet'
☼ ◊ Z4–8

MONARDA • 79

M. DIDYMA
Habit Bushy, clump-forming, rhizomatous, herbaceous perennial.
Flowers Tubular, 2-lipped, borne from summer to early autumn. Scarlet or pink, with red-tinted bracts.
Leaves Oval to lance-shaped, hairy beneath. Dull mid-green.
• HEIGHT 36in (90cm) or more.
• SPREAD indefinite.

M. didyma
Oswego tea, Bee balm, Bergamot
☼ ◐ Z4–8

M. 'Mahogany'
Habit Clump-forming, rhizomatous, herbaceous perennial.
Flowers Tubular, 2-lipped, borne in terminal whorls over long periods during summer. Burgundy-red, with reddish brown bracts.
Leaves Oval, toothed. Dark green.
• HEIGHT 36in (90cm).
• SPREAD indefinite.

M. 'Mahogany'
☼ ◐ Z4–8

M. 'Beauty of Cobham'
Habit Clump-forming, rhizomatous, herbaceous perennial.
Flowers Tubular, 2-lipped, borne in terminal whorls over long periods during summer. Pale pinkish lilac, with purple-brown bracts.
Leaves Oval, toothed. Dark purplish-green.
• HEIGHT 36in (90cm).
• SPREAD indefinite.

M. 'Beauty of Cobham'
☼ ◐ Z4–8

M. 'Prärienacht'
Habit Clump-forming, rhizomatous, herbaceous perennial.
Flowers Tubular, 2-lipped, borne in terminal whorls during summer. Purple-lilac, with red-tinged bracts.
Leaves Oval, toothed. Dark green.
• OTHER NAME
M. 'Prairie Night'.
• HEIGHT 36in (90cm).
• SPREAD indefinite.

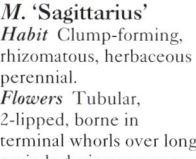

M. 'Prärienacht'
☼ ◐ Z4–8

M. 'Sagittarius'
Habit Clump-forming, rhizomatous, herbaceous perennial.
Flowers Tubular, 2-lipped, borne in terminal whorls over long periods during summer. Pink-purple.
Leaves Oval, toothed. Dark green.
• OTHER NAME
M. 'Bowman'.
• HEIGHT 36in (90cm).
• SPREAD indefinite.

M. 'Sagittarius'
☼ ◐ Z4–8

M. PUNCTATA
Habit Clump-forming, rhizomatous, herbaceous perennial.
Flowers Tubular, 2-lipped, borne in dense whorls from summer to autumn. Yellow, spotted purple, with green-white bracts, flushed pale purple or pink.
Leaves Lance-shaped, toothed. Dark green.
• HEIGHT 36in (90cm).
• SPREAD indefinite.

M. punctata
Horsemint
☼ ○ Z3–9

Pelargonium

The genus *Pelargonium* consists of 230 species of evergreen perennials, sub-shrubs, shrubs, and succulents that are found in a range of habitats, from desert to mountainside, mostly in South Africa. The numerous named cultivars are subdivided into six main groups, including the scented-leaved geraniums that are described here.

Scented-leaved geraniums are shrubby evergreen perennials and subshrubs, grown mainly for their foliage. The flowers are attractive but often very small. The leaves are variable and release a distinctive scent when crushed. Most of them make fragrant additions to potpourri or herb pillows when dried, while a few have culinary uses – in teas, jellies, jams, vinegars, and sauces – and some are used medicinally. *P. capitatum*, *P.* 'Graveolens' and *P.* Radula Group, among others, are grown commercially for geranium oil.

Geraniums can be grown permanently outdoors only in areas that are frost-free, but elsewhere they are ideal container plants for the home or conservatory and may be moved outdoors during the warm summer months.

Under glass, grow in soilless or soil-based potting mix in full light. Provide some shade from the hottest mid-day sun, and ensure that there is good ventilation. Water moderately and apply a balanced liquid fertilizer every 10–14 days when in active growth. Water sparingly during winter. If kept almost dry, geraniums will tolerate winter temperatures of 36°F (2°C) under glass, but at 45–50°F (7–10°C) they may even produce a few winter flowers. Cut back hard in early spring to keep plants compact and to produce the best foliage.

Propagate by stem-tip cuttings taken between spring and autumn.

P. ODORATISSIMUM
Habit Low-growing, evergreen perennial.
Flowers Tiny, borne in trailing, branched clusters of 5–10 in late spring and summer. White, with red veins on upper petals.
Leaves Apple-scented, rounded, with wavy margins. Light green.
• HEIGHT 8–10in (20–25cm).
• SPREAD 18–24in (45–60cm).

P. odoratissimum
Apple geranium
☼ ◊ Min. 36°F/2°C
⚱ ⚘ ⚶

P. 'Fragrans Variegatum'
Habit Bushy, evergreen perennial.
Flowers Small, star-shaped, borne from spring to summer. White, marked with 2 red lines.
Leaves Nutmeg-pine scented, rounded, silky-hairy. Gray-green, variegated creamy white.
• HEIGHT 8–10in (20–25cm).
• SPREAD to 8in (20cm).

P. 'Fragrans Variegatum'
☼ ◊ Min. 36°F/2°C
⚱ ⚘ ⚶

P. 'Fragrans'
Habit Bushy, evergreen perennial.
Flowers Small, star-shaped, borne in clusters from spring to summer. White, marked with 2 red lines.
Leaves Nutmeg-pine scented, rounded, silky-hairy. Gray-green.
• HEIGHT 8–10in (20–25cm).
• SPREAD 6–8in (15–20cm).

P. 'Fragrans'
Nutmeg geranium
☼ ◊ Min. 36°F/2°C
⚱ ⚘ ⚶

P. ABROTANIFOLIUM
Habit Evergreen, woody subshrub.
Flowers Star-shaped, borne in clusters of up to 5 from spring to summer. White or pink.
Leaves Scented like southernwood, rounded, finely divided, with linear lobes. Gray-green.
• HEIGHT 12–16in (30–40cm).
• SPREAD 12in (30cm).

P. abrotanifolium
Southernwood-scented geranium
☼ ◊ Min. 36°F/2°C
⚱ ⚶

P. CRISPUM
Habit Upright, evergreen subshrub.
Flowers Small, star-shaped, borne in clusters in spring and summer. Pale pink.
Leaves Lemon-scented, small, kidney-shaped to 3-lobed, coarse-crinkled. Mid-green.
• HEIGHT 24–28in (60–70cm).
• SPREAD 12–18in (30–45cm).

P. crispum
Lemon geranium
☼ ◊ Min. 36°F/2°C

⚬ ⚭

P. CITRONELLUM
Habit Upright, evergreen subshrub.
Flowers Small, borne in clusters of 5–8 in summer. Purple-pink, marked deep purple.
Leaves Lemon-scented, deeply cut into toothed lobes. Fresh green.
• HEIGHT 4–6ft (1.2–2m).
• SPREAD 3ft (1m).

P. citronellum
☼ ◊ Min. 36°F/2°C

⚬ ⚭

P. 'Sweet Mimosa'
Habit Vigorous, upright, branching perennial.
Flowers Trumpet-shaped, borne in clusters, in summer. Shell-pink with red marks.
Leaves Sweetly fruit-scented, deeply lobed. Fresh green.
• HEIGHT 3–4ft (1–1.2m).
• SPREAD 3–4ft (1–1.2m).

P. 'Sweet Mimosa'
☼ ◊ Min. 36°F/2°C

⚬ ⚭

P. 'Fair Ellen'
Habit Evergreen, bushy, shrubby perennial.
Flowers Small, delicate, irregularly star-shaped, borne in clusters in summer. Pale mauve-pink, marked dark pink.
Leaves Balsam-scented and deeply lobed. Fresh green with dark midrib.
• HEIGHT 12–24in (30–60cm).
• SPREAD 24–36in (60–90cm).

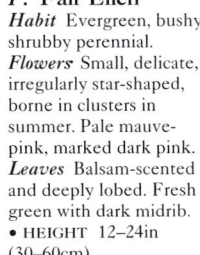
P. 'Fair Ellen'
☼ ◊ Min. 36°F/2°C

⚬

P. 'Clorinda'
Habit Vigorous, upright, evergreen perennial.
Flowers Large, single, borne in clusters, from spring to summer. Rose-pink.
Leaves Cedar-rose scented, crinkled, 3-lobed. Mid-green.
• HEIGHT 18–20in (45–50cm) or more.
• SPREAD 8–10in (20–25cm).

P. 'Clorinda'
☼ ◊ Min. 36°F/2°C

⚬

P. Radula Group
Habit Subshrubby, evergreen perennials.
Flowers Small, borne in clusters from spring through to summer. Pale pink to deepest purple-pink.
Leaves Camphor-rose scented, triangular and deeply cut. Bright green.
• HEIGHT 3–5ft (1–1.5m).
• SPREAD 2–5ft (0.6–1.5m).

P. Radula Group
☼ ◊ Min. 36°F/2°C

⚬ ⚭

P. 'Rober's Lemon Rose'
Habit Vigorous, bushy, evergreen subshrub.
Flowers Small, star-shaped, borne in clusters from spring to summer. Mauve-pink.
Leaves Lemon-rose scented, irregularly lobed. Grayish green.
• HEIGHT 18–20in (45–50cm).
• SPREAD 8–10in (20–25cm).

P. 'Rober's Lemon Rose'
☼ ◊ Min. 36°F/2°C

⚬ ⚭

P. 'Prince of Orange'
Habit Slender, upright, evergreen perennial.
Flowers Small, single, borne in clusters from early summer to autumn. Pale mauve-pink, with purple veins.
Leaves Orange-scented, fan-shaped. Mid-green.
• HEIGHT 10–12in (25–30cm).
• SPREAD 6–8in (15–20cm).

P. 'Prince of Orange'
☼ ◊ Min. 36°F/2°C

⚬ ⚭

P. 'Galway Star'
Habit Subshrubby evergreen perennial.
Flowers Small, borne in clusters from spring to summer. Pink, marked cerise and purple.
Leaves Lemon-scented, small, deeply lobed and cut. Mid-green with cream margins.
- HEIGHT 18–24in (45–60cm).
- SPREAD 12–18in (30–45cm).

P. 'Galway Star'
☼ ◊ Min. 36°F/2°C

P. 'Lady Plymouth'
Habit Vigorous, bushy, evergreen subshrub.
Flowers Small, delicate, borne in clusters in summer and autumn. Pale pink or white, with darker lines.
Leaves Scented, deeply lobed, triangular. Gray-green, cream margins.
- HEIGHT 12–16in (30–40cm).
- SPREAD 6–8in (15–20cm).

P. 'Lady Plymouth'
☼ ◊ Min. 36°F/2°C

P. 'Filicifolium'
Habit Compact, evergreen, subshrubby perennial.
Flowers Borne in small clusters from spring to summer. Pale mauve.
Leaves Balsam-scented, fernlike, finely divided. Mid-green.
- HEIGHT 10–12in (25–30cm).
- SPREAD 5–6in (12–15cm).

P. 'Filicifolium'
☼ ◊ Min. 36°F/2°C

P. QUERCIFOLIUM
Habit Upright, sticky, evergreen subshrub.
Flowers Small, borne in clusters during spring and summer. Purple-pink with darker markings.
Leaves Balsam-scented, triangular, deeply lobed or cut. Mid-green.
- HEIGHT 1½–5ft (0.45–1.5m).
- SPREAD 1½–3ft (45–90cm).

P. quercifolium
Oak-leaved geranium
☼ ◊ Min. 36°F/2°C

P. CAPITATUM
Habit Spreading, erect to arching, evergreen perennial.
Flowers Small, borne in compact clusters in summer and autumn. Mauve-pink.
Leaves Rose-scented, lobed, velvety, crinkled margins. Light green.
- HEIGHT 12–36in (30–90cm).
- SPREAD 1½–5ft (0.45–1.5m).

P. capitatum
Wild rose geranium
☼ ◊ Min. 36°F/2°C

P. 'Mabel Grey'
Habit Vigorous, upright, evergreen subshrub.
Flowers Small, delicate, star-shaped, borne in clusters from summer to autumn. Mauve-purple with darker markings.
Leaves Lemon-scented, lobed, diamond-shaped. Bright green.
- HEIGHT 12–14in (30–35cm).
- SPREAD 5–6in (12–15cm).

P. 'Mabel Grey'
☼ ◊ Min. 36°F/2°C

P. CRISPUM 'Variegatum'
Habit Upright, bushy, evergreen subshrub.
Flowers Small, star-shaped, borne in clusters from summer to autumn. Pale lilac.
Leaves Lemon-scented, 3-lobed, crinkled. Mid-green edged pale yellow.
- HEIGHT 14–18in (35–45cm).
- SPREAD 5–6in (12–15cm).

P. crispum 'Variegatum'
☼ ◊ Min. 36°F/2°C

PELARGONIUM • 83

P. 'Attar of Roses'
Habit Compact, sub-shrubby, evergreen perennial.
Flowers Small, borne in clusters from spring to summer. Mauve.
Leaves Rose-scented, 3-lobed. Mid-green.
• HEIGHT 20–24in (30–60cm).
• SPREAD 10–12in (25–30cm).

P. 'Attar of Roses'
☼ ◊ Min. 36°F/2°C

☼ ☙

P. TOMENTOSUM
Habit Vigorous, sprawling, evergreen perennial.
Flowers Small, butterfly-shaped, borne in clusters from spring to summer. White.
Leaves Peppermint-scented, velvety, lobed, heart-shaped. Mid-green.
• HEIGHT 30–36in (75–90cm).
• SPREAD 24–30in (60–75cm).

P. tomentosum
Peppermint geranium
☼ ◊ Min. 36°F/2°C

☼ ☙ ⊲

P. 'Old Spice'
Habit Bushy, upright, evergreen perennial.
Flowers Small, star-shaped, borne in clusters in summer. Pale pink.
Leaves Spice-scented, rounded, lobed, softly hairy, with slightly crisped margins. Light green.
• HEIGHT 10–12in (25–30cm).
• SPREAD 5–6in (12–15cm).

P. 'Old Spice'
☼ ◊ Min. 36°F/2°C

☼

P. 'Chocolate Peppermint'
Habit Evergreen, sub-shrubby perennial.
Flowers Small, borne in clusters from spring to summer. Pink with darker markings.
Leaves Peppermint-scented, velvety, lobed. Mid-green with a central chocolate-brown blotch.
• HEIGHT to 3ft (1m).
• SPREAD 18–24in (45–60cm).

P. 'Chocolate Peppermint'
☼ ◊ Min. 36°F/2°C

☼

P. 'Graveolens'
Habit Vigorous, bushy, evergreen subshrub.
Flowers Small, borne in small clusters in spring and summer. Pale pink, marked dark purple.
Leaves Rose-lemon scented, triangular, lobed and cut, rough-textured. Bright green.
• HEIGHT 45–60cm (30–36in).
• SPREAD 20–40cm (18–16in).

P. 'Graveolens'
Rose geranium
☼ ◊ Min. 36°F/2°C

☼ ☙ ⊲

P. 'Royal Oak'
Habit Subshrubby, evergreen perennial.
Flowers Relatively large, borne in clusters from spring to summer. Pink-purple with darker spots.
Leaves Balsam-scented, lobed, oak-leaf-shaped. Dark green with darker central marks.
• HEIGHT 12–16in (30–40cm).
• SPREAD 10–12in (25–30cm).

P. 'Royal Oak'
☼ ◊ Min. 36°F/2°C

☼

Capsicum

The genus *Capsicum* consists of about 10 species of annuals and often short-lived perennials, found in forest margins in tropical North and South America. Most are cultivated as crop plants for their vitamin-rich and sweet- or hot-flavored fruits. The small, bell-shaped flowers are insignificant. *C. annuum* var. *annuum* has been superseded in cultivation by numerous cultivars. Some of these are dwarf in habit, attractive in fruit, and suit windowboxes and other containers. The cultivars are subdivided into five main groups based on shape, color, and flavor.
Cherry peppers have hot-flavored, rounded fruits and are available in shades of red, yellow, or purple.
Cone peppers have erect, conical, hot-flavored, white or green fruits that ripen to red or purple.
Red cone peppers produce upright, conical, hot-flavored, red fruits.
Bell peppers include sweet, bell, or salad peppers, with egg- to bell-shaped fruits in shades of green, yellow, red, or purple.
Cayenne or chili peppers are long, tapering, drooping fruits, and include hot cayenne and very hot chili peppers.

All hot peppers should be handled carefully since they are known to cause inflammation on contact with broken skin, eyes, and mucous membranes.

Outdoors, peppers grow best in fertile, well-drained soil in a sunny site. Under glass, they need fertile, freely draining, soilless or soil-based potting mix in bright, filtered light. Water freely during growth, and apply a balanced liquid fertilizer every 10 days. Maintain high humidity and a growing temperature of 70–77°F (21–25°C). Mist the flowers daily to encourage the fruit to set.

Propagate by seed sown in late winter or early spring at 70°F (21°C).

C. ANNUUM var. *ANNUUM*
'Chili Serrano'
Habit Vigorous, bushy, free-fruiting cultivar, grown as an annual.
Fruits Hot-flavored, slender, drooping, cone-shaped. Green, ripening to scarlet-red.
Leaves Lance-shaped to oval. Mid-green.
• HEIGHT 24in (60cm).
• SPREAD 15in (38cm).

C. annuum var. *annuum* 'Chili Serrano'
☼ ◊ ANNUAL

C. ANNUUM var. *ANNUUM*
'Super Cayenne'
Habit Vigorous, bushy, free-fruiting F1 hybrid, grown as an annual.
Fruits Hot-flavored, slender, drooping, slim, cone-shaped. Green, ripening to deep red.
Leaves Lance-shaped to oval. Mid-green.
• HEIGHT to 30in (75cm).
• SPREAD 18in (45cm).

C. annuum var. *annum* 'Super Cayenne'
☼ ◊ ANNUAL

C. BACCATUM
Habit Spreading, shrubby perennial.
Fruits Hot-flavored, small, upright, rounded. Green, maturing to red.
Leaves Lance-shaped to oval. Mid-green.
• HEIGHT 10ft (3m).
• SPREAD 5–6ft (1.5–2m).

C. baccatum
☼ ◊ ANNUAL

C. ANNUUM var. ***ANNUUM*** 'Jalapeño'
Habit Vigorous, bushy, high-yielding cultivar, grown as an annual.
Fruits Hot-flavored, slender, drooping, narrowly cone-shaped. Dark green, ripening to red.
Leaves Lance-shaped to oval. Mid-green.
• HEIGHT 24in (60cm).
• SPREAD 18in (45cm).

C. annuum var. *annuum* 'Jalapeño'
☼ ◊ ANNUAL

C. ANNUUM var. ***ANNUUM*** 'Anaheim'
Habit Vigorous, bushy, early-fruiting cultivar, grown as an annual.
Fruits Mildly hot, slender, drooping, cone-shaped. Green, ripening to red.
Leaves Lance-shaped to oval. Mid-green.
• TIPS Use fresh, since fruit do not dry well.
• HEIGHT 24in (60cm).
• SPREAD 15in (38cm).

C. annuum var. *annuum* 'Anaheim'
☼ ◊ ANNUAL

C. ANNUUM var. ***ANNUUM*** 'Hungarian Wax'
Habit Short-lived perennial, grown as an annual.
Fruits Mildly hot, slender, drooping, cone-shaped, with a waxy skin. Yellow, ripening to red.
Leaves Lance-shaped to oval. Mid-green.
• HEIGHT 18in (45cm).
• SPREAD 12in (30cm).

C. annuum var. *annuum* 'Hungarian Wax'
☼ ◊ ANNUAL

C. FRUTESCENS 'Tabasco'
Habit Upright, woody-based perennial, grown as an annual.
Fruits Hot-flavored, small, upright, conical. Green, ripening to red.
Leaves Oval. Mid-green.
• TIPS Used in hot-flavored condiments.
• HEIGHT 36in (90cm).
• SPREAD 24in (60cm).

C. frutescens 'Tabasco'
☼ ◊ ANNUAL

Liliaceae	GARLIC

ALLIUM SATIVUM

Habit Bulbous perennial. **Flowers** Bell-shaped, borne in clusters, often with bulbils, in summer. White. **Leaves** Linear. Gray-green.
• NATIVE HABITAT Probably central Asia.
• CULTIVATION Grow in deep, fertile, well-drained soil, in a warm, sunny site. Bulbs may be harvested during late summer and early autumn. They should be air-dried and then stored in frost-free conditions.
• PROPAGATION Plant bulbs or individual cloves 2–4in (5–10cm) deep in autumn.

Z4–9

Height 12–36in (30–90cm)

Spread to 12in (30cm)

Boraginaceae	VARIEGATED RUSSIAN COMFREY

SYMPHYTUM × UPLANDICUM 'Variegatum'

Habit Bristly perennial. **Flowers** Tubular, borne in heads, from late spring to summer. Pale lilac. **Leaves** Coarse, oblong to lance-shaped. Gray-green with broad, cream margins.
• NATIVE HABITAT Garden origin.
• CULTIVATION Grow in any moist soil in part-shade. Exposure to full sun causes leaf scorch.
• PROPAGATION By division in spring.
• WARNING Leaves and roots harmful if eaten. Contact with foliage may irritate skin.

Z4–9

Height 36in (90cm)

Spread 24in (60cm)

Verbenaceae	VERVAIN

VERBENA OFFICINALIS

Habit Woody-based perennial.
Flowers Tiny, borne in slender spikes during summer. Pale lilac. **Leaves** Oval, often cut into lobes. Dark green.
• NATIVE HABITAT Dry grassland in Europe, western Asia, and N. Africa.
• CULTIVATION Grow in well-drained, moderately fertile soil in a sunny site. Suitable for growing in a border as a contrast to large-leaved herbs.
• PROPAGATION By seed in autumn or spring, or by division in spring.

Z4–8

Height 32in (80cm)

Spread 24in (60cm)

Asteraceae	MILK THISTLE

SILYBUM MARITIMUM

Habit Rosette-forming biennial. **Flowers** Thistle-like, slightly scented, borne from summer to autumn. Purple-pink. **Leaves** Spiny, deeply lobed, glossy. Dark green, marbled and veined white.
• NATIVE HABITAT Stony places from southwest Europe to Afghanistan and N. Africa.
• CULTIVATION Grow in poor to moderately fertile, well-drained, neutral to alkaline soil, in full sun.
• PROPAGATION Sow seed *in situ*, either in spring as an annual, or in early summer or autumn as a biennial.

Z7–8

Height 3–4ft (0.9–1.2m) or more

Spread 24–36in (60–90cm)

| Asteraceae | PURPLE CONEFLOWER |

ECHINACEA PURPUREA
Habit Upright rhizomatous perennial.
Flowers Daisylike, with cone-shaped disk, borne in late summer. Purplish red, with golden-brown disk. *Leaves* Oval, toothed. Mid-green.
• NATIVE HABITAT Grasslands in the US.
• CULTIVATION Grow in fertile, moist but well-drained soil in a sunny site.
• PROPAGATION By seed at 55°F (13°C) in spring, by division in autumn or spring, or by root cuttings taken in late autumn to early winter.
• OTHER NAME *Rudbeckia purpurea*.

Z3–10

HEIGHT
3–4ft
(0.9–1.2m)

SPREAD
18in (45cm)

| Chenopodiaceae | RED ORACHE |

ATRIPLEX HORTENSIS var. *RUBRA*
Habit Upright annual. *Flowers* Small, borne in terminal spikes in summer. Blood-red to rust-brown. *Leaves* Edible, succulent, lance-shaped. Gray-green, flushed pink to beet-red.
• NATIVE HABITAT Waste and saline soils in Asia. Widely naturalized elsewhere.
• CULTIVATION Grow in moist but well-drained fertile soil in sun. Keep well watered during the growing season to prevent premature bolting.
• PROPAGATION Sow seed *in situ* in succession between spring and early summer. May self-seed.

ANNUAL

HEIGHT
to 4ft
(1.2m)

SPREAD
to 12in
(30cm)

| Lamiaceae | ANISE HYSSOP |

AGASTACHE FOENICULUM
Habit Upright perennial. *Flowers* Tubular, borne in dense spikes, from mid- to late summer. Blue, with violet bracts. *Leaves* Anise-scented, oval to lance-shaped. Mid-green, white-downy beneath.
• NATIVE HABITAT Dry hills in N. America.
• CULTIVATION Grow in fertile, well-drained soil in a sunny site.
• PROPAGATION Sow seed at 64°F (18°C) in early spring, divide in spring, or take stem-tip cuttings in summer. May self-seed.
• OTHER NAMES *A. anethiodora*, *A. anisata*.

Z6–9

HEIGHT
24–48in
(60–120cm)

SPREAD
18in (45cm)

| Lamiaceae | CURLY BEEFSTEAK PLANT |

PERILLA FRUTESCENS 'Crispa'
Habit Vigorous annual. *Flowers* Tiny, 2-lipped, borne in upright spikes in late summer and autumn. Pink. *Leaves* Edible, aromatic, broadly oval, pointed, with crisped margins. Dark green, purple, or bronze.
• NATIVE HABITAT Garden origin.
• CULTIVATION Grow in fertile, moist but well-drained soil in a sunny or partially shaded site.
• PROPAGATION Sow seed at 55–64°F (13–18°C) in spring.
• OTHER NAME *P. frutescens* var. *nankinensis*.

ANNUAL

HEIGHT
to 36in
(90cm)

SPREAD
12in (30cm)

Asteraceae	CHICORY

CICHORIUM INTYBUS

Habit Taprooted, clump-forming perennial. **Flowers** Daisylike, borne on long stems in summer. Clear blue, sometimes white or pink. **Leaves** Lance-shaped, toothed, mostly basal. Mid-green.
- NATIVE HABITAT Mediterranean region.
- CULTIVATION Grow in fertile, moist but well-drained, neutral to alkaline soil in full sun.
- PROPAGATION Sow seed in a cold frame in autumn or spring. Deadhead regularly, since it often self-seeds to the point of nuisance.

Z3–10

Height 4ft (1.2m)

Spread 24in (60cm)

Geraniaceae	ALUM ROOT, CRANESBILL

GERANIUM MACULATUM

Habit Erect perennial. **Flowers** Cupped, upward-facing, borne in late spring to mid-summer. Lilac to bright pink. **Leaves** Glossy, divided into 5–7 lobes. Mid-green.
- NATIVE HABITAT Woodlands and meadows in eastern N. America.
- CULTIVATION Grow in moist to boggy soil in sun or part shade. Suitable for growing in a mixed or herbaceous border or in a wild garden.
- PROPAGATION By seed in early autumn or spring or by division when dormant.

Z3–9

Height 24–30in (60–75cm)

Spread 18in (45cm)

Polemoniaceae	GREEK VALERIAN, JACOB'S LADDER

POLEMONIUM CAERULEUM

Habit Clump-forming perennial. **Flowers** Bell-shaped, borne in loose sprays, in early to mid-summer. Lavender blue or, rarely, pure white. **Leaves** Divided, lance-shaped. Bright green.
- NATIVE HABITAT Meadows, northern and central Europe, northern Asia, and western N. America.
- CULTIVATION Grow in fertile, moist but well-drained soil in sun or light shade. Suitable for growing in mixed or herbaceous borders.
- PROPAGATION By seed in a cold frame in autumn or spring, or by division in spring.

Z3–9

Height 12–36in (30–90cm)

Spread 12in (30cm)

Iridaceae	BLUE FLAG, WILD IRIS

IRIS VERSICOLOR

Habit Rhizomatous perennial. **Flowers** Beardless falls, borne on branching stems in early and mid-summer. Purple to lavender blue, veined white and yellow. **Leaves** Sword-shaped. Bright green.
- NATIVE HABITAT Watersides in eastern N. America.
- CULTIVATION Grow in fertile, moist to boggy soil, or in shallow water, in a sunny site.
- PROPAGATION By seed in autumn in a cold frame, or by division in late summer.
- WARNING All parts are harmful if eaten.

Z3–8

Height to 32in (80cm)

Spread indefinite

Boraginaceae	BORAGE

BORAGO OFFICINALIS
Habit Vigorous annual. ***Flowers*** Star-shaped, borne in branched heads throughout summer. Bright blue. ***Leaves*** Coarse, bristly-hairy, lance-shaped to oval. Dull mid-green.
• NATIVE HABITAT Rocky places in Europe.
• CULTIVATION Grow in any well-drained soil, including poor, dry types, in sun or dappled shade.
• PROPAGATION Sow seed *in situ* in spring. Self-sows freely.

ANNUAL

HEIGHT
24in (60cm)

SPREAD
18in (45cm)

Asteraceae	BACHELOR'S BUTTONS, CORNFLOWER

CENTAUREA CYANUS
Habit Upright annual. ***Flowers*** Hemispherical, with a hairy base, borne in summer. Deep blue, with violet-blue inner petals. ***Leaves*** Lance-shaped, sparsely lobed. Mid-green, with woolly-hairy underside.
• NATIVE HABITAT Grassland in northern temperate regions.
• CULTIVATION Grow in any well-drained soil in a sunny site.
• PROPAGATION Sow seed *in situ* in autumn or spring. May self-seed.

ANNUAL

HEIGHT
8–32in
(20–80cm)

SPREAD
6in (15cm)

Lamiaceae	HYSSOP

HYSSOPUS OFFICINALIS
Habit Aromatic, semi-evergreen shrub. ***Flowers*** Funnel-shaped, 2-lipped, borne in slender, whorled spikes, from mid-summer to autumn. Deep blue. ***Leaves*** Narrowly lance-shaped or oblong. Mid-green.
• NATIVE HABITAT Dry, rocky places in southern Europe.
• CULTIVATION Grow in fertile soil that is neutral to alkaline, in full sun.
• PROPAGATION By seed in autumn or spring, or by softwood cuttings taken in summer.

Z3–9

HEIGHT
18–24in
(45–60cm)

SPREAD
24–36in
(60–90cm)

LAVANDULA

The genus *Lavandula* consists of about 24 species of aromatic evergreen shrubs and subshrubs, which are native to dry, rocky, open habitats in the Mediterranean, the Canary Islands, and from North Africa to southwest Asia and India.

Commonly known as lavender, these plants are grown for their strongly scented foliage and spikes of fragrant flowers, which are an important source of nectar for bees and other beneficial insects. The flowers may be air dried for use in winter arrangements and potpourri. Those of *L. angustifolia* yield oils with medicinal properties; along with *L.* × *intermedia*, the flowers are also widely used in cosmetics and perfumery.

Lavenders are invaluable in mixed or herbaceous borders. The lower-growing types are ideal for rock gardens, containers, and as low edging, while taller species and cultivars may be used in informal hedging.

Grow in well-drained, moderately fertile soil in full sun. Species and cultivars that are less than fully hardy need a warm site with shelter from harsh winter winds. In cold-winter climates, tender types can be grown in pots and overwintered under glass in frost-free conditions. *L. lanata* needs sharp drainage and prefers a top-dressing of grit or gravel.

Deadhead and lightly trim plants after flowering; trim hedges and specimen plants in spring. Lavenders tolerate fairly close clipping, but this must be performed annually to maintain a dense habit, since they will not re-grow from old wood (see p. 148). Harvest flowers for drying before they are fully open, and hang them upside down in a cool, airy place (see p. 156).

Sow seed in containers in a cold frame or cool greenhouse in early autumn or spring. Stratify for more reliable germination. Root semi-ripe cuttings during summer.

L. STOECHAS f. *LEUCANTHA*
Habit Compact, bushy shrub.
Flowers Tubular, 2-lipped, in oval to oblong spikes, borne during summer. White, with white bracts.
Leaves Linear. Light gray-green.
• HEIGHT 12–36in (30–90cm).
• SPREAD 12–36in (30–90cm).

L. stoechas f. *leucantha*
☼ ◊ Z8–9

☗ ⚘

L. ANGUSTIFOLIA 'Nana Alba'
Habit Compact, upright, bushy shrub.
Flowers Tubular, 2-lipped, borne in short spikes, during summer. White.
Leaves Linear. Gray-green.
• TIPS Good for rock gardens, containers, and as border edging.
• HEIGHT 12in (30cm).
• SPREAD 12in (30cm).

L. angustifolia 'Nana Alba'
☼ ◊ Z5–8

☗ ⚘

L. ANGUSTIFOLIA 'Rosea'
Habit Compact, upright, bushy shrub.
Flowers Tubular, 2-lipped, borne in short spikes during summer. Pink.
Leaves Linear. Green.
• TIPS Good for mixed and herbaceous borders.
• HEIGHT 9–18in (23–45cm).
• SPREAD 12–18in (30–45cm).

L. angustifolia 'Rosea'
☼ ◊ Z5–8

☗ ⚘

LAVANDULA • 91

L. × *INTERMEDIA* Dutch Group
Habit Robust, rounded, low-branching shrub.
Flowers Slightly fragrant, tubular, 2-lipped, borne in dense spikes in mid-summer. Lavender-blue.
Leaves Large, narrowly oblong. Gray.
• TIPS Suitable for mixed borders.
• HEIGHT to 4ft (1.2m).
• SPREAD 16in (40cm).

L. × *intermedia*
Dutch Group
☼ ◊ Z5–7
❆

L. STOECHAS
Habit Compact, bushy shrub.
Flowers Tubular, 2-lipped, borne in dense, egg-shaped to oblong spikes from late spring through to summer. Dark purple, topped with rose-purple bracts.
Leaves Linear. Gray-green.
• HEIGHT 24in (60cm).
• SPREAD 24in (60cm).

L. STOECHAS subsp. *PEDUNCULATA*
Habit Compact, bushy shrub.
Flowers Tubular, 2-lipped, in oval to oblong spikes, borne above the foliage on long stems during summer. Dark purple with long maroon bracts.
Leaves Linear. Light gray-green.
• HEIGHT 30in (75cm).
• SPREAD 30in (75cm).

L. stoechas
French lavender
☼ ◊ Z8–9
❆ ✂

L. stoechas subsp.
pedunculata
Spanish lavender
☼ ◊ Z8–9
❆ ✂

L. DENTATA
Habit Bushy, spreading shrub.
Flowers Tubular, 2-lipped, borne in dense spikes from mid- to late summer. Dark purple.
Leaves Linear to lance-shaped, toothed. Gray-green, with white-woolly undersides.
• HEIGHT 24–36in (60–90cm).
• SPREAD 24–36in (60–90cm).

L. dentata
Fringed lavender
☼ ◊ Z8–9
❆

L. × *INTERMEDIA* 'Grappenhall'
Habit Robust, rounded, low-branching shrub.
Flowers Slightly fragrant, tubular, 2-lipped, borne in dense spikes in mid-summer. Lavender-blue.
Leaves Narrowly oblong. Gray-green.
• TIPS Good for mixed borders or low hedging.
• HEIGHT 36in (90cm).
• SPREAD 5ft (1.5m).

L. × *intermedia*
'Grappenhall'
☼ ◊ Z5–9
❆

L. ANGUSTIFOLIA
Habit Compact, bushy shrub.
Flowers Fragrant, tubular, 2-lipped, borne in dense, narrow spikes in mid- to late summer. Pale to deep purple.
Leaves Linear, downy. Gray-green.
• TIPS Suitable for growing in borders and as low hedging.
• HEIGHT 36in (90cm).
• SPREAD 4ft (1.2m).

L. angustifolia
Common lavender
☼ ◊ Z5–8
❆ ✂

L. PINNATA
Habit Bushy, spreading shrub.
Flowers Fragrant, tubular, 2-lipped, borne in slender spikes in late summer. Blue-purple.
Leaves Pinnate. Gray-green, with white hairs.
• TIPS Grow in a warm, sheltered site. Produces some flowers all year in warm climates.
• HEIGHT 36in (90cm).
• SPREAD 36in (90cm).

L. pinnata
☼ ◊ Z9–10
🌡

L. ANGUSTIFOLIA 'Folgate'
Habit Compact, bushy, spreading shrub.
Flowers Very fragrant, tubular, 2-lipped, borne in loose spikes in summer. Violet.
Leaves Linear, downy. Gray-green.
• TIPS Suitable for edging and for mixed and herbaceous borders.
• HEIGHT 20in (50cm).
• SPREAD 30in (75cm).

L. angustifolia 'Folgate'
☼ ◊ Z5–8
🌡 ✂

L. ANGUSTIFOLIA 'Hidcote'
Habit Compact, erect, bushy shrub.
Flowers Scented, tubular, 2-lipped, borne in dense spikes in early summer. Deep purple.
Leaves Linear, downy. Silver-gray.
• TIPS Suitable for edging or hedging.
• HEIGHT 24in (60cm).
• SPREAD 30in (75cm).

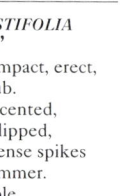

L. angustifolia 'Hidcote'
☼ ◊ Z5–8
🌡 ✂

L. ANGUSTIFOLIA 'Imperial Gem'
Habit Compact, erect, bushy shrub.
Flowers Scented, tubular, 2-lipped, borne in dense spikes throughout summer. Deep purple.
Leaves Linear, downy. Gray-green.
• TIPS Suitable for edging or hedging.
• HEIGHT 24in (60cm).
• SPREAD 24in (60cm).

L. angustifolia 'Imperial Gem'
☼ ◊ Z5–8
🌡 ✂

L. ANGUSTIFOLIA 'Munstead'
Habit Very compact, bushy, upright shrub.
Flowers Very fragrant, tubular, 2-lipped, borne in loose spikes in early summer. Blue-purple.
Leaves Linear, downy. Gray-green.
• TIPS Suitable for edging or hedging.
• HEIGHT 12–18in (30–45cm).
• SPREAD 30in (75cm).

L. angustifolia 'Munstead'
☼ ◊ Z5–8
🌡 ✂

L. × INTERMEDIA 'Seal'
Habit Vigorous, rounded shrub.
Flowers Slightly fragrant, tubular, 2-lipped, borne in dense spikes in mid-summer. Pale purple.
Leaves Narrowly lance-shaped. Mid-green.
• TIPS Good for mixed borders or hedging.
• HEIGHT 5ft (1.5m).
• SPREAD 4ft (1.2m).

L. × *intermedia* 'Seal'
☼ ◊ Z5–9
🌡

LAVANDULA • 93

L. × INTERMEDIA
Old English Group
Habit Vigorous, rounded shrub.
Flowers Tubular, 2-lipped, borne in long-stemmed spikes in summer. Pale lavender to violet.
Leaves Narrowly lance-shaped. Gray-green.
• TIPS Good for a mixed border or edging.
• HEIGHT 20in (50cm).
• SPREAD 20in (50cm).

L. × *intermedia*
Old English Group
☼ ◊ Z5–8
⚥

L. × INTERMEDIA
'Twickel Purple'
Habit Vigorous, bushy, rather untidy shrub.
Flowers Scented, tubular, 2-lipped, borne in long spikes in summer. Dark purple.
Leaves Narrowly oblong. Grey-green, often flushed purple in winter.
• TIPS Suitable for a mixed border.
• HEIGHT 24in (60cm).
• SPREAD 36in (90cm).

L. × *intermedia*
'Twickel Purple'
☼ ◊ Z5–9
⚥

L. 'Sawyers'
Habit Robust, rounded shrub.
Flowers Large, tubular, 2-lipped, borne in dense, long-stemmed spikes in summer. Purple, from lavender-blue buds.
Leaves Linear to lance-shaped. Gray.
• TIPS Suitable for low hedging.
• HEIGHT 18–30in (45–70cm).
• SPREAD 4ft (1.2m).

L. 'Sawyers'
(hybrid of *L. lanata* × *L. angustifolia*)
☼ ◊ Z7–9
⚥

L. × ALLARDII
Habit Vigorous shrub.
Flowers Tubular, 2-lipped, borne in large, long-stemmed spikes from summer to autumn. Violet-purple.
Leaves Broadly linear, with scalloped margins. Gray-green.
• TIPS Needs a warm, well-drained site.
• HEIGHT 3–5ft (0.9m–1.5m).
• SPREAD 4ft (1.2m).

L. × *allardii*
Giant lavender
☼ ◊ Z8–9
⚥

L. LANATA
Habit Rounded, bushy shrub.
Flowers Fragrant, tubular, 2-lipped, borne in dense, long-stemmed spikes in mid- to late summer. Deep purple.
Leaves Linear to lance-shaped. Densely white-woolly.
• TIPS Must have sharp drainage.
• HEIGHT 30in (75cm).
• SPREAD 36in (90cm).

L. lanata
Woolly lavender
☼ ◊ Z8–9
⚥

L. × INTERMEDIA
Habit Robust, rounded shrub.
Flowers Tubular, 2-lipped, borne in long spikes in summer. Violet to light blue.
Leaves Oblong to lance- or spoon-shaped. Gray green, with silver hairs.
• HEIGHT 12–20in (30–50cm).
• SPREAD 12–20in (30–50cm).

L. × *intermedia*
Lavandin
☼ ◊ Z5–7
⚥

L. VIRIDIS
Habit Bushy, upright shrub.
Flowers Small, tubular, 2-lipped, borne in dense, short-stemmed spikes in mid- to late summer. White, with green bracts.
Leaves Lemon-scented, oblong. Fresh green.
• TIPS Needs a warm, sheltered site with well-drained soil.
• HEIGHT 24in (60cm).
• SPREAD 30in (75cm).

L. viridis
Green lavender
☼ ◊ Z9–10
⚥

SALVIA

The genus *Salvia* consists of about 900 species of annuals, biennials, herbaceous and evergreen perennials and shrubs, which are found throughout the drier temperate and tropical zones, usually in sunny and open habitats. Commonly known as sages, most *Salvia* are aromatic. They bear hooded, tubular, 2-lipped flowers, often with conspicuous or colorful bracts, in interrupted spikes, and frequently have hairy or woolly foliage.

Many shrubby and perennial species are ideal for growing in an herb garden and for a mixed or herbaceous border, where they can provide foliar contrasts of form and color. The flowers are rich in nectar and are attractive to bees and other beneficial insects in the garden.

The foliage of several species, such as *S. coccinea* and *S. dorisiana*, can be dried for use in potpourri, while *S. officinalis* and its variants are invaluable for culinary use.

Some sages, like *S. viridis* and *S. sclarea*, produce flowers that are suitable for cutting and may be used either fresh or dried in floral arrangements.

Grow in well-drained, neutral to alkaline soil in a warm, sunny site. In cold areas, overwinter tender species in a greenhouse or conservatory. Use soil-based potting mix and provide full light with good ventilation. Water freely and apply a balanced liquid fertilizer monthly when in growth; water sparingly during winter. Trim any straggly growth in spring to keep the plant compact, but avoid cutting into old wood. Sparse or leggy plants need to be replaced every 2–7 years.

Sow seed *in situ* in spring for perennials or at 61–64°F (16–18°C) for annual cultivars, or in a cold frame in summer for biennials. *S. officinalis* Purpurascens Group may come true from seed. Take stem-tip cuttings in spring or summer.

S. OFFICINALIS 'Albiflora'
Habit Subshrubby, evergreen perennial.
Flowers Two-lipped, borne in spikes in summer. White, with green bracts.
Leaves Narrowly oval. Gray-green.
• HEIGHT 24–32in (60–80cm).
• SPREAD 36in (90cm).

S. officinalis 'Albiflora'
☼ ◊ Z5–8

S. SCLAREA var. TURKESTANICA
Habit Upright, branched biennial or perennial.
Flowers Two-lipped, borne from spring through to summer. White, flecked pink, with pink bracts.
Leaves Large, strong smelling, wrinkled, heart-shaped at the base, oval, toothed. Mid-green.
• HEIGHT 36in (90cm).
• SPREAD 24in (60cm).

S. sclarea var. *turkestanica*
☼ ◊ Z4–9

S. OFFICINALIS 'Tricolor'
Habit Subshrubby, evergreen perennial.
Flowers Two-lipped, borne in summer. Pale lilac-blue.
Leaves Oblong to oval. Gray-green, with cream, pink, and purple zones.
• HEIGHT 18–24in (45–60cm).
• SPREAD to 24in (60cm).

S. officinalis 'Tricolor'
☼ ◊ Z7–9

S. COCCINEA
Habit Slender, upright annual or short-lived perennial.
Flowers Two-lipped, borne in long, slender, open, terminal spikes from summer to autumn. Scarlet to dark red.
Leaves Oval to heart-shaped, toothed, hairy. Dark green.
• HEIGHT 12–18in (30–45cm).
• SPREAD 12in (30cm).

S. coccinea
Scarlet sage, Red sage, Indian fire
☼ ◊ Z8–10

SALVIA • 95

S. COCCINEA 'Lady in Red'
Habit Compact, bushy annual or short-lived perennial.
Flowers Two-lipped, borne in slender terminal spikes in summer to autumn. Brilliant red.
Leaves Oval to heart-shaped, toothed, hairy. Dark green.
• HEIGHT 12–15in (30–38cm).
• SPREAD 12in (30cm).

S. coccinea 'Lady in Red'
☼ ◊ Z8–10
⌀

S. ELEGANS 'Scarlet Pineapple'
Habit Subshrubby, herbaceous perennial.
Flowers Two-lipped, long-tubed, borne in clusters from winter to spring. Rich scarlet.
Leaves Pineapple-scented, triangular, softly hairy. Mid-green.
• OTHER NAME *S. rutilans*.
• HEIGHT 6ft (2m).
• SPREAD 3ft (0.9m).

S. elegans 'Scarlet Pineapple'
Pineapple sage
☼ ◊ Z9–10
⌀ ⌂

S. FRUTICOSA
Habit Bushy, white-hairy, evergreen shrub.
Flowers Two-lipped, borne in terminal or axillary spikes in summer. Mauve to pink, rarely white.
Leaves Simple or trilobed. Gray-green with white, downy undersides.
• OTHER NAME *S. triloba*.
• HEIGHT 36in (90cm).
• SPREAD 36in (90cm).

S. fruticosa
Greek sage
☼ ◊ Z8–9
⌀ ⌂ ⚘

S. SCLAREA
Habit Upright, branched biennial or perennial.
Flowers Two-lipped, borne from spring to summer. Cream and lilac to pink or blue, with lilac bracts.
Leaves Strong-smelling, wrinkled, heart-shaped at the base, oval to oblong, toothed. Mid-green.
• HEIGHT 36in (90cm).
• SPREAD 24in (60cm).

S. sclarea
Clary sage
☼ ◊ Z4–9
⌀ ⌂ ⚘

S. OFFICINALIS Purpurascens Group
Habit Subshrubby, evergreen perennial.
Flowers Two-lipped, borne during summer. Purple-blue, with red-purple bracts.
Leaves Oblong to oval. Grayish red-purple.
• HEIGHT 24–32in (60–80cm).
• SPREAD 36in (90cm).

S. officinalis Purpurascens Group
Purple sage, Red sage
☼ ◊ Z7–9
⌀ ⌂ ⚘

S. VIRIDIS
Habit Bushy, upright annual.
Flowers Tiny, enclosed in papery bracts, borne in summer. Pink to lilac, with dark-veined pink, purple, or white bracts.
Leaves Oval to oblong, notched, hairy. Mid-green.
• OTHER NAME *S. horminum*.
• HEIGHT 18in (45cm).
• SPREAD 8in (20cm).

S. viridis
Annual clary
☼ ◊ ANNUAL
⌀ ⌂ ⚘

S. VIRIDIS 'Claryssa'
Habit Bushy, compact annual.
Flowers Tiny, enclosed in papery bracts, borne in summer. Pink to lilac or in mixed shades, with rose-pink, blue, purple, or white bracts, with dark veins.
Leaves Oval to oblong, notched, and hairy. Mid-green.
• HEIGHT 16in (40cm).
• SPREAD 8in (20cm).

S. viridis 'Claryssa'
☼ ◊ ANNUAL
⌀ ⌂ ⚘

S. APIANA
Habit Downy-stemmed, evergreen shrub.
Flowers Two-lipped, borne in erect, branching clusters in summer. White to pale lavender.
Leaves Large, oval, sometimes notched. Silver-white hairy.
• TIPS Needs to be grown in a sharply drained site.
• HEIGHT to 10ft (3m).
• SPREAD 6ft (2m).

S. apiana
California white sage, Bee sage
☼ ◊ Z8–9
⚱ ⌂ ✂

S. DORISIANA
Habit Shrubby, evergreen perennial.
Flowers Two-lipped, borne in spikes in winter. Magenta to rose-pink.
Leaves Fruit-scented, large, oval, narrowly pointed, velvety-hairy. Mid-green with conspicuous veins.
• HEIGHT 3–5ft (0.9–1.5m).
• SPREAD 3–5ft (0.9–1.5m).

S. dorisiana
Fruit-scented sage
☼ ◊ Z10–11
⚱ ⌂

S. LAVANDULIFOLIA
Habit Woody-based, shrubby perennial.
Flowers Two-lipped, borne in terminal and axillary spikes in summer. Blue-violet.
Leaves Lavender-balsam scented, narrowly oblong, mostly basal. Gray to white-woolly.
• OTHER NAME *S. hispanica*.
• HEIGHT 20in (50cm).
• SPREAD 24in (60cm).

S. lavandulifolia
Narrow-leaved sage, Spanish sage
☼ ◊ Z5–9
⚱ ⌂ ✂

S. OFFICINALIS 'Icterina'
Habit Subshrubby, evergreen perennial.
Flowers Two-lipped, borne in spikes in summer. Lilac-blue.
Leaves Oblong to oval, velvety. Grayish green, variegated yellow.
• HEIGHT 32in (80cm).
• SPREAD 36in (90cm).

S. officinalis **'Icterina'**
☼ ◊ Z7–9
⚱ ⌂ ✂

S. OFFICINALIS
Habit Subshrubby, evergreen perennial.
Flowers Two-lipped, borne in axillary and terminal spikes in summer. Lilac-blue, pink, rarely white.
Leaves Oblong to oval, velvety-woolly. Pale gray-green.
• HEIGHT 32in (80cm).
• SPREAD 36in (90cm).

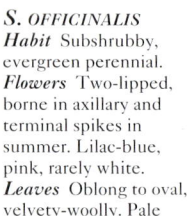

S. officinalis
Common sage
☼ ◊ Z5–8
⚱ ⌂ ✂

S. OFFICINALIS 'Kew Gold'
Habit Compact, evergreen perennial.
Flowers Two-lipped, borne in spikes in summer. Mauve.
Leaves Oblong to oval, velvety. Golden-yellow, flecked green.
• HEIGHT 12in (30cm).
• SPREAD 18in (45cm).

S. officinalis **'Kew Gold'**
☼ ◊ Z7–9
⚱ ⌂ ✂

S. OFFICINALIS 'Berggarten'
Habit Dense, compact, evergreen perennial.
Flowers Two-lipped, borne in axillary and terminal spikes in summer. Purple-blue.
Leaves Rounded, velvety-woolly. Pale gray-green.
• HEIGHT 18in (45cm).
• SPREAD 36in (90cm).

S. officinalis **'Berggarten'**
☼ ◊ Z5–8
⚱ ⌂ ✂

ARTEMISIA

The genus *Artemisia* consists of about 300 species of aromatic, evergreen or deciduous annuals, perennials, and shrubs, which are native to dry fields and scrub, mostly in the northern hemisphere, with a few species found in South Africa and western South America.

Artemisias are grown primarily for their foliage, which is usually deeply cut and often silver or white. Most types have insignificant, dull-colored flowers that may be removed for the best foliage effect. The foliage of many white- or silver-leaved species is used in floral arrangements and often lends a distinctive fragrance when used fresh. Artemisias also suit mixed or herbaceous borders, whether to provide foliage contrast, to form the backbone of a white- or silver-themed border, or for use in Mediterranean-style plantings. Several are bitter herbs with medicinal uses, especially in the treatment of fevers and intestinal worms, hence the common name wormwood. *A. dracunculus* (tarragon) is grown mainly for culinary use. Although *A. d.* subsp. *dracunculoides* is hardier and more vigorous, it has a less pleasant flavor that is said to improve with age.

Grow in well-drained fertile soil in full sun, although most species tolerate poor, dry soils. *A. lactiflora* and its cultivars prefer moisture-retentive soils and tolerate partial shade. Cut back shrubby species hard in spring to keep them compact and to produce the most attractive foliage. Harvest tarragon shoots during the growing season. Whole plants may be cut and dried at flowering time for herbal use.

Propagate by sowing seed in containers in a cold frame or cool greenhouse in autumn or spring. Divide clump-forming species in spring or autumn. Take heeled greenwood or semi-ripe cuttings from shrubby species in early to mid-summer.

A. LACTIFLORA
Habit Vigorous, upright, clump-forming perennial.
Flowers Tiny, borne in long, open, plume-shaped clusters in late summer. Creamy white.
Leaves Deeply lobed, jaggedly toothed. Dark green.
• TIPS Best grown in moist but well-drained soil.
• HEIGHT 5ft (1.5m).
• SPREAD 24in (60cm).

A. lactiflora
White mugwort
☼ ◐ Z5–8

A. LACTIFLORA Guizhou Group
Habit Upright, clump-forming, maroon-stemmed perennial.
Flowers Tiny, borne in plume-shaped clusters during late summer. Cream.
Leaves Deeply lobed, toothed. Dark green.
• OTHER NAME *A. kitadakensis* 'Guizhou'.
• HEIGHT to 5ft (1.5m).
• SPREAD 24in (60cm).

A. lactiflora
Guizhou Group
☼ ◐ Z5–8

A. ARBORESCENS
Habit Upright, rounded, semi-evergreen or evergreen shrub.
Flowers Tiny, borne in one-sided clusters from summer to early autumn. Yellow-brown.
Leaves Fernlike, finely cut. Silver-white.
• TIPS Good for a mixed border. Use cut stems in flower arrangements.
• HEIGHT 12in (30cm).
• SPREAD 5ft (1.5m).

A. arborescens
Tree wormwood
☼ ◊ Z8–9
🌡

A. PEDEMONTANA
Habit Tufted, evergreen or semi-evergreen, sub-shrubby perennial.
Flowers Tiny, globose, borne in summer. Yellow.
Leaves Finely divided, fernlike. Silver-hairy.
• OTHER NAMES
A. assoana, *A. caucasica*, *A. lanata*.
• HEIGHT 6–12in (15–30cm).
• SPREAD 6–12in (15–30cm).

A. pedemontana
☼ ◊ Z3–7

🌡

A. 'Powis Castle'
Habit Upright, shrubby, semi-evergreen or evergreen perennial.
Flowers Insignificant, and rarely produced.
Leaves Feathery, finely cut. Silver-white.
• TIPS Best grown in sharply drained, poor soil.
• OTHER NAME *A. arborescens* 'Brass Band'.
• HEIGHT 24in (60cm).
• SPREAD to 4ft (1.2m).

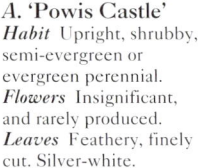

A. 'Powis Castle'
☼ ◊ Z6–9
🌡

A. LUDOVICIANA
Habit Clump-forming, rhizomatous perennial.
Flowers Tiny, borne in white-woolly clusters in mid-summer. Brown-yellow.
Leaves Lance-shaped, toothed or entire. Silver-white to gray-green.
• TIPS Good in a white or silver border and for use in flower arrangements.
• HEIGHT to 4ft (1.2m).
• SPREAD indefinite.

A. ludoviciana
Western mugwort, White sage, Cudweed
☼ ◊ Z4–9
🌡

A. LUDOVICIANA
'Valerie Finnis'
Habit Clump-forming, rhizomatous perennial.
Flowers Tiny, borne in white-woolly clusters in mid-summer. Yellow.
Leaves Lance-shaped, sometimes with sharply cut margins. Silver-gray.
• TIPS Suitable for a white or silver border.
• HEIGHT to 24in (60cm).
• SPREAD 24in (60cm) or more.

A. ludoviciana
'Valerie Finnis'
☼ ◊ Z4–9

🌡

ARTEMISIA • 99

A. ABROTANUM
Habit Upright, semi-evergreen or deciduous shrub.
Flowers Tiny, borne in clusters in late summer but seldom borne during cool summers. Dull yellow.
Leaves Deeply cut into linear lobes. Gray-green.
• TIPS Suitable as a low, informal hedge.
• HEIGHT 36in (90cm).
• SPREAD 24in (60cm).

A. abrotanum
Lad's love, Old man, Southernwood
☼ ◊ Z6–10
❆ ⛁ ✄

A. ABSINTHIUM
Habit Clump-forming, woody-based perennial.
Flowers Tiny, globose, borne in loose clusters during summer. Yellow-gray.
Leaves Finely cut, finely hairy. Silvery gray.
• TIPS Good for a mixed border. Cut stems suit flower arrangements.
• HEIGHT 36in (90cm).
• SPREAD 24–36in (60–90cm).

A. absinthium
Absinthe, Wormwood
☼ ◊ Z3–9
❆ ✄

A. PONTICA
Habit Rhizomatous, evergreen perennial.
Flowers Tiny, borne in loose clusters in early summer. Gray-white.
Leaves Finely cut and woolly-hairy. Gray-green.
• TIPS Good for growing at the front of a mixed or silver-themed border.
• HEIGHT 16–32in (40–80cm).
• SPREAD indefinite.

A. pontica
Roman wormwood, Small absinthe
☼ ◊ Z5–9
❆ ✄

A. DRACUNCULUS
Habit Clump-forming, subshrubby perennial.
Flowers Tiny, borne in nodding clusters during summer. Yellow-green.
Leaves Mint-anise flavored, linear. Bright green.
• TIPS Prefers stony soils. Protect in severe winter weather.
• HEIGHT 5ft (1.5m).
• SPREAD 24in (60cm).

A. dracunculus
Estragon, French tarragon
☼ ◊ Z4–7
❆ ⛁ ✄

A. VULGARIS
Habit Upright perennial with red-purple stems.
Flowers Tiny, borne in clusters in late summer. Red-brown.
Leaves Pinnate. Dark green, with white-downy undersides.
• TIPS Suitable for growing in a wild garden.
• HEIGHT to 5½ft (1.7m).
• SPREAD to 36in (90cm).

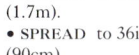

A. vulgaris
Mugwort, Felon herb
☼ ◊ Z4–10
❆ ⛁ ✄

TANACETUM

The genus *Tanacetum* consists of 70 species of annuals and evergreen or herbaceous perennials and subshrubs, which grow on dry slopes, meadows, and mountain cliffs in northern temperate regions. Some species were formerly included in other genera, namely *Balsamita*, *Chrysanthemum*, *Matricaria*, and *Pyrethrum*.

Commonly known as tansies, *Tanacetum* bear daisy- or buttonlike flowerheads and are ideal for herb gardens. The cultivars of *T. parthenium* are good for low edging, while the low carpet of foliage and the tall flower clusters of *T. balsamita* can be used at the front of a herbaceous or mixed border. Some species, such as *T. vulgare* and *T. parthenium*, may be invasive.

Many *Tanacetum* are strongly aromatic. When cut and dried, their leaves make an aromatic addition to potpourri. The flowers and leaves of *T. cinerariifolium* and *T. vulgare* contain insecticidal compounds; the latter was once used as a strewing herb. *T. parthenium* is used in the treatment of migraine and rheumatism. The leaves of *T. vulgare* are used to symbolize bitter Passover herbs and are also used to flavor cakes eaten at Easter time. Contact with the foliage may irritate the skin.

Grow in well-drained, preferably sandy soil in full sun. Most species tolerate a range of soil types, including dry, stony soils. *T. balsamita* and *T. parthenium* will grow in partial or dappled shade, and gray-leaved species need good drainage. Deadhead *T. parthenium* after flowering to prevent excessive self-seeding.

Propagate by seed sown at 55–61°F (10–18°C) in late winter or early spring. *T. parthenium* and its cultivars self-seed easily, or softwood cuttings can be taken in early summer. Root basal cuttings of *T. vulgare*, *T. balsamita*, and their cultivars during spring. Divide in spring or autumn.

T. PARTHENIUM 'Plenum'
Habit Short-lived, woody-based perennial.
Flowers Double, daisylike, borne in dense heads in summer. White.
Leaves Aromatic and deeply cut into scalloped segments. Fresh green.
• TIPS Suitable for use as border edging. Tolerates light shade.
• HEIGHT 14in (35cm).
• SPREAD 12in (30cm).

T. parthenium 'Plenum'
☼ ◊ Z4–9
☼ ⚘

T. CINERARIIFOLIUM
Habit Slender, hairy-stemmed perennial.
Flowers Solitary, daisylike, borne from early summer through to early autumn. White, with a yellow disk.
Leaves Lance-shaped to oblong, finely divided. Dark green, with white-hairy undersides.
• HEIGHT 12–30in (30–75cm).
• SPREAD 12in (30cm).

T. cinerariifolium
Pyrethrum, Dalmatian pellitory
☼ ◊ Z4–9
☼ ⚘

T. BALSAMITA
Habit Rhizomatous, mat-forming perennial.
Flowers Long-stemmed, daisylike, borne in heads in late summer and early autumn. White, with a central yellow disk.
Leaves Mint-scented, oblong, scalloped. Gray-green, with silver hairs.
• TIPS Suitable for use as border edging.
• HEIGHT 36in (90cm).
• SPREAD 18in (45cm).

T. balsamita
Alecost, Costmary
☼ ◊ Z4–8
☼ ⚘

T. BALSAMITA* subsp. *BALSAMETOIDES
Habit Rhizomatous, mat-forming perennial.
Flowers Daisylike, borne in late summer and early autumn. White, with a yellow disk.
Leaves Scented, oblong to oval, scalloped. Gray-green with silver hairs.
• OTHER NAME *T. b.* var. *tomentosum*.
• HEIGHT 36in (90cm).
• SPREAD 36in (90cm).

T. balsamita subsp. *balsametoides*
Camphor plant
☼ ◊ Z4–8
♂ ♀

***T. PARTHENIUM* 'Aureum'**
Habit Short-lived, woody-based perennial.
Flowers Daisylike, borne during summer. White, with a yellow disk.
Leaves Aromatic, deeply cut. Golden-yellow.
• TIPS Suitable for use as border edging. Tolerates shade.
• HEIGHT 18in (45cm).
• SPREAD 12in (30cm).

T. parthenium 'Aureum'
☼ ◊ Z4–9
♂ ♀

T. PARTHENIUM
Habit Short-lived, woody-based perennial.
Flowers Daisylike, borne in dense heads in summer. White, with a yellow disk.
Leaves Aromatic, deeply scalloped. Fresh green.
• TIPS Suitable for use as border edging. Tolerates shade.
• HEIGHT 18–24in (45–60cm).
• SPREAD 12in (30cm).

T. parthenium
Feverfew
☼ ◊ Z4–9
♂ ♀

T. VULGARE* var. *CRISPUM
Habit Vigorous, upright, rhizomatous perennial.
Flowers Small, button-like, borne in flat-topped heads from late summer through to autumn. Bright yellow.
Leaves Aromatic, oblong, pinnate, in deeply lobed or toothed segments. Fresh green.
• HEIGHT 24in (60cm).
• SPREAD indefinite.

T. vulgare var. *crispum*
Fern-leaved tansy
☼ ◊ Z4–9
♂ ♀ ♂

***T. PARTHENIUM* 'Golden Moss'**
Habit Short-lived, carpet-forming perennial.
Flowers Daisylike, borne in summer. White, with a yellow disk.
Leaves Aromatic, moss-like, with scalloped edges. Golden-yellow.
• TIPS Suitable for use as border edging and bedding.
• HEIGHT 6in (15cm).
• SPREAD 6in (15cm).

T. parthenium 'Golden Moss'
☼ ◊ Z4–9
♂ ♀

T. VULGARE
Habit Vigorous, upright, rhizomatous perennial.
Flowers Small, button-like, borne in flat-topped heads from late summer to autumn. Bright yellow.
Leaves Scented, oblong, pinnate, toothed or lobed segments. Dark green.
• TIPS Tends to be very invasive.
• HEIGHT 24–36in (60–90cm).
• SPREAD 18in (45cm).

T. vulgare
Tansy
☼ ◊ Z4–9
♂ ♀ ♂

| Lamiaceae | LEMON BALM, MELISSA |

MELISSA OFFICINALIS

Habit Dense, bushy, upright perennial.
Flowers Small, tubular, 2-lipped, borne in irregular spikes, over long periods in summer. Pale yellow, fading to white or lilac-tinted white.
Leaves Strongly lemon-scented, oval, toothed, wrinkled. Bright green.
• NATIVE HABITAT Scrub, shady places, and on disturbed and cultivated ground in Europe, and naturalized in gardens elsewhere.
• CULTIVATION Grow in poor to moderately fertile, moist but well-drained soil in a sunny or lightly shaded site. Ideal for growing in an herb garden, in containers, or in mixed or herbaceous borders. The plant is very attractive to bees and other beneficial insects. Harvest leaves for culinary and medicinal use before flowering. Cut back at or just after flowering to produce fresh young leaves. The dried leaves are excellent for use in potpourri and herb pillows.
• PROPAGATION Sow seed in containers in a cold frame in spring, or divide in spring as growth begins, or divide in autumn.

Z4–9

HEIGHT
24–48in
(60–120cm)

SPREAD
18in (45cm)

Apiaceae	VARIEGATED GOUTWEED

Aegopodium podagraria 'Variegata'

Habit Vigorous, rhizomatous perennial.
Flowers Tiny, borne in flat clusters in early summer. Creamy white. ***Leaves*** Divided, oval. Deep green, heavily splashed creamy white.
• NATIVE HABITAT Garden origin.
• CULTIVATION Grow in any soil in a sunny or partially shaded site. Deadhead regularly to prevent seeding, although not as invasive as the species. Suitable for use as deciduous groundcover in poor and dry soils.
• PROPAGATION Divide in autumn or spring.

Z5–8

Height
24in (60cm)

Spread
indefinite

Brassicaceae	HORSERADISH

Armoracia rusticana

Habit Taprooted perennial. ***Flowers*** Cross-shaped, borne in terminal clusters, from late spring to late summer. White. ***Leaves*** Oval to oblong, toothed, puckered, coarse, shiny. Dark green.
• NATIVE HABITAT Southeast Europe.
• CULTIVATION Grow in deep, light, moist but well-drained, fertile soil in sun or light shade.
• PROPAGATION Divide or take root cuttings in winter, or sow seed *in situ* in spring.

Z3–10

Height
36in (90cm)

Spread
18in (45cm)

Fabaceae	FENUGREEK

Trigonella foenum-graecum

Habit Upright, aromatic annual. ***Flowers*** Pea-like, solitary or paired, borne in summer. Creamy yellow, tinted violet at the base. ***Leaves*** Edible, aromatic, divided into 3 leaflets. Mid-green. ***Fruits*** Beaked pod with pale brown seeds.
• NATIVE HABITAT Southern Europe to Asia. Widely cultivated.
• CULTIVATION Grow in fertile, well-drained soil in a sunny site.
• PROPAGATION Sow seed *in situ* in spring. Seed sold for culinary use may be used for propagation.

Annual

Height
24in (60cm)

Spread
12–18in (30–45cm)

Pedaliaceae	SESAME

Sesamum indicum

Habit Upright annual. ***Flowers*** Bell-shaped, borne in summer. Off-white. ***Leaves*** Strongly scented, large, broadly oval, irregularly toothed. Mid-green. ***Fruits*** Capsule. Creamy white seeds.
• NATIVE HABITAT Tropical Asia. Widely grown.
• CULTIVATION Grow in sandy, well-drained soil in a warm, sunny site.
• PROPAGATION Sow seed *in situ* in spring, when danger of frost has passed, or in autumn in frost-free areas. Untoasted seed bought for culinary use may be used for propagation.

Annual

Height
36in (90cm)

Spread
18–36in (45–90cm)

| Lamiaceae | PATCHOULI |

POGOSTEMON CABLIN
Habit Aromatic perennial. **Flowers** Borne in terminal and axillary spikes throughout the year. Violet, marked white. **Leaves** Oval to triangular, irregularly toothed, velvety. Dark green.
• NATIVE HABITAT India and Malaysia.
• CULTIVATION Grow in moist, fertile soil, in high humidity and full sun. Under glass, use a soil-based mix. Water freely when in growth.
• PROPAGATION By heeled greenwood cuttings in late spring, or by stem-tip cuttings rooted in water.
• OTHER NAME *P. patchouli*.

Min. 61–64°F (16–18°C)

HEIGHT 36in (90cm)

SPREAD 36in (90cm)

| Chenopodiaceae | GOOD KING HENRY |

CHENOPODIUM BONUS-HENRICUS
Habit Upright perennial. **Flowers** Small, borne in terminal spikes in summer. Green. **Leaves** Edible, succulent, triangular to diamond-shaped. Deep green.
• NATIVE HABITAT Waste and bare ground in central and southern Europe.
• CULTIVATION Grow in moist but well-drained fertile soil in sun. Keep well watered during the growing season to prevent premature bolting.
• PROPAGATION Sow seed *in situ* between spring and early summer, or divide in autumn or spring.

Z5–9

HEIGHT 30in (75cm)

SPREAD 20in (50cm)

| Polygonaceae | COMMON SORREL |

RUMEX ACETOSA
Habit Perennial. **Flowers** Small, borne in branched or unbranched spikes during summer. Red-green. **Leaves** Sharp, acidic-flavored, arrow-shaped. Mid- to bright green.
• NATIVE HABITAT Meadows in Europe.
• CULTIVATION Grow in moist, fertile soil in sun or light shade. Harvest young leaves for culinary use in the growing season. Remove flower stems before flowering to prolong leaf production.
• PROPAGATION Sow seed *in situ* in spring, or divide in autumn or spring.

Z4–8

HEIGHT 24–36in (60–90cm)

SPREAD to 18in (45cm)

| Buxaceae | EDGING BOXWOOD |

BUXUS SEMPERVIRENS 'Suffruticosa'
Habit Compact, slow-growing shrub. **Flowers** Small, star-shaped, male and female borne on same plant in spring. Yellow-green. **Leaves** Oval to oblong, glossy. Dark green.
• NATIVE HABITAT Garden origin.
• CULTIVATION Grow in well-drained soil that is neutral to alkaline, in sun or part shade. Tolerates hard clipping and may be shaped for topiary.
• PROPAGATION By semi-ripe cuttings in summer.
• WARNING All parts of the plant are toxic if eaten. Contact with foliage may irritate skin.

Z6–8

HEIGHT 36in (90cm)

SPREAD 5ft (1.5m)

| Zingiberaceae | TURMERIC |

Curcuma longa

Habit Rhizomatous, aromatic perennial.
Flowers Conelike, borne in spring. Yellow, tinted pink, with pale green lower bracts.
Leaves Shiny, pointed, oval to oblong, up to 50cm (20in) long. Bright green.
• NATIVE HABITAT Seasonally dry forests in India.
• CULTIVATION Grow in moist, fertile soil, in high humidity and shade. Suitable for use as groundcover in warm climates. Under glass, use a soil-based mix. Admit bright filtered light. Water freely when in growth, but keep almost dry during dormancy. Apply a balanced liquid fertilizer monthly.
• PROPAGATION By seed sown at 70°F (21°C) in autumn, or by division during the dormant period.
• OTHER NAME *C. domestica*.

Min. 59–64°F (15–18°C)

HEIGHT 36in (90cm)

SPREAD 36in (90cm)

Araceae	VARIEGATED SWEET FLAG

ACORUS CALAMUS 'Variegatus'

Habit Aromatic, rhizomatous, aquatic perennial.
Flowers Insignificant, borne in a spike in midsummer. Green. **Leaves** Aromatic, strap-shaped. Bright green, with creamy white stripes.
• NATIVE HABITAT Garden origin.
• CULTIVATION Grow in fertile, boggy soil or in the muddy margins of a pond or stream, in full sun. Use an aquatic container to restrict spread.
• PROPAGATION Divide in spring as growth begins. Pot up divisions and grow on, but set out only when they are well established.

Z3–9

HEIGHT
24–36in
(60–90cm)

SPREAD
24in (60cm)

Liliaceae	BARBADOS ALOE

ALOE VERA

Habit Evergreen, clumping, suckering perennial.
Flowers Tubular, borne in spikes in summer. Yellow. **Leaves** Fleshy, lance-shaped. Gray-green.
• NATIVE HABITAT Origin unknown.
• CULTIVATION Grow in sharply drained soil and full sun. Under glass, use a soil-based mix with added sharp sand or perlite.
Water moderately and keep almost dry in winter.
• PROPAGATION By offsets in spring or early summer, or by seed sown at 70°F (21°C) in spring.
• OTHER NAMES *A. arabica, A. barbadensis, A. indica*.

Min. 41°F (5°C)

HEIGHT
24in (60cm)

SPREAD
indefinite

Araceae	SWEET FLAG, CALAMUS

ACORUS CALAMUS

Habit Aromatic, rhizomatous, aquatic perennial.
Flowers Insignificant, borne in a spike in midsummer. Green. **Leaves** Aromatic, strap-shaped. Bright green.
• NATIVE HABITAT Shallow, fresh water in Asia and southeast US. Naturalized elsewhere.
• CULTIVATION Grow in fertile, boggy soil or in the muddy margins of a pond or stream, in full sun. Use an aquatic container to restrict spread.
• PROPAGATION Divide in spring as growth begins. Pot up and grow on until established.

Z3–9

HEIGHT
24–36in
(60–90cm)

SPREAD
24in (60cm)

MEDIUM • 107

Rutaceae	VARIEGATED RUE

RUTA GRAVEOLENS 'Variegata'
Habit Rounded shrub. *Flowers* Cup-shaped, 4-petaled, borne in heads, in summer. Dull yellow. *Leaves* Aromatic, evergreen, divided into oval lobes. Blue-green, variegated creamy white.
• NATIVE HABITAT Garden origin.
• CULTIVATION Grow in moderately fertile, well-drained soil in sun. Tolerates hot, dry sites.
• PROPAGATION By semi-ripe cuttings taken in summer, or by seed sown in a cold frame in spring.
• WARNING Contact with foliage in sunlight may cause skin to blister.

Z4–8

HEIGHT
24in (60cm)

SPREAD
24in (60cm)

Lamiaceae	GOLDEN LEMON BALM

MELISSA OFFICINALIS 'Aurea'
Habit Bushy perennial. *Flowers* Small, tubular, 2-lipped, borne in spikes, in summer. Pale yellow, fading to white or lilac-tinted white. *Leaves* Lemon-scented, oval, toothed, wrinkled. Bright green, with golden-yellow variegation.
• NATIVE HABITAT Garden origin.
• CULTIVATION Grow in poor to moderately fertile, moist but well-drained soil in a sunny or lightly shaded site. Cut back at flowering to produce fresh young leaves.
• PROPAGATION Divide in spring.

Z4–9

HEIGHT
24–48in
(60–120cm)

SPREAD
18in (45cm)

Brassicaceae	VARIEGATED HORSERADISH

ARMORACIA RUSTICANA 'Variegata'
Habit Taprooted perennial. *Flowers* Cross-shaped, borne in terminal sprays, from late spring to late summer. White. *Leaves* Oval to oblong, toothed. Dark green, variegated creamy white.
• NATIVE HABITAT Garden origin.
• CULTIVATION Grow in deep, light, moist but well-drained, fertile soil, in sun or light shade. Leaves are prone to scorch when exposed to full sun. Less vigorous than the species.
• PROPAGATION Divide or take root cuttings in winter.

Z3–10

HEIGHT
36in (90cm)

SPREAD
18in (45cm)

| Asteraceae | LAVENDER COTTON |

SANTOLINA CHAMAECYPARISSUS

Habit Dense, rounded shrub. **Flowers** Tiny, bright yellow in rounded heads, on long, slender stems. Mid- to late summer. **Leaves** Evergreen, aromatic. Narrowly oblong, finely divided into slender, toothed divisions. Gray-white.
• NATIVE HABITAT Dry, rocky sites around the Mediterranean.
• CULTIVATION Grow in poor to moderately fertile, well-drained soil in full sun. Tolerates poor and dry soils. Cut back annually in spring to maintain a neat, dense habit. Deadhead and trim lightly after flowering. Excellent for a herbaceous or mixed border, especially one with a silver-leaved or Mediterranean theme. May be used as low hedging or edging in the herb garden. Suitable for creating a knot garden. The flowers dry well for winter arrangements, and the dried leaves may be used in potpourris.
• PROPAGATION Sow seed in a cold frame during autumn or spring. Root semi-ripe cuttings taken in summer.
• OTHER NAME *S. incana*.

Z6–8

HEIGHT 24in (60cm)

SPREAD 36in (90cm)

Asteraceae	CURRY PLANT

Helichrysum italicum

Habit Bushy subshrub. *Flowers* Small, borne in heads from summer to autumn. Dark yellow. *Leaves* Curry-scented, evergreen, linear. Silver-gray to yellow-green.
• NATIVE HABITAT Dry scrub in southern Europe.
• CULTIVATION Grow in well-drained soil in a warm, sunny site. Cut back hard in spring.
• PROPAGATION Sow seed in a cold frame in autumn or spring, or root semi-ripe cuttings taken in summer.
• OTHER NAME *H. angustifolium*.

Z7–9

HEIGHT
24in (60cm)

SPREAD
36in (90cm)

Apiaceae	

Anethum graveolens 'Mammoth'

Habit Aromatic, sturdy, upright annual. *Flowers* Tiny, borne in flat clusters, in summer. Yellow. *Leaves* Finely divided, threadlike. Blue-green. *Fruits* Egg-shaped, aromatic seeds.
• NATIVE HABITAT Garden origin.
• CULTIVATION Grow in well-drained soil that is neutral to slightly acidic, in a sunny site. Likely to bolt rapidly in poor, dry soils.
• PROPAGATION Sow seed *in situ* in succession between spring and summer.
• OTHER NAME *Peucedanum graveolens* 'Mammoth'.

ANNUAL

HEIGHT
4ft (1.2m)

SPREAD
18in (45cm)

Rutaceae	HERB OF GRACE, RUE

Ruta graveolens

Habit Rounded shrub. *Flowers* Cup-shaped, 4-petaled, borne in heads in summer. Dull yellow. *Leaves* Aromatic, evergreen, divided into oval lobes. Blue-green.
• NATIVE HABITAT Dry rocks in southeast Europe.
• CULTIVATION Grow in moderately fertile, light, well-drained soil in sun. Tolerates hot, dry sites.
• PROPAGATION By seed sown in a cold frame in spring, or by semi-ripe cuttings taken in summer.
• WARNING Contact with foliage in sunlight may cause skin to blister.

Z4–8

HEIGHT
24in (60cm)

SPREAD
24in (60cm)

Apiaceae	DILL

Anethum graveolens

Habit Aromatic, sturdy, upright annual. *Flowers* Tiny, borne in flattened clusters in summer. Yellow. *Leaves* Finely divided, threadlike. Blue-green. *Fruits* Egg-shaped, flattened seeds.
• NATIVE HABITAT Probably southwest Asia, India.
• CULTIVATION Grow in well-drained soil that is neutral to slightly acidic, in a sunny site. Likely to bolt rapidly in poor, dry soils.
• PROPAGATION Sow seed *in situ* in succession between spring and summer.
• OTHER NAME *Peucedanum graveolens*.

ANNUAL

HEIGHT
4ft (1.2m)

SPREAD
18in (45cm)

| Apiaceae | ALEXANDERS, BLACK LOVAGE |

Smyrnium olusatrum

Habit Aromatic, stout perennial.
Flowers Tiny, borne in flattened clusters in late spring and early summer. Yellow-green.
Leaves Oval to rectangular, divided, shiny with toothed margins. Dark green. **Fruits** Aromatic seeds. Black.
• NATIVE HABITAT Coastal areas in western and southern Europe and the Mediterranean.
• CULTIVATION Grow in moist, rich, sandy soil in a sunny site. Suitable for growing beside a pond. All parts of the plant have a celery-like aroma and flavor. The leaves, young stems and shoots, and roots are edible as cooked vegetables. The seeds may be ground for flavoring soups and stews. The cut flowers make an unusual addition to flower arrangements.
• PROPAGATION Sow seed as soon as ripe in late summer, or in early spring.

Z7–10

Height
24–48in
(60–120cm)
or more

Spread
12–36in
(30–60cm)

MEDIUM • 111

Fabaceae	YELLOW SWEET CLOVER, MELILOT

MELILOTUS OFFICINALIS

Habit Slender biennial. ***Flowers*** Small, pealike, honey-scented, borne in slender spikes during summer. Yellow. ***Leaves*** Three-lobed. Mid-green.
• NATIVE HABITAT Fields and waste ground in Eurasia and N. Africa.
• CULTIVATION Grow in well-drained soil that is neutral or alkaline, in a sunny site.
• PROPAGATION Sow seed in spring or autumn.
• OTHER NAME *M. arvensis*.

Z3–8

HEIGHT
24–48in
(60–120cm)

SPREAD
24–36in
(60–90cm)

Asteraceae	GOLDENROD

SOLIDAGO VIRGAUREA

Habit Rhizomatous perennial. ***Flowers*** Small, daisylike, borne in branched spikes from late summer to autumn. Yellow. ***Leaves*** Oval to lance-shaped, toothed. Mid-green.
• NATIVE HABITAT Woods, scrub, heaths, and grassland in Europe.
• CULTIVATION Grow in poor to moderately fertile, sandy, moist but well-drained soil in sun. Attractive to bees and other beneficial insects.
• PROPAGATION Divide in autumn or spring. Sow seed in spring in a cold frame.

Z3–9

HEIGHT
32in (80cm)

SPREAD
24in (60cm)

Papaveraceae	GREATER CELANDINE, SWALLOW WORT

CHELIDONIUM MAJUS

Habit Clump-forming perennial. ***Flowers*** Small, 4-petaled, borne in loose, terminal clusters in spring. Yellow. ***Leaves*** Lobed, cut, or divided, scalloped. Pale to blue-green.
• NATIVE HABITAT Woodlands in Europe and western Asia.
• CULTIVATION For best results, grow in moist but well-drained soil that is enriched with organic matter, in a partially shaded site. Tolerates almost any soil in a sunny or shaded site.
• PROPAGATION Sow seed *in situ* in early spring.

Z4–8

HEIGHT
24in (60cm)

SPREAD
8in (20cm)

Clusiaceae	PERFORATE ST JOHN'S WORT

HYPERICUM PERFORATUM

Habit Upright, rhizomatous perennial. ***Flowers*** Star-shaped, with long stamens, borne in summer. Bright yellow. ***Leaves*** Oval to linear. Mid-green, with translucent dots.
• NATIVE HABITAT Scrub and grassland in Europe and western Asia.
• CULTIVATION Grow in well-drained soil in a sunny or partially shaded site.
• PROPAGATION Sow seed or divide plants in autumn or spring.
• WARNING Foliage is harmful if eaten.

Z4–8

HEIGHT
24–42in
(60–110cm)

SPREAD
24in (60cm)

Papaveraceae	

Chelidonium majus
'Laciniatum Flore Pleno'

Habit Clump-forming perennial.
Flowers Double, with small, finely cut petals, borne in loose clusters during spring. Yellow.
Leaves Finely cut. Pale to blue-green.
• NATIVE HABITAT Garden origin.
• CULTIVATION For best results, grow in moist but well-drained soil that is enriched with organic matter, in a partially shaded site. Tolerates almost any soil in a sunny or shaded site.
• PROPAGATION Sow seed *in situ* in early spring.

Z4–8

HEIGHT
16in (40cm)

SPREAD
8in (20cm)

Asteraceae	GUM PLANT, TAR WEED

Grindelia camporum

Habit Resinous annual or short-lived perennial.
Flowers Daisylike, with resinous buds, borne in summer. Bright yellow. *Leaves* Narrowly oblong, toothed. Dark green.
• NATIVE HABITAT Dry sites in California.
• CULTIVATION Grow in well-drained soil in a warm, sunny site.
• PROPAGATION Sow seed in spring or summer at 61–66°F (16–19°C). May self-seed.

ANNUAL

HEIGHT
20–48in
(50–120cm)

SPREAD
30in (75cm)

Compositae	BLESSED THISTLE, HOLY THISTLE

Cnicus benedictus

Habit Spiny, taprooted annual. *Flowers* Thistle-like, with bristly bracts, borne during summer. Yellow. *Leaves* Prickly, divided into lobes or toothed. Gray-green.
• NATIVE HABITAT Disturbed ground around the Mediterranean. Widely naturalized in Europe.
• CULTIVATION Grow in any well-drained soil in sun. Deadhead to prevent self-sown seedlings. Suitable for growing in an herb or wild garden.
• PROPAGATION Sow seed *in situ* in spring. Self-sows freely.

ANNUAL

HEIGHT
30in (70cm)

SPREAD
12in (30cm)

Scrophulariaceae — WOOLLY FOXGLOVE

DIGITALIS LANATA

Habit Clump-forming biennial or short-lived perennial. **Flowers** Tubular to bell-shaped, borne in dense, leafy spikes, from mid- to late summer. Pale cream or fawn, with brown or violet-brown veins and paler cream lower lips. **Leaves** Oblong tapering to a point at the base, with toothed margins. Mid-green.
• NATIVE HABITAT Open woodlands in eastern Europe.
• CULTIVATION Grow in moist but well-drained soil that is neutral to acidic and enriched with organic matter, in partial or dappled shade or in part-day sun. Deadhead after flowering to prevent self-seeding. Suitable for growing in a woodland garden or a mixed or herbaceous border. Susceptible to crown and root rots in overly moist soils.
• PROPAGATION Sow seed in a cold frame in autumn or spring. May self-seed, but seldom to the point of nuisance.
• WARNING All parts are highly toxic if eaten. Contact with foliage may irritate skin.

Z4–10

Height
24in (60cm)

Spread
12in (30cm)

| Asteraceae | SWEET MACE, MEXICAN MARIGOLD |

TAGETES LUCIDA

Habit Aromatic, slender perennial, usually grown as an annual. *Flowers* Single, borne in flat-topped clusters, in late summer. Yellow. *Leaves* Narrowly lance-shaped, sharply toothed. Bright green.
• NATIVE HABITAT Hot, dry slopes and valley bottoms in Mexico and Guatemala.
• CULTIVATION Grow in moderately fertile, well-drained soil in a sunny site. Tolerates poor, dry soils. Deadhead to prolong flowering.
• PROPAGATION Sow seed in spring at 64°F (18°C). Set out when danger of frost has passed.

ANNUAL

HEIGHT
12–32in
(30–80cm)

SPREAD
18in (45cm)

| Asteraceae | FALSE SAFFRON, SAFFLOWER |

CARTHAMUS TINCTORIUS

Habit Upright annual. *Flowers* Thistlelike, with spiny bracts, borne in summer. Red, yellow, orange, or cream. *Leaves* Oval to linear, wavy margined or cut, often spine-toothed. Gray-green.
• NATIVE HABITAT Dry, sunny places, probably in western Asia. Long cultivated.
• CULTIVATION Grow in light, well-drained soil in a sunny site. Flowers are good for cutting and drying, and are long-lasting.
• PROPAGATION Sow seed *in situ* between early and late spring.

ANNUAL

HEIGHT
24–36in
(60–90cm)

SPREAD
12–15in
(30–38cm)

| Asclepiadaceae | BUTTERFLY WEED |

ASCLEPIAS TUBEROSA

Habit Tuberous perennial. *Flowers* Small, borne in clusterlike heads, from mid-summer to autumn. Orange-red to yellow. *Leaves* Lance-shaped, spiraling up the stem. Mid-green.
Fruits Spindle-shaped, with seeds covered in long silky-white hairs.
• NATIVE HABITAT Dry scrub and grassland in eastern and southern N. America.
• CULTIVATION Grow in sandy soil that is neutral to acidic, in a sunny site. Resents being disturbed.
• PROPAGATION Sow seed in spring at 59°F (15°C).

Z4–9

HEIGHT
36in (90cm)

SPREAD
12in (30cm)

SMALL • 115

Lamiaceae	WINTER SAVORY

SATUREJA MONTANA
Habit Dwarf, aromatic, semi-evergreen subshrub. **Flowers** Tiny, tubular, 2-lipped, borne in whorled spikes during summer. White to pale pink. **Leaves** Narrowly lance-shaped, leathery. Mid-green.
• NATIVE HABITAT Dry habitats, southern Europe.
• CULTIVATION Grow in well-drained, neutral to alkaline soil, in sun. Suitable for growing at the front of a mixed or herbaceous border, or for use as edging in an herb garden.
• PROPAGATION Sow seed in autumn or spring, or take greenwood cuttings in summer.

☼ ◊

Z5–8

HEIGHT
16in (40cm)

SPREAD
8in (20cm)

Lamiaceae	WHITE HOREHOUND

MARRUBIUM VULGARE
Habit Aromatic, woody-based perennial. **Flowers** Tubular, 2-lipped, borne in axillary whorls in summer. Off-white. **Leaves** Rounded to oval, scalloped, rough-textured. Gray-green.
• NATIVE HABITAT Dry, stony, open sites throughout Eurasia and N. Africa.
• CULTIVATION Grow in very well-drained, neutral to alkaline soil in full sun. Trim after flowering.
• PROPAGATION By seed in spring (although germination may be erratic), by division in spring, or by softwood cuttings taken in summer.

☼ ◊

Z4–8

HEIGHT
8–24in
(20–60cm)

SPREAD
8–24in
(20–60cm)

Scrophulariaceae	GRATIOLE, HEDGE HYSSOP

GRATIOLA OFFICINALIS
Habit Rhizomatous perennial. **Flowers** Solitary, axillary, tubular, with spreading petal lobes, borne in leafy spikes in summer. White, veined purple-red. **Leaves** Linear to lance-shaped. Mid-green.
• NATIVE HABITAT Damp grassland in Europe.
• CULTIVATION Grow in moist but well-drained, alkaline soil, in a sunny site. Suitable for growing in herbaceous borders.
• PROPAGATION By seed in containers in a cold frame, or by division, both in spring.
• WARNING All parts are highly toxic if eaten.

☼ ●

Z5–8

HEIGHT
12–24in
(30–60cm)

SPREAD
8–16in
(20–40cm)

Apiaceae	CUMIN

CUMINUM CYMINUM
Habit Slender annual. **Flowers** Tiny, borne in clusters in mid-summer. White to pale pink. **Leaves** Oval, divided into threadlike segments. Mid-green. **Fruits** Ribbed, oval, and hairy.
• NATIVE HABITAT Rocky scrub from eastern Mediterranean to central Asia.
• CULTIVATION Grow in fertile, well-drained soil in a sunny site. Needs 3–4 warm months in summer to produce a good crop of seeds, which can be harvested in late summer.
• PROPAGATION By seed in spring.

☼ ◊

ANNUAL

HEIGHT
12in (30cm)

SPREAD
12in (30cm)

Apiaceae	ANISE

PIMPINELLA ANISUM

Habit Slender, aromatic annual. *Flowers* Tiny, borne in open clusters during summer. White. *Leaves* Kidney-shaped, toothed or divided, basal, finely divided at stem. Mid-green. *Fruits* Ribbed and oblong. Pale green, ripening to dark brown.
• NATIVE HABITAT Hedges, grassland, and woods from Russia to central and southern Europe.
• CULTIVATION Grow in fertile, well-drained, slightly acidic to slightly alkaline soil, in a sunny site. A long, hot summer is needed to ripen seeds.
• PROPAGATION By seed in spring.

ANNUAL

HEIGHT
20in (50cm)

SPREAD
to 18in (45cm)

Saururaceae	

HOUTTUYNIA CORDATA

Habit Spreading, rhizomatous perennial. *Flowers* Tiny, borne in short, dense spikes in spring. Yellow-green, with 4–6 white bracts at the base. *Leaves* Aromatic, oval to heart-shaped. Dull bluish to grayish green, with red-tinted margins.
• NATIVE HABITAT Damp, shaded woods or marshland in China and Japan.
• CULTIVATION Grow in wet, fertile soil in sun or dappled shade. Mulch in areas with cold winters.
• PROPAGATION By seed when ripe, or by division in spring or autumn.

Z6–10

HEIGHT
6–12in (15–30cm)

SPREAD
indefinite

Liliaceae	

ALLIUM SCHOENOPRASUM
'Wallington White'

Habit Bulbous, rhizomatous perennial. *Flowers* Tiny, bell-shaped, borne in dense, almost spherical heads in summer. White. *Leaves* Hollow, cylindrical. Mid- to deep green.
• NATIVE HABITAT Garden origin.
• CULTIVATION Grow in moist, fertile soil in a sunny site. Tolerates light, dappled shade. Leaves suit culinary use in the growing season.
• PROPAGATION By seed in spring, or by division in autumn or spring. May not come true from seed.

Z3–9

HEIGHT
12–24in (30–60cm)

SPREAD
2in (5cm)

Rosaceae	WILD STRAWBERRY

FRAGARIA VESCA

Habit Stoloniferous perennial. *Flowers* Single, 5-petaled, borne in sprays in early summer. White. *Leaves* Palmate, in basal clumps. Bright green. *Fruits* Small, sweet-tasting, ½in (1cm) long. Red.
• NATIVE HABITAT Woods and meadows in Europe, western Asia, and N. America.
• CULTIVATION Grow in moist but well-drained, fertile soil that is rich in organic matter, in sun or dappled shade. Suitable for use as edging in an herb garden, or in a mixed or herbaceous border.
• PROPAGATION By seed in autumn or spring.

Z5–9

HEIGHT
to 12in (30cm)

SPREAD
8in (20cm)

| Asteraceae | GERMAN CHAMOMILE, SCENTED MAYWEED |

Matricaria recutita

Habit Upright or ascending, well-branched, sweetly aromatic annual or biennial.
Flowers Single, daisylike, with ray florets that reflex downward at maturity, borne from summer to early autumn. White, with a central, conical, yellow disk. **Leaves** Finely divided into slender, bristle-tipped segments. Fresh green.

- NATIVE HABITAT Cultivated, arable, and waste ground, usually on sandy or loamy soils at low altitudes throughout Europe, western Asia, and India.
- CULTIVATION Grow in moist or dry, well-drained soil that is neutral to slightly acid, in a sunny site. Suitable for an herb or wild garden. Harvest the flower heads when they are first fully open and use fresh, frozen, or dried for teas and infusions.
- PROPAGATION By seed in autumn or spring. Self-seeds freely.
- OTHER NAMES *M. chamomilla, Chamomilla recutita*.

ANNUAL

HEIGHT
6–24in
(15–60cm)

SPREAD
4–16in
(10–40cm)

| Lamiaceae | SUMMER SAVORY |

SATUREJA HORTENSIS

Habit Dense, bushy, aromatic annual. **Flowers** Tubular, 2-lipped, borne in dense or loose whorled spikes in summer. White to lilac. **Leaves** Linear to narrowly lance-shaped. Fresh green.
- NATIVE HABITAT Stony or sandy areas, fields, and roadsides in the Mediterranean region.
- CULTIVATION Grow in well-drained, neutral to alkaline soil, in sun. Suitable for an herb garden, or at the front of a mixed or herbaceous border.
- PROPAGATION By seed in spring, or in autumn for winter crops under glass.

ANNUAL

HEIGHT 10in (25cm)

SPREAD 12in (30cm)

| Lamiaceae | |

CALAMINTHA NEPETA subsp. *NEPETA*

Habit Robust, rhizomatous perennial. **Flowers** Tubular, 2-lipped, borne in branched sprays in summer. White to lilac. **Leaves** Scented, oval, shallow-toothed. Mid- to dark green.
- NATIVE HABITAT Scrub, grassland, or woods in Eurasia and N. Africa.
- CULTIVATION Prefers a sunny site with well-drained soil that is neutral to alkaline.
- PROPAGATION By seed sown in autumn or spring, by stem-tip cuttings taken in summer, or by division in spring.

Z5–10

HEIGHT 18–24in (45–60cm)

SPREAD 24–36in (60–90cm)

| Brassicaceae | |

CARDAMINE PRATENSIS 'Flore Pleno'

Habit Compact, clumping, rhizomatous perennial. **Flowers** Double, borne in sprays in late spring or early summer. Lilac-pink. **Leaves** Pinnate, with kidney-shaped, oval, or round leaflets. Dark green.
- NATIVE HABITAT Garden origin. Species grows in Europe, northern Asia, and N. America.
- CULTIVATION Grow in moist soil that is enriched with organic matter, in sun or dappled shade.
- PROPAGATION Divide in spring or after flowering. Root leaf-tip cuttings or plantlets that develop in the basal leaf clusters in mid-summer.

Z3–9

HEIGHT 8in (20cm)

SPREAD 8in (20cm)

Brassicaceae	CUCKOO FLOWER, LADY'S SMOCK

CARDAMINE PRATENSIS

Habit Spreading, rhizomatous perennial.
Flowers Four-petaled, borne in loose clusters in late spring or early summer. White or lilac.
Leaves Pinnate, kidney-shaped. Dark green.
• NATIVE HABITAT Damp meadows in Europe, northern Asia, and N. America.
• CULTIVATION Grow in moist soil that is rich in organic matter, in sun or dappled shade.
• PROPAGATION By division in spring or after flowering. Root leaf-tip cuttings or plantlets that develop in the basal leaf clusters in mid-summer.

Z3–9

HEIGHT
12–18in
(30–45cm)

SPREAD
12in (30cm)

Lamiaceae	WALL GERMANDER

TEUCRIUM CHAMAEDRYS

Habit Shrubby, evergreen perennial.
Flowers Tubular, 2-lipped, borne in spikes from summer to autumn. Pink or purple, rarely white.
Leaves Oblong, lobed or toothed. Dark green.
• NATIVE HABITAT Dry grasslands, bare ground, or open woods from Europe to the Caucasus.
• CULTIVATION Grow in well-drained soil that is neutral to alkaline, in a sunny site. Suitable for use as edging in borders and on patios.
• PROPAGATION By seed in autumn or spring, or by stem-tip cuttings in summer.

Z5–9

HEIGHT
to 10in
(25cm)

SPREAD
10in (25cm)

Polygonaceae	BISTORT, SNAKEWEED, ENGLISH SERPENTARY

PERSICARIA BISTORTA

Habit Vigorous, clumping, rhizomatous perennial.
Flowers Tiny, narrowly bell-shaped, borne in dense spikes from summer to autumn. White or pink. ***Leaves*** Pointed, broadly oval. Mid-green.
• NATIVE HABITAT Damp woods, meadows, and by streams in Europe and northern and western Asia.
• CULTIVATION Grow in fertile, moist but well-drained soil in sun or dappled shade.
• PROPAGATION By seed or division, both in autumn or spring.
• OTHER NAME *Polygonum bistorta*.

Z3–9

HEIGHT
to 30in
(75cm)

SPREAD
36in (90cm)

| Scrophulariaceae | CHINESE FOXGLOVE |

REHMANNIA GLUTINOSA

Habit Sticky, tuberous-rooted perennial with slender runners. **Flowers** Drooping, tubular, foxglove-like, borne in few-flowered spikes from mid-spring to summer. Pale, dull purple-brown, with red-purple veining and yellow-brown lips. **Leaves** Oval, scalloped or coarsely toothed. Mid-green, with conspicuous veining.
- NATIVE HABITAT Woods and stony places, distributed throughout China.
- CULTIVATION Grow in well-drained, sandy soil that is rich in organic matter, in a sheltered site in sun. In mild, damp winter climates without reliable cold or snow cover, lift the plant in autumn. Pot up and overwinter in a cool, dry place. Alternatively, grow the plant permanently under glass in soil-based potting mix, in bright filtered light. Water freely and apply a balanced liquid fertilizer every 4 weeks when in growth, but keep the soil mix just moist during winter.
- PROPAGATION Sow seed in late winter at 55–64°F (13–18°C). Take root cuttings in autumn, or basal cuttings in spring. Separate runners in spring.

Z8–10

Height
6–12in
(15–30cm)

Spread
12in (30cm)

Lamiaceae	

TEUCRIUM × LUCIDRYS

Habit Shrubby, upright, evergreen perennial.
Flowers Tubular, 2-lipped, borne in whorled spikes from summer to autumn. Pink to purple.
Leaves Oblong, lobed, leathery. Deep green.
• NATIVE HABITAT Garden origin.
• CULTIVATION Grow in well-drained soil that is neutral to alkaline soil, in a sunny site. Trim in early spring. Suitable for use as low hedging and edging.
• PROPAGATION By stem-tip cuttings taken in summer and rooted with gentle heat below.

Z6–9

HEIGHT
to 10in
(25cm)

SPREAD
10in (25cm)

Caryophyllaceae	CLOVE PINK, WILD CARNATION

DIANTHUS CARYOPHYLLUS

Habit Tufted, woody-based perennial. **Flowers** Single, clove-scented, tubular, with 5 fringed, spreading petals, borne solitary or in loose, few-flowered sprays in early summer. Purple-pink.
Leaves Linear to lance-shaped. Grayish-green.
• NATIVE HABITAT Rocky places, southern Europe.
• CULTIVATION Grow in well-drained, neutral to alkaline soil, in full sun. Suitable for potpourri.
• PROPAGATION By seed in containers in a cold frame in spring, by stem-tip cuttings in summer, or by layering in late summer.

Z5–8

HEIGHT
8–20in
(20–50cm)

SPREAD
4–10in
(10–25cm)

Saxifragaceae	ALUMROOT, AMERICAN SANICLE

HEUCHERA AMERICANA

Habit Mound-forming perennial. **Flowers** Tiny, borne in long sprays in early summer. Purplish green. **Leaves** Oval to heart-shaped, glossy, and leathery. Dark green, marbled copper-green.
• NATIVE HABITAT Woodlands in central and eastern N. America.
• CULTIVATION For best results, grow in moist but well-drained, fertile soil, in a sunny or partially shaded site.
• PROPAGATION Sow seed or divide the plant in spring or autumn.

Z4–9

HEIGHT
12–36in
(30–90cm)

SPREAD
to 18in
(45cm)

Iridaceae	SAFFRON CROCUS

CROCUS SATIVUS

Habit Cormous perennial. **Flowers** Widely funnel-shaped, borne in autumn. Rich lilac, veined deep purple, with dark red styles. **Leaves** Linear, emerging with, or just after, flowers. Dull green.
- NATIVE HABITAT Origin uncertain.
- CULTIVATION Grow in well-drained, poor to moderately fertile soil, in a warm site in full sun.
- PROPAGATION Sow seed as soon as ripe in containers in a cold frame. Separate offsets when dormant in late spring.
- OTHER NAME *C. sativus* var. *cashmirianus*.

Z4–8

Height 2–4in (5–10cm)

Spread 2–4in (5–10cm)

Lamiaceae	THYME-LEAVED SAVORY

SATUREJA THYMBRA

Habit Dwarf, aromatic, semi-evergreen, wiry-stemmed subshrub. **Flowers** Tiny, tubular, 2-lipped, borne in whorled spikes during spring and summer. Pink. **Leaves** Minty, thymelike scent, linear to spoon-shaped. Gray-green.
- NATIVE HABITAT Dry, sunny habitats, Balkans.
- CULTIVATION Grow in well-drained, neutral to alkaline soil, in sun. Suits edging or border fronts.
- PROPAGATION By seed sown in autumn or spring, or by softwood cuttings taken in summer.

Z8–9

Height to 16in (40cm)

Spread 16in (40cm)

Lamiaceae	LESSER CALAMINT

CALAMINTHA NEPETA

Habit Robust, rhizomatous perennial. **Flowers** Tubular, 2-lipped, borne in branched sprays in summer. Mauve or pink. **Leaves** Peppermint-scented, oval, shallow-toothed. Mid- to dark green.
- NATIVE HABITAT Scrub, grassland, or woods in Eurasia and N. Africa.
- CULTIVATION Grow in well-drained soil that is neutral to alkaline, in a sunny site.
- PROPAGATION By seed sown in autumn or spring, by division in spring, or by stem-tip cuttings taken in summer.

Z5–10

Height 8–30in (20–75cm)

Spread 24–36in (60–90cm)

Liliaceae	CHIVES

ALLIUM SCHOENOPRASUM

Habit Bulbous, rhizomatous perennial. **Flowers** Tiny, bell-shaped, borne in dense, almost spherical heads in summer. Pale purple. **Leaves** Hollow, cylindrical. Mid- to deep green.
- NATIVE HABITAT Grassy places, in Europe, Asia, and N. America.
- CULTIVATION Grow in moist, fertile soil in full sun or light, dappled shade. Leaves are suitable for culinary use in the growing season.
- PROPAGATION By seed sown in spring, or by division in autumn or spring.

Z3–9

Height 12–24in (30–60cm)

Spread 2in (5cm)

Lamiaceae	BETONY, BISHOPSWORT

STACHYS OFFICINALIS

Habit Upright, sparsely branched, smooth to densely hairy perennial. **Flowers** Tubular, 2-lipped, borne in dense, interrupted, oblong spikes from summer to autumn. Deep red-purple, pink, or white. **Leaves** Oval to oblong, heart-shaped at the base, scalloped, wrinkled. Dark green with conspicuous veining.
• NATIVE HABITAT Grassy places, heathlands, and open woodlands, usually on light soils, in Europe.
• CULTIVATION Grow in light, well-drained soil that is moderately fertile, in full sun or light, dappled shade. Suitable for growing in an herb garden, and effective when used as an ornamental plant in a mixed or herbaceous border. It is also good for naturalizing in light woodland or short grass. The flowers are very attractive to bees and other beneficial insects. They may be harvested in summer and dried for use in infusions.
• PROPAGATION By seed in autumn or spring, sown in containers in a cold frame, or by division in spring as growth begins.
• OTHER NAMES *S. betonica, Betonica officinalis.*

Z4–8

Height
24in (60cm)

Spread
12in (30cm)

| Lamiaceae | VIRGINIA SKULLCAP, MAD DOG SKULLCAP |

Scutellaria lateriflora

Habit Rhizomatous perennial. *Flowers* Tubular, 2-lipped, borne in one-sided spikes during summer. Blue, occasionally white or pink. *Leaves* Narrowly oval, toothed. Mid-green.
• NATIVE HABITAT Damp habitats throughout N. America.
• CULTIVATION Grow in moist, moderately fertile soil in a sunny site.
• PROPAGATION By seed sown in autumn or spring, by semi-ripe cuttings taken in summer, or by division in autumn or spring.

Z4–8

HEIGHT
6–30in
(15–75cm)

SPREAD
18in (45cm)

| Lamiaceae | ROCK HYSSOP |

Hyssopus officinalis subsp. *ARISTATUS*

Habit Dwarf, aromatic, semi-evergreen shrub. *Flowers* Tubular, borne in spikes in late summer. Blue. *Leaves* Lance-shaped. Fresh green.
• NATIVE HABITAT Stony sites in southern Europe.
• CULTIVATION Grow in well-drained soil that is neutral to alkaline, in a sunny site. Suitable for growing in a rock garden or containers, or for use as low hedging.
• PROPAGATION By seed in spring or autumn, or by softwood cuttings taken in early summer.

Z3–9

HEIGHT
12in (30cm)

SPREAD
24in (60cm)

| Boraginaceae | JERUSALEM COWSLIP, LUNGWORT |

Pulmonaria officinalis

Habit Rhizomatous, clump-forming, evergreen perennial. *Flowers* Funnel-shaped, borne in spring. Opening from pink buds, maturing through red-violet to blue. *Leaves* Oval, bristle-haired. Bright green, with white spots.
• NATIVE HABITAT Woodlands in Europe.
• CULTIVATION Grow in moist but well-drained soil rich in leaf mold, in partial or deep shade.
• PROPAGATION Sow ripe seed, divide in autumn or after flowering, or take root cuttings in winter.
• WARNING All parts are irritant and allergenic.

Z3–9

HEIGHT
10in (25cm)

SPREAD
18in (45cm)

| Plantaginaceae | RED GREATER PLANTAIN |

Plantago major 'Rubrifolia'

Habit Rosette-forming perennial. *Flowers* Minute, borne in dense, long-stemmed heads, in summer. Yellow-green. *Leaves* Broadly oval, ribbed, entire or toothed. Deep maroon.
• NATIVE HABITAT Garden origin.
• CULTIVATION Grow in moist, poor to moderately fertile soil that is neutral to slightly acidic, in a partially shaded site.
• PROPAGATION Sow seed in spring, in containers in a cold frame. May self-seed prolifically.
• OTHER NAME *P. major* 'Atropurpurea'.

Z3–9

HEIGHT
12–16in
(30–40cm)

SPREAD
12–16in
(30–40cm)

| Ranunculaceae | BLACK CUMIN, NUTMEG FLOWER |

NIGELLA SATIVA

Habit Upright, freely branching annual.
Flowers Small, borne in summer. Palest blue.
Leaves Feathery, finely cut into linear segments. Bright green. *Fruits* Inflated capsules with 3–7 fused, horned segments, with shiny black seeds.
• NATIVE HABITAT Dry, open habitats in southwest Asia; widely naturalized elsewhere.
• CULTIVATION Grow in well-drained soil in full sun. Harvest the spicy-flavored seeds when ripe.
• PROPAGATION Sow seed *in situ* in spring or autumn. May self-seed.

ANNUAL

HEIGHT
12in (30cm)

SPREAD
9in (23cm)

| Polemoniaceae | ABSCESS ROOT, GREEK VALERIAN |

POLEMONIUM REPTANS

Habit Upright or spreading, rhizomatous perennial. *Flowers* Widely bell-shaped, borne in few-flowered sprays in late spring and early summer. Blue. *Leaves* Divided into 7–19 oval leaflets. Fresh green.
• NATIVE HABITAT Damp woods in eastern US.
• CULTIVATION Grow in moist but well-drained, fertile soil, in sun or dappled shade. Suitable for a herb garden or a mixed or herbaceous border.
• PROPAGATION By seed in containers in a cold frame in autumn or spring, or by division in spring.

Z3–9

HEIGHT
6–12in
(15–30cm)

SPREAD
15in (38cm)

| Apiaceae | ERYNGO, SEA HOLLY |

ERYNGIUM MARITIMUM

Habit Short-lived, tufted perennial.
Flowers Tiny, borne in dense, rounded heads in summer. Powder-blue with a ruff of spiny, blue-gray bracts. *Leaves* Stiff, leathery, rounded, with 3–5 wavy-edged spiny lobes. Glaucous, blue-gray.
• NATIVE HABITAT Coastal sand or gravel, Europe.
• CULTIVATION Grow in dry, well-drained, sandy or stony soil, in a sunny site. Flower heads are suitable for drying for use in winter arrangements.
• PROPAGATION By seed in containers in a cold frame as soon as ripe, or by root cuttings in winter.

Z6–9

HEIGHT
12–18in
(30–45cm)

SPREAD
12–18in
(30–45cm)

OCIMUM

A genus of 65 species of highly aromatic annuals and evergreen perennials and shrubs, *Ocimum* are found growing wild in dry scrub in tropical regions of Africa and Asia. They have opposite, paired, linear to almost round leaves and bear tubular, 2-lipped flowers in whorled spikes during summer. *O. basilicum*, commonly known as basil, is an annual or short-lived perennial.

O. basilicum is widely grown as an annual herb and has both culinary and medicinal uses. The flavor is volatile and, when used in hot dishes, the leaves are best added at the end of the cooking period. Basils are ideal for growing in greenhouses, windowboxes, and containers. Outdoors, they are most suited to herb gardens in areas with warm summers. The purple-leaved variants are particularly attractive, providing foliage contrast in mixed or herbaceous borders, or in a potager. In temperate areas with cool summers, the best crops are obtained under glass in a cold frame or greenhouse. Basils are very sensitive to cold: their growth will be checked or they may fail to survive if sown too early or in too cool conditions. A temperature of no less than 50–59°F (10–15°C) is required for good growth.

Grow in light, well-drained soil that is slightly acidic to slightly alkaline in a warm, sheltered site in full sun. Keep well-watered during dry spells in summer. Pinch out the growing tips as plants reach about 6in (15cm) high to promote a bushy habit, and remove flower spikes as they appear to prolong leaf production.

Propagate by seed sown in containers under glass during spring, at a minimum temperature of 55°F (13°C). In warm areas, seed may also be sown *in situ* in late spring or early summer. Basil can also be increased by stem-tip cuttings taken in spring, which will root easily in water.

O. BASILICUM
'Genovese'
Habit Bushy, upright annual or perennial.
Flowers Small, tubular, borne in summer. White.
Leaves Narrowly oval. Dark green, often with purple veining.
• TIPS Good for use in pesto or tomato dishes.
• HEIGHT 18–24in (45–60cm).
• SPREAD 12–15in (30–38cm).

O. basilicum
'Genovese'
Perfume basil
☼ ◊ ANNUAL

O. BASILICUM var.
CITRIODORUM
Habit Bushy annual or perennial.
Flowers Tubular, 2-lipped, borne in summer. White.
Leaves Lemon-scented, oval. Gray-green.
• TIPS Good in vinegars and with fish and poultry.
• HEIGHT 45–60cm (18–24in).
• SPREAD 25–35cm (10–14in).

O. basilicum
var. *citriodorum*
Lemon basil
☼ ◊ ANNUAL

O. BASILICUM
Habit Upright, bushy, well-branched annual or perennial.
Flowers Small, tubular, 2-lipped, borne in slender, terminal spikes from summer to early autumn. White.
Leaves Sweet-scented, oval. Bright green.
• HEIGHT 8–24in (20–60cm).
• SPREAD 6–18in (15–45cm).

O. basilicum
Basil, Sweet basil
☼ ◊ ANNUAL

O. BASILICUM 'Mexican'

Habit Vigorous, bushy annual or perennial.
Flowers Tubular, 2-lipped, borne in terminal spikes in summer. White.
Leaves Cinnamon-scented, oval, glossy. Dark green.
• TIPS Retains flavor and scent when dried.
• HEIGHT 36in (90cm).
• SPREAD 18in (45cm).

O. basilicum 'Mexican'
Mexican basil
☀ ◊ ANNUAL

O. TENUIFLORUM

Habit Shrubby, softly hairy perennial, usually grown as an annual.
Flowers Tubular, 2-lipped, borne in spikes in summer. White or violet.
Leaves Scented, oval, downy. Dark green.
• OTHER NAME
O. sanctum.
• HEIGHT 18–24in (45–60cm).
• SPREAD 36in (to 90cm).

O. tenuiflorum
Holy basil, Sacred basil
☀ ◊ ANNUAL

O. BASILICUM 'Cinnamon'

Habit Upright, sturdy annual or perennial.
Flowers Small, tubular, 2-lipped, borne in terminal spikes from summer to early autumn. Deep rose-pink.
Leaves Cinnamon-clove scented, oval. Mid-green, flushed red-purple.
• HEIGHT 30in (75cm).
• SPREAD 12–18in (30–45cm).

O. basilicum 'Cinnamon'
☀ ◊ ANNUAL

O. BASILICUM var. *PURPURASCENS*

Habit Upright, bushy, well-branched annual or perennial.
Flowers Small, tubular, 2-lipped, borne in spikes from summer to early autumn. Pink.
Leaves Scented, oval. Purple-flushed.
• HEIGHT 8–24in (20–60cm).
• SPREAD 6–18in (15–45cm).

O. basilicum var. *purpurascens*
Purple basil
☀ ◊ ANNUAL

O. BASILICUM 'Red Rubin'

Habit Upright, bushy, well-branched annual or perennial.
Flowers Small, tubular, 2-lipped, borne in spikes from summer to early autumn. Red.
Leaves Scented, oval, crinkle-edged. Purple-black.
• HEIGHT 24in (60cm).
• SPREAD 12in (30cm).

O. basilicum 'Red Rubin'
☀ ◊ ANNUAL

O. BASILICUM
'Dark Opal'
Habit Upright, bushy, well-branched annual or perennial.
Flowers Small, tubular, 2-lipped, borne in terminal spikes from summer to early autumn. Cerise-pink.
Leaves Strongly scented, pepper-tasting, narrowly oval. Purple-black.
• HEIGHT 24in (60cm).
• SPREAD 12in (30cm).

O. basilicum
'Dark Opal'
☼ ◊ ANNUAL

O. BASILICUM
'Purple Ruffles'
Habit Bushy annual or perennial.
Flowers Tubular, 2-lipped, borne in terminal spikes in summer. Deep pink.
Leaves Oval, shiny, with fringed, ruffled margins. Deep purple.
• HEIGHT 18–24in (45–60cm).
• SPREAD 18–24in (45–60cm).

O. basilicum
'Purple Ruffles'
☼ ◊ ANNUAL

O. BASILICUM
'Green Ruffles'
Habit Bushy annual or perennial.
Flowers Tubular, 2-lipped, borne in terminal spikes in summer. White.
Leaves Oval, shiny, with fringed, ruffled margins. Bright green.
• HEIGHT 18–24in (45–60cm).
• SPREAD 18–24in (45–60cm).

O. basilicum
'Green Ruffles'
☼ ◊ ANNUAL

O. BASILICUM 'Horapha'
Habit Vigorous annual or perennial.
Flowers Tubular, 2-lipped, borne in spikes in summer. Pale purple.
Leaves Scented, oval. Green, purple-stemmed.
- OTHER NAMES
O. basilicum 'Glycyrrhiza', O. basilicum 'Thai'.
- HEIGHT 24–36in (60–90cm).
- SPREAD 18in (45cm).

O. basilicum 'Horapha'
☼ ◊ ANNUAL

O. BASILICUM var. MINIMUM
Habit Dwarf, bushy annual or perennial.
Flowers Tiny, 2-lipped, borne in short spikes from summer to autumn. White.
Leaves Strong-smelling, small, narrowly oval. Bright green.
- HEIGHT 6–12in (15–30cm).
- SPREAD 6–12in (15–30cm).

O. basilicum var. minimum
Bush basil, Greek basil
☼ ◊ ANNUAL

O. CAMPECHIANUM
Habit Annual or short-lived perennial.
Flowers Small, tubular, 2-lipped, borne in spikes from summer to autumn. Greenish white to pale violet.
Leaves Aromatic, hairy, oval, slightly toothed. Bright green.
- OTHER NAME
O. micranthum.
- HEIGHT 24in (60cm).
- SPREAD 18in (45cm).

O. campechianum
Peruvian basil, Duppy basil
☼ ◊ ANNUAL

O. AMERICANUM
Habit Annual or short-lived perennial.
Flowers Small, tubular, 2-lipped, borne in spikes from summer to autumn. White or mauve.
Leaves Scented, hairy, oval. Gray-green.
- OTHER NAMES
O. canum, O. 'Spice', O. 'Meng Luk'.
- HEIGHT 8–24in (20–60cm).
- SPREAD 18in (45cm).

O. americanum
Hoary basil, Spice basil
☼ ◊ ANNUAL

O. BASILICUM 'Spicy Globe'
Habit Rounded, dense, compact annual or perennial.
Flowers Tiny, tubular, 2-lipped, borne in short spikes in late summer. White.
Leaves Scented, oval. Bright green.
- TIPS Suitable for containers or edging.
- HEIGHT 8–10in (20–25cm).
- SPREAD 12in (30cm).

O. basilicum 'Spicy Globe'
☼ ◊ ANNUAL

O. BASILICUM 'Green Bouquet'
Habit Compact, bushy annual or perennial.
Flowers Small, tubular, 2-lipped, borne in short spikes in late summer. White.
Leaves Strongly spice-scented, small. Mid-green.
- HEIGHT 18in (45cm).
- SPREAD 12–15in (30–38cm).

O. basilicum 'Green Bouquet'
☼ ◊ ANNUAL

| Polygonaceae | |

RUMEX SCUTATUS 'Silver Shield'

Habit Low-branching, mat-forming perennial.
Flowers Tiny, borne in branched spikes in summer. Greenish red. *Leaves* Pleasantly acidic-tasting, spear-shaped, long-stalked. Silvery green.
• NATIVE HABITAT Garden origin.
• CULTIVATION Grow in moist soil in a sunny or partially shaded site. Harvest young leaves before flowering for use in salads and other dishes. Suitable for groundcover, but may be invasive.
• PROPAGATION By seed sown *in situ* in spring, or by division in autumn or spring.

Z4–8

HEIGHT
6–20in
(15–50cm)

SPREAD
to 4ft
(1.2m)

| Apiaceae | SEA FENNEL |

CRITHMUM MARITIMUM

Habit Succulent, slightly woody-based perennial.
Flowers Tiny, borne in flat-topped clusters in summer. Yellow-green. *Leaves* Divided into thick, fleshy, linear segments. Dark green.
• NATIVE HABITAT Coastal sites in Europe (Atlantic coast), Mediterranean, and Black Sea.
• CULTIVATION Grow in well-drained soil in sun, with winter mulch protection in colder areas. Harvest fresh young leaves in late spring.
• PROPAGATION Sow seed as soon as ripe in containers in a cold frame, or divide in spring.

Z7–9

HEIGHT
6–12in
(15–30cm)

SPREAD
6–12in
(15–30cm)

| Polygonaceae | BUCKLER-LEAF SORREL |

RUMEX SCUTATUS

Habit Low-branching, mat-forming perennial.
Flowers Tiny, borne in branched spikes, during summer. Greenish red. *Leaves* Pleasantly acidic-tasting, spear-shaped, long-stalked. Mid-green.
• NATIVE HABITAT Rocky or stony sites in Europe, western Asia, and N. Africa.
• CULTIVATION Grow in moist but well-drained soil, in sun or partial shade. Harvest young leaves before flowering for culinary use.
• PROPAGATION By seed *in situ* in spring, or by division in autumn or spring.

Z4–8

HEIGHT
6–20in
(15–50cm)

SPREAD
to 4ft
(1.2m)

| Ranunculaceae | GOLDENSEAL, YELLOWROOT |

HYDRASTIS CANADENSIS

Habit Rhizomatous perennial. *Flowers* Tiny, solitary, borne in late spring. Greenish white. *Leaves* Palmate, toothed. Mid-green.
Fruits Inedible, in globose clusters. Dark red.
• NATIVE HABITAT Peaty, sandy soils in N. America.
• CULTIVATION Grow in moist, well-drained fertile soil that is slightly acidic to neutral, in a shady site.
• PROPAGATION By seed sown in containers in a cold frame as soon as ripe, or by division in autumn.

Z4–8

HEIGHT
8–15in
(20–38cm)

SPREAD
6–12in
(15–30cm)

SMALL • 131

| Portulacaceae | PURSLANE |

Portulaca oleracea

Habit Fleshy, mat-forming annual with soft, thick, trailing stems. **Flowers** Small, solitary, cup-shaped, produced from early summer to autumn. Yellow. **Leaves** Iron-rich, with a mildly acidic flavor, succulent, spoon-shaped to oval. Mid-green.
• NATIVE HABITAT Cultivated and waste ground throughout warm temperate regions, and naturalized elsewhere, including Europe.
The form usually cultivated as a pot herb is *P. oleracea* var. *sativa*, commonly known as kitchen-garden purslane.

• CULTIVATION Grow in moist but well-drained, fertile soil in a sunny, sheltered site. Young leaves taken before flowering are suitable for culinary use. Begin harvesting about 6–8 weeks after sowing, and deadhead flowers to prevent self-seeding.
• PROPAGATION Sow seed *in situ* in succession from early summer onward. Earlier sowings can be made under glass to be set out when all danger of frost has passed.

Annual

Height
8–18in
(20–45cm)

Spread
18–24in
(45–60cm)

Brassicaceae	WASABI

WASABIA JAPONICA

Habit Rhizomatous perennial. ***Flowers*** Small, cross-shaped, borne in spikes in summer. White. ***Leaves*** Kidney-shaped, long-stalked. Fresh green.
• NATIVE HABITAT Mountain streamsides in Japan.
• CULTIVATION Grow in constantly moist soil or, preferably, in clean running water. Harvest the horseradish-like roots for culinary use, either fresh or dried, 15–24 months after planting.
• PROPAGATION By seed in spring, or by division in autumn, when harvesting the roots.
• OTHER NAME *Eutrema wasabia*.

Z6–9

HEIGHT
8–16in
(20–40cm)

SPREAD
12in (30cm)

Lamiaceae	AMERICAN PENNYROYAL

HEDEOMA PULEGIOIDES

Habit Bushy, aromatic annual. ***Flowers*** Tiny, tubular, 2-lipped, borne in loose, axillary sprays during summer. Pale lilac. ***Leaves*** Mint-scented, oval. Fresh green.
• NATIVE HABITAT Open woodlands in eastern US.
• CULTIVATION Grow in well-drained, preferably sandy, fertile soil, in a sunny site. Suitable for growing in an herb garden, for siting near seats and entrances, or for planting in containers.
• PROPAGATION By seed sown *in situ* in spring.

ANNUAL

HEIGHT
4–16in
(10–40cm)

SPREAD
3–10in
(7–24cm)

Apiaceae	COMMON CHERVIL

ANTHRISCUS CEREFOLIUM

Habit Slender, upright biennial grown as an annual. ***Flowers*** Tiny, borne in clusters in mid-summer. White. ***Leaves*** Pinnate, divided into oval leaflets. Fresh green.
• NATIVE HABITAT Europe and western Asia.
• CULTIVATION Grow in light, moist but well-drained soil in partial or dappled shade. Bolts rapidly in hot, dry conditions. For culinary use, harvest young leaves before flowering.
• PROPAGATION Sow seed *in situ*, in succession between early spring and mid-summer.

Z3–8

HEIGHT
to 20in
(50cm)

SPREAD
10in (24cm)

SMALL • 133

Apiaceae	FRENCH PARSLEY, ITALIAN PARSLEY

PETROSELINUM CRISPUM var. NEAPOLITANUM

Habit Clump-forming biennial. *Flowers* Tiny, borne in flat-topped clusters in summer. Yellow-green. *Leaves* Divided, flat. Fresh green.
• NATIVE HABITAT Grassy places in southern Europe.
• CULTIVATION Grow in fertile, moist but well-drained soil in sun or part shade.
• PROPAGATION Sow seed in succession between spring and late summer.
• OTHER NAME *P. crispum* 'Italian'.

Z6–9

HEIGHT
15–24in
(38–60cm)

SPREAD
15–24in
(38–60cm)

Apiaceae	PARSLEY

PETROSELINUM CRISPUM

Habit Clump-forming biennial. *Flowers* Tiny, star-shaped, borne in flat-topped clusters in summer. Yellow-green. *Leaves* Pinnate, divided into oval, toothed, shiny segments, variably curled. Fresh green.
• NATIVE HABITAT Grassy places, southern Europe.
• CULTIVATION Grow in fertile, moist but well-drained soil, in sun or part shade.
• PROPAGATION Sow seed in succession between spring and late summer. As with cultivars, pre-soaking in hot water speeds germination.

Z6–9

HEIGHT
to 32in
(80cm)

SPREAD
24in (60cm)

Apiaceae	

PETROSELINUM CRISPUM 'Afro'

Habit Upright, clump-forming biennial. *Flowers* Tiny, borne in flat-topped clusters in summer. Yellow-green. *Leaves* Divided into tightly curled segments. Dark green.
• NATIVE HABITAT Garden origin.
• CULTIVATION Grow in fertile, moist but well-drained soil in a sunny or partially shaded site.
• PROPAGATION By seed sown in succession between spring and late summer. As with the species, pre-soaking the seed in hot water speeds germination.

Z6–9

HEIGHT
15–24in
(38–60cm)

SPREAD
15–24in
(38–60cm)

Asteraceae	

SANTOLINA CHAMAECYPARISSUS
'Lemon Queen'
Habit Compact, aromatic, evergreen shrub.
Flowers Pomponlike, borne on long, wiry stems in summer. Pale creamy yellow. *Leaves* Narrowly oblong, finely cut into segments. Gray-green.
• NATIVE HABITAT Garden origin.
• CULTIVATION Grow in well-drained, poor to moderately fertile soil in sun. Deadhead after flowering, and trim back hard in spring. Leaves may be dried for use in potpourri.
• PROPAGATION By semi-ripe cuttings in summer.

Rubiaceae	LADY'S BEDSTRAW, CHEESE RENNET

GALIUM VERUM
Habit Creeping, rhizomatous perennial.
Flowers Tiny, fragrant, star-shaped, borne in dense, whorled clusters in early summer. Bright yellow. *Leaves* Linear, whorled. Bright green.
• NATIVE HABITAT Meadows and hedgerows from Europe to western Asia and N. America.
• CULTIVATION Grow in well-drained soil that is neutral to alkaline, in a sunny site. Leaves are highly aromatic when dried.
• PROPAGATION Sow seed as soon as ripe in a cold frame, or divide in autumn or spring.

Z6–8

HEIGHT
24in (60cm)

SPREAD
24in (60cm)

Z3–8

HEIGHT
6–16in
(15–40cm)

SPREAD
indefinite

Solanaceae	MANDRAKE, DEVIL'S APPLES

MANDRAGORA OFFICINARUM
Habit Rosette-forming, taprooted perennial.
Flowers Tubular, bell-shaped, upward-facing, borne in spring. Greenish to bluish white.
Leaves Oval to lance-shaped, with wavy margins. Dark green.
• NATIVE HABITAT Stony places, Mediterranean.
• CULTIVATION Grow in deep, well-drained soil enriched with organic matter, in a sunny site.
• PROPAGATION Sow seed in autumn or spring, or take root cuttings in winter.
• WARNING All parts of the plant are toxic if eaten.

Rosaceae	LION'S FOOT

ALCHEMILLA XANTHOCHLORA
Habit Clump-forming perennial with a woody rootstock. *Flowers* Tiny, star-shaped, borne in sprays from early to late summer. Yellow-green.
Leaves Kidney-shaped, with 9–11 shallow, finely toothed lobes. Bright yellow-green.
• NATIVE HABITAT Mountain meadows, Europe.
• CULTIVATION Grow in moist but well-drained, preferably acidic soil in sun or dappled shade.
• PROPAGATION By seed sown *in situ* or by division, both in autumn or spring. Self-seeds freely.
• OTHER NAME *A. vulgaris*.

Z6–8

HEIGHT
6in (15cm)

SPREAD
12in (30cm)

Z4–8

HEIGHT
20in (50cm)

SPREAD
24in (60cm)

| Primulaceae | PRIMROSE |

PRIMULA VULGARIS
Habit Rosetted, evergreen or semi-evergreen perennial. ***Flowers*** Fragrant, saucer-shaped, solitary, borne in spring. Pale yellow. ***Leaves*** Lance-shaped to oval. Bright green.
• NATIVE HABITAT Shady banks in Europe.
• CULTIVATION Grow in moist but well-drained soil enriched with organic matter, in a sunny or partially shaded site.
• PROPAGATION By seed sown when ripe, or by division in early autumn or after flowering, in late spring.

Z5–9

HEIGHT
8in (20cm)

SPREAD
14in (35cm)

| Ranunculaceae | LESSER CELANDINE, PILEWORT |

RANUNCULUS FICARIA
Habit Tuberous perennial. ***Flowers*** Solitary, shallow-cupped, borne in spring. Shiny, bright yellow. ***Leaves*** Heart-shaped, glossy. Dark green.
• NATIVE HABITAT Grassy places in Europe, northwest Africa, and southwest Asia.
• CULTIVATION Grow in moist, neutral to alkaline soil, in sun. Likely to be invasive in shade, which encourages bulbil production at the leaf bases.
• PROPAGATION By seed when ripe in summer, or by division in autumn or spring.
• WARNING Contact with sap may irritate skin.

Z4–9

HEIGHT
2in (5cm)

SPREAD
12in (30cm)

| Primulaceae | COWSLIP, PAIGLE |

PRIMULA VERIS
Habit Rosette-forming, evergreen or semi-evergreen perennial. ***Flowers*** Nodding, fragrant, saucer-shaped, borne in clusters in spring. Yellow. ***Leaves*** Oblong to oval. Bright green.
• NATIVE HABITAT Grassland in Europe and western Asia.
• CULTIVATION Grow in well-drained or dry soil that is neutral to alkaline, in a sunny or partially shaded site.
• PROPAGATION Sow seed when ripe, or divide in early autumn or after flowering, in late spring.

Z5–9

HEIGHT
10in (25cm)

SPREAD
10in (25cm)

| Violaceae | HEARTSEASE, WILD PANSY |

VIOLA TRICOLOR
Habit Tufted annual, biennial, or short-lived perennial. ***Flowers*** Flat-faced, short-spurred, borne from spring to early autumn. Combinations of purple, lilac, white, and yellow. ***Leaves*** Oval to heart-shaped, and toothed. Mid-green.
• NATIVE HABITAT Grassy places and waste ground in Europe and Asia.
• CULTIVATION Grow in moist but well-drained soil in sun or dappled shade.
• PROPAGATION Sow seed when ripe or in spring, take basal cuttings in spring, or divide in autumn.

Z4–9

HEIGHT
3–5in
(8–12cm)

SPREAD
4–6in
(10–15cm)

| Ranunculaceae | | Asteraceae | FRENCH MARIGOLD |

RANUNCULUS FICARIA
var. FLORE PLENO
Habit Tuberous perennial. *Flowers* Solitary, double, shallow-cupped, borne in spring. Bright yellow. *Leaves* Heart-shaped, glossy. Dark green.
• NATIVE HABITAT Grassy places in Europe, northwest Africa, and southwest Asia.
• CULTIVATION Grow in moist soil that is neutral to alkaline, in a sunny or shady site. Likely to be less invasive than the species.
• PROPAGATION By division in autumn or spring.
• WARNING Contact with sap may irritate skin.

TAGETES PATULA
Habit Bushy annual. *Flowers* Single, daisylike, borne throughout summer. Yellow, orange, or red-brown. *Leaves* Aromatic, deeply divided into toothed segments. Bright green.
• NATIVE HABITAT Dry slopes and valley beds in Mexico.
• CULTIVATION Grow in fertile, well-drained soil in sun. Deadhead regularly to prolong flowering. May be used to repel slugs in organic gardens.
• PROPAGATION Sow seed in spring at 64°F (18°C).
• WARNING Contact with foliage may irritate skin.

Z4–9

HEIGHT
2–6in
(5–15cm)

SPREAD
12in (30cm)

ANNUAL

HEIGHT
12in (30cm)

SPREAD
12in (30cm)

| Asteraceae | ARNICA, MOUNTAIN TOBACCO | Asteraceae | POT MARIGOLD |

ARNICA MONTANA
Habit Clump-forming, aromatic, rhizomatous perennial. *Flowers* Solitary, daisylike, borne in summer. Deep yellow to orange-yellow. *Leaves* Oval to lance-shaped, mostly basal. Mid-green.
• NATIVE HABITAT From Europe to western Asia.
• CULTIVATION Grow in moist but well-drained soil enriched with organic matter, in a sunny site.
• PROPAGATION By seed sown in autumn or by division in spring.
• WARNING Contact with foliage may irritate skin. All parts may cause severe discomfort if eaten.

CALENDULA OFFICINALIS
Habit Upright, aromatic annual. *Flowers* Daisy-like, borne throughout summer. Bright yellow to orange. *Leaves* Lance-shaped. Bright green.
• NATIVE HABITAT Origin uncertain. Naturalized in rocky places and on cultivated and waste land, especially around the Mediterranean.
• CULTIVATION Grow in any well-drained soil in a sunny site. Deadhead regularly to prolong flowering and to prevent excessive self-seeding.
• PROPAGATION Sow seed in autumn or spring. Self-sows freely.

Z6–9

HEIGHT
to 20in
(50cm)

SPREAD
12in (30cm)

ANNUAL

HEIGHT
20–28in
(50–70cm)

SPREAD
20–28in
(50–70cm)

ORIGANUM

A genus of about 20 species of aromatic herbaceous perennials and evergreen or semi-evergreen subshrubs and shrubs, *Origanum* usually occurs in dry, open, sunny habitats. It can be found growing in the hills and mountains around the Mediterranean and in southwest Asia.

Commonly known as oregano or marjoram, *Origanum* bears tubular to funnel-shaped, 2-lipped flowers, often with conspicuous bracts, in whorled, clusterlike spikes during summer and into autumn.

Some species are grown primarily for ornamental purposes; those described here are highly aromatic and are also grown for culinary use. They are suitable for growing in an herb garden or in a herbaceous or mixed border. Compact variants are especially suited to growing in containers.

Most species and variants dislike the combination of cold with winter moisture and need good drainage; they do well in raised beds. *O. dictamnus* is especially sensitive to winter moisture and must have sharp drainage. In cold areas, it is best overwintered, or grown permanently, in a cold greenhouse or alpine house.

Grow in well-drained, neutral to alkaline soil that is poor to moderately fertile in a warm site in full sun. Most golden-leaved variants are prone to scorch in hot sun and are best sited where there is mid-day shade. Cut fresh leaves throughout the growing season for culinary use; most species dry well for winter use. Commercial, dried oregano is produced from several species, including *O. vulgare* and *O. vulgare* subsp. *hirtum*.

Propagate species by seed sown in containers in a cold frame in autumn, or in spring at 55–61°F (13–16°C). All species may be increased by division in spring, or by basal or stem-tip cuttings of nonflowering shoots in early summer.

O. × MAJORICUM
Habit Upright, evergreen subshrub.
Flowers Tubular, 2-lipped, borne in sprays in early to late summer. Pink or white.
Leaves Strongly aromatic, oval, softly hairy. Grayish green.
• TIPS May be used in place of *O. majorana* for culinary purposes.
• HEIGHT 24in (60cm).
• SPREAD 18in (45cm).

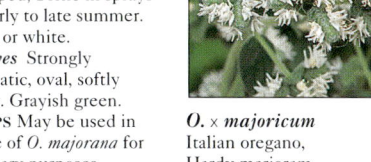

O. × *majoricum*
Italian oregano,
Hardy marjoram
☼ ◊ Z6–9
🌡 ❄

O. VULGARE var. ALBUM
Habit Bushy, woody-based perennial.
Flowers Tubular, 2-lipped, borne in whorls, in dense sprays from mid-summer to autumn. White with green bracts.
Leaves Rounded to oval. Bright green.
• HEIGHT 10in (25cm).
• SPREAD 10in (25cm).

O. vulgare var. *album*
☼ ◊ Z5–9

❄ 🌡 ❄

O. ONITES
Habit Mounded, semi-evergreen subshrub.
Flowers Tubular, borne in dense whorls during late summer. White with green bracts.
Leaves Thyme-scented, oval, heart-shaped at the base. Bright green.
• OTHER NAME *Majorana onites*.
• HEIGHT 24in (60cm).
• SPREAD 12in (30cm).

O. onites
Greek oregano,
Pot marjoram
☼ ◊ Z8–10
🌡 ❄

O. MAJORANA
Habit Erect, evergreen subshrub, usually grown as an annual or biennial.
Flowers Tubular, 2-lipped, borne in sprays in early to late summer. Pink or white, with gray-green bracts.
Leaves Oval, softly hairy. Gray-green.
• HEIGHT 32in (to 80cm).
• SPREAD 18in (45cm).

O. majorana
Sweet marjoram,
Knotted marjoram
☼ ◊ Z9–10
🌡 ❄ ❄

O. VULGARE
Habit Rhizomatous, woody-based perennial.
Flowers Tubular, 2-lipped, borne in dense, terminal clusters from mid-summer to autumn. Pink-purple to white, usually with whorls of purple-tinged bracts.
Leaves Rounded to oval. Dark green.
• HEIGHT 18in (45cm).
• SPREAD 18in (45cm).

O. vulgare
Oregano, Wild marjoram
☼ ◊ Z6–9
⛊ ⌂ ⚘

***O. VULGARE* 'Nanum'**
Habit Compact, dwarf, rhizomatous perennial.
Flowers Tubular, borne from mid-summer to autumn. Purple with green bracts.
Leaves Rounded to oval. Dark green.
• TIPS Suitable for container plantings and edging.
• HEIGHT 6in (15cm).
• SPREAD 12in (30cm).

O. vulgare 'Nanum'
☼ ◊ Z6–9
⛊ ⌂ ⚘

O. VULGARE* subsp. *HIRTUM
Habit Compact, hairy, rhizomatous perennial.
Flowers Tubular, 2-lipped, borne in late summer. White.
Leaves Rounded to oval, hairy. Dark green.
• OTHER NAME
O. heracleoticum.
• HEIGHT 12–28in (30–70cm).
• SPREAD 8–18in (20–45cm).

O. vulgare subsp. *hirtum*
☼ ◊ Z6–9
⛊ ⌂ ⚘

***O. VULGARE* 'Aureum Crispum'**
Habit Rhizomatous, spreading perennial.
Flowers Tubular, borne from summer to autumn. Pale lavender or white.
Leaves Rounded, curly. Yellow-green.
• TIPS Less vigorous than the species.
• OTHER NAME
O. 'Curly Gold'.
• HEIGHT 12in (30cm).
• SPREAD 18in (45cm).

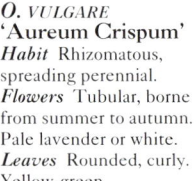
O. vulgare 'Aureum Crispum'
☼ ◊ Z6–9
⛊ ⌂ ⚘

***O. VULGARE* 'Compactum'**
Habit Dense, compact, rhizomatous perennial.
Flowers Tubular, borne in summer and autumn. Pink-violet, with green, purple-tinted bracts.
Leaves Small, rounded to oval. Dark green.
• TIPS Suitable for container plantings.
• HEIGHT 6in (15cm).
• SPREAD 12in (30cm).

O. vulgare 'Compactum'
Compact marjoram
☼ ◊ Z7–9
⛊ ⌂ ⚘

***O. VULGARE* 'Polyphant'**
Habit Rhizomatous, woody-based perennial.
Flowers Tubular, 2-lipped, borne from mid-summer to autumn. White, with green bracts.
Leaves Rounded. Mid-green, variegated white.
• TIPS Suitable for growing in containers.
• HEIGHT 12in (30cm).
• SPREAD 12in (30cm).

O. vulgare 'Polyphant'
☼ ◊ Z8–9
⛊ ⌂ ⚘

O. DICTAMNUS
Habit Dome-shaped, evergreen subshrub.
Flowers Small, funnel-shaped, with hoplike bracts, borne in drooping whorls in mid- to late summer. Pink with purple bracts.
Leaves Rounded, white-hairy. Gray-green.
• TIPS Needs a sharply drained soil.
• HEIGHT 6in (15cm).
• SPREAD 8in (20cm).

O. dictamnus
Cretan dittany, Hop marjoram
☼ ◊ Z8–9
⛊

ORIGANUM • 139

O. VULGARE 'County Cream'
Habit Rhizomatous, woody-based perennial.
Flowers Tubular, borne from mid-summer to autumn. White with green bracts.
Leaves Rounded. Mid-green, with creamy white variegation.
• TIPS Good for border edging and containers.
• HEIGHT 12in (30cm).
• SPREAD 12in (30cm).

O. vulgare 'County Cream'
☼ ◊ Z7–9

O. VULGARE 'Aureum'
Habit Rhizomatous, spreading perennial.
Flowers Tubular, 2-lipped, borne from mid-summer to autumn. Lavender-pink.
Leaves Rounded. Bright golden-yellow.
• TIPS Protect from the hottest mid-day sun to prevent leaf scorch.
• HEIGHT 12in (30cm).
• SPREAD 12in (30cm).

O. vulgare 'Aureum'
Golden marjoram
☼ ◊ Z6–9

O. VULGARE 'Gold Tip'
Habit Rhizomatous, spreading perennial.
Flowers Tubular, borne from summer to autumn. Lavender-pink.
Leaves Rounded. Dark green, with bright golden-yellow tips during spring.
• OTHER NAME
O. vulgare 'Variegatum'.
• HEIGHT 16in (40cm).
• SPREAD 18in (45cm).

O. vulgare 'Gold Tip'
☼ ◊ Z8–9

O. ONITES 'Aureum'
Habit Mounded, semi-evergreen subshrub.
Flowers Tubular, borne in dense whorls in late summer. White with green bracts.
Leaves Thyme-scented, heart-shaped at the base, oval. Bright golden-yellow.
• TIPS Shows some resistance to sun scorch.
• HEIGHT 24in (60cm).
• SPREAD 24in (60cm).

O. onites 'Aureum'
☼ ◊ Z8–10

O. 'Norton Gold'
Habit Rhizomatous, spreading perennial.
Flowers Tubular, 2-lipped, borne from mid-summer through to autumn. Pink.
Leaves Rounded. Golden-yellow.
• HEIGHT 10in (25cm).
• SPREAD 18in (45cm).

O. 'Norton Gold'
☼ ◊ Z7–10

O. VULGARE 'Acorn Bank'
Habit Rhizomatous, spreading perennial.
Flowers Tubular, borne from mid-summer to autumn. White with pink stamens.
Leaves Oval, taper-pointed, with incurved margins. Golden-yellow.
• TIPS Suitable for mixed or herbaceous borders.
• HEIGHT 24in (60cm).
• SPREAD 36in (90cm).

O. vulgare 'Acorn Bank'
☼ ◊ Z6–9

Caring for Herbs

The first step when planning which herbs to grow is to choose plants that suit the situation, since herbs vary greatly in size, habit, and requirements. Some of the most popular herbs are incompatible with each other: angelica and lovage both have lush foliage and large leaves and need deep, rich soil, while thyme and savory have tiny leaves and thrive on shallow, dry soils.

However, there is no need to grow most herbs in a special herb garden, since most of them are easily raised among other plants. Shrubby herbs, herbaceous perennials, and some of the more colorful annuals make a valuable contribution when included in border plantings, although several of them tend to be invasive. Soapwort, yarrow, and common tansy (*Tanacetum vulgare*) have fast-spreading rhizomes, while both red plantain (*Plantago major* var. *rubra*) and red orache (*Atriplex hortensis* var. *rubra*) self-sow freely, often to the point of nuisance, especially in lawns.

For the vegetable plot, choose herbs that you use regularly and best sown in succession or grown as a permanent, neat, and attractive edging. Parsley, dill, common chervil (*Anthriscus cerefolium*), cilantro, and purslane can be "catch-cropped"; between rows of vegetables, while chives (*Allium schoenoprasum*) and basil serve as useful perimeter plants.

Buying herbs

Many common herbs are available as young plants from garden centers, but specialty herb nurseries offer a wider range, larger specimens, and expert advice. They also supply herbs that may be needed in large quantities, such as boxwood or lavender for hedging, or chamomile for lawns. Short-lived herbs, and those that are used regularly, are best grown from seed as they are expensive to buy repeatedly and may not transplant well. Quite often, if you let a few plants go to seed, they will sow themselves. This usually happens with calendulas, borage (*Borago officinalis*), coriander, and salad rocket (*Eruca vesicaria* subsp. *sativa*).

Before buying, check plants for pests and diseases, and choose the ones that have the best shape and condition. Look for healthy, colorful foliage and plenty of growth or new shoots rather than a showy display of flowers that may tempt you to buy an inferior specimen. A young plant in an 3in (8cm) pot has enough nutrients for only a few weeks, so small plants are best bought and planted out as soon as they become available. For chives, parsley, dill, and basil, several seedlings are sometimes potted up together to look better at the point of sale. If the roots can be easily separated, divide the plants. Grow them on in individual pots, allowing them to reestablish before planting out. This reduces the risk of gray mold (see p. 150), and produces larger yields.

Choosing Herbs

POT-BOUND CONTAINER PLANT

Roots coiled tightly around the root ball

Avoid plants with compacted root balls and numerous roots protruding through the drainage holes of the container. Once they have been placed in the ground, such plants are unlikely ever to do well.

SOIL PREPARATION AND PLANTING

Ideally, a herb garden should have a sunny, open but sheltered site with well-drained, fertile soil that is neutral to slightly alkaline. These conditions suit the majority of common herbs, such as lavenders, sages, and thymes, which are largely Mediterranean in origin. If you are planning a new herb garden and the site has serious drawbacks, it is worth considering professional help to clear, drain, and landscape the area.

When deciding where to plant different species, note the soil conditions and the amount of shade or sun, and the proximity of surrounding plants, which may cast shade or encroach later in the growing season. If you intend to crop the herbs, make sure that they are accessible for harvesting without having to stand on the surrounding soil. Wide beds might need subdividing by a path or stepping stones to give easier access.

PREPARING AN HERB GARDEN

1 *Prepare the ground thoroughly before planting. Clear any weeds and rake the surface of the soil to produce a fine tilth. Using string and stakes to outline the design, mark out the planting design for the herb garden, including any paths or paved areas on the site.*

2 *Position the plants in their pots to check the overall effect and spacing. Dense planting achieves the desired results quickly.*

3 *Once the design is laid out, sink boards at the edges of beds to keep gravel or mulch paths contained. Plant and water the herbs.*

4 *Spread mulch or gravel evenly between the boards marking the edges of the paths. Level out the surface with a straightedge.*

5 *Keep the herb garden watered and weeded. Prune plants as necessary, pinching out growing tips to promote bushy growth.*

Planting Seeds in Paving

Aromatic herbs, such as creeping thyme, release their scent when crushed and suit patios and paths. Sow seeds in moist soil mix laid between the paving stones.

Planting in Crevices

Choose seedlings or small-rooted cuttings (here, houseleeks) for drystone walls. Using a thin blade, insert the plant in position and pack well with soil mix.

Planting out

Before planting out herbs, it is best to set them in their final positions to check for effect and spacing. It is easy to underestimate the eventual size of young plants, so as a rule, allow more rather than less, space between them. Shrubby herbs and perennials are often better planted in groups of three or five for greater coverage in the first year. Seedlings of smaller herbs and annuals may be planted more densely and thinned out later. Vigorous herbs are best grown in a small bed on their own or in a large container, while seed is the easiest way of establishing herbs in crevices and gravel where it is not feasible to insert young plants. Grow medicinal and culinary herbs away from possible contamination by pets, roadside pollution, and agricultural sprays, and site toxic herbs carefully in gardens used by young children. Container herbs can be planted throughout the growing season, but they establish more quickly in spring, when there is regular rainfall.

Choose a calm, damp day for planting, since sunny, windy conditions tend to encourage leaf scorch and moisture loss. Use a wooden board for standing on at

Planting Invasive Herbs in Open Ground

Tansies, sweet woodruff (*Galium odoratum*), and mints tend to encroach on neighboring plants in open ground. To contain the spread of vigorous herbs, grow them in sunken pots, old buckets, or heavy-duty plastic bags. Lift and divide the plants each spring and replant young shoots in fresh soil mix.

1 *Make drainage holes in the pot, then sink it in the ground. Fill with a mixture of soil and compost.*

2 *Plant the herb (here, mint) in the pot, firm in well, and water. Conceal the rim of the pot with soil mix.*

the planting site. This avoids trampling and compacting the soil, which restricts root growth. Water the herbs well before planting, since root balls are difficult to wet thoroughly when underground. If the root ball is very dry, lift the plant from the pot and soak it in a bucket of water. Most commercially produced herbs need to be hardened off for at least a few days before planting out, since they have usually been raised under protective cover.

In some areas, evergreen herbs, such as sage, thyme, and savory, can be harvested nearly all year, while spearmint (*Mentha spicata*), tarragon (*Artemisia dracunculus*), and other herbaceous perennials may be "forced" to ensure supplies until the following spring. To force herbs, lift the plants at intervals when dormant and pot them up under glass to produce tender new shoots in frost-free conditions.

Conditioning the soil

When digging holes for planting, allow extra space for additional soil mix and grit if the soil is less than ideal. On heavy clay soil it is important to improve texture and drainage by forking in sand or grit and organic matter, such as leaf mold. Adding organic matter in and around the planting holes rather than through the whole area is also advisable for sandy soils to improve moisture retention. Whatever the weather, water well to settle the soil around the plants and provide evenly moist conditions for new root growth. A layer of grit beneath low-growing herbs will help to prevent mud splashing and prolonged contact with wet soil.

Although many Mediterranean herbs, such as lavenders, thrive in alkaline soils, other species prefer neutral or slightly acidic conditions. If the pH is below 6.5, a dressing of lime in the recommended quantity may be needed. It is not advisable to feed Mediterranean herbs with fertilizers, since it produces soft growth with poor aroma and little resistance to pests, diseases, and cold.

FORCING TENDER HERBS FOR FRESH WINTER USE

1 *Using a fork, lift a clump of herbs (here, chives). It is best to choose a dry day in early autumn for harvesting.*

2 *Divide the clump of herbs into smaller pieces, and shake loose as much soil as possible from the roots.*

3 *Pot up the divided pieces in soil mix. Water well, cut back any top growth, and place in a light, frost-free site.*

4 *Harvest the leaves regularly when they reach 4in (10cm), to ensure a supply of new growth.*

Container and Greenhouse Herbs

Although herbs grown in containers need more care than those planted in open ground, the reward of any attractive display makes the effort worthwhile. Containers filled with herbs are especially effective when arranged in groups and are useful for decorating small or paved areas. Compared with those raised in beds, container-grown herbs are more accessible for harvesting, and allow unsightly or poor specimens to be removed and replaced easily.

Containers are often the best choice for growing marginally hardy and tender herbs. They also suit species such as checkerberry (*Gaultheria procumbens*) which have special soil requirements that cannot be provided in open ground. Mints and other invasive herbs can be restrained in containers, while succulent herbs can be protected from slugs.

Choosing the right container

There is a limitless range of containers available for herbs. At one time, most containers had to be taken indoors or moved under glass during cold winters. Fortunately, many of them now are frostproof, allowing container gardening to become a year-round activity. Frostproof terracotta pots are particularly well suited, since they age beautifully to complement a plant's foliage, color, and texture. Strawberry jars are specially made pots with planting pockets through which the plants can grow. Rarely filled with strawberries alone, they can be planted up with a selection of culinary herbs or trailing, ornamental plants. Strawberry jars also suit themed collections of plants, such as herbs used in home remedies. Segmented containers and wagon wheels bedded

Planting Herbs in Containers

An elegant standard
For a strong focal point, a standard boxwood (Buxus sempervirens) *has been positioned amid an attractive base of creeping and bushy herbs (here, thyme).*

Herbs on different levels
A collection of container plants makes an attractive display on patios and paved areas. For best effect, choose herbs with contrasting foliage, such as sages and artemisias.

Planting up a Windowbox

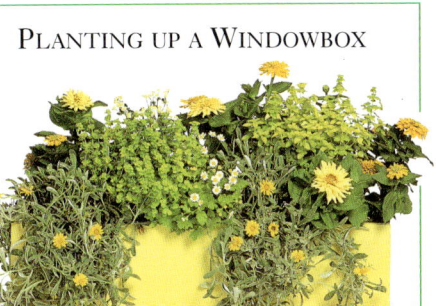

Choose a color theme for a windowbox display and use trailing herbs to soften the outline. Here, Origanum vulgare 'Aureum' and Tanacetum parthenium enhance the yellow planting design.

Growing Herbs on a Windowsill

Grown in containers placed on windowsills, culinary herbs, such as marjoram, chives, purple sage, and apple mint (Mentha suaveolens), can be kept close for easy use when preparing dishes.

into the soil allow different kinds of herb to be separated into triangular compartments. They are very effective when planted with thymes to form bold blocks of color and texture. A half-barrel or rectangular Versailles box provides ample space for a formal clipped bay or boxwood, while hanging baskets, windowboxes, and improvised containers (such as a chimney pot, old wheelbarrow, or jardinière) make excellent display bases.

Selecting the right herb

The key to successful container gardening is to plant the right kind of herbs and in appropriate numbers. Overplanted pots can easily become top heavy; in addition, the soil dries out quickly and is soon exhausted of nutrients. When choosing herbs for a mixed planting or strawberry jar, look for dwarf cultivars and naturally small-growing herbs, such as houseleeks, creeping savory (*Satureja spicigera*), and heartsease (*Viola tricolor*). Bugles, creeping thymes, and other prostrate or trailing herbs are useful for softening outlines, but avoid invasive or large, deep-rooted herbs, such as tansies, which may outgrow their neighbors and cause overcrowding.

Large plants, such as bay and rosemary, are best grown as single specimens in patio tubs. They make attractive focal points when placed on terraces and can be used to add height to displays.

Composts for container gardening

The choice of compost for containers is an important consideration. Soilless composts are lightweight and well suited to windowboxes, hanging baskets, and large patio tubs that may need moving. However, they need careful watering since they are difficult to wet when dried out and are prone to waterlogging if overwatered. Adding moisture-retaining granules reduces the amount of watering needed, while the inclusion of vermiculite will improve both water retention and aeration. Soil-based mixes are heavier than soilless ones and retain moisture better, reducing the need for frequent watering and making the pot more stable in strong winds.

To minimize evaporation, shield containers from prevailing wind and full sun, and stand them in trays of water during hot, dry weather. Before filling a container with soil mix, insert a layer of drainage material, such as stones or broken pieces of terracotta pot or polystyrene to improve drainage.

Container Herbs for Culinary Use

Culinary hanging basket
Use soilless mix to reduce the weight of a hanging basket, and add moisture-retaining granules to prevent the soil mix from drying out rapidly, especially in summer.

Growing watercress
Take 3–4 cuttings of watercress (Nasturtium officinale) *and plant them in rich soil mix in a 6in (15cm) pot. Stand the pot in a saucer of water that is changed daily.*

Greenhouse climber
Grapes (Vitis vinifera) *can be trained to grow along the roof a greenhouse. The plant benefits from the warmth and sunlight of this position and fruits well under glass. It also provides shade for the plants growing below.*

Growing herbs under glass

A greenhouse is the ideal place in which to grow tender herbs, such as Arabian jasmine (*Jasminum sambac*), galangal (*Alpinia galanga*), and scented geraniums, as well as for producing crops of popular culinary herbs, such as spearmint and chives, out of season. It provides good levels of light, constant warmth, and shelter from extreme weather conditions and wind. Although the warm, sheltered atmosphere of greenhouses makes plants more prone to infestations such as spider mites (see p. 150), the enclosed environment allows pest control to be more accurate.

In areas with cool, short summers, herbs such as *Perilla frutescens* 'Crispa' and basils usually perform far better in a greenhouse than in open ground, while peppers are more likely to bear ripe fruits under glass. A greenhouse is also invaluable for raising herbs from seeds and cuttings. However, young plants that have been raised under glass, including most commercially produced herbs, have no resistance to frost and need to be given a period of hardening off in a colder, more airy site before being transplanted outdoors.

Routine Care

An herb garden needs regular care to keep its appearance and remain productive throughout the growing season. As well as routine maintenance, such as watering, feeding, and weeding, plants need individual attention, too. Tasks such as deadheading, pruning, and training give you the opportunity to check for problems and also to enjoy the aromas, colors, and textures of herbs at close quarters.

Watering and feeding

Newly planted herbs need regular watering until strong new growth is apparent. Always water thoroughly, rather than little and often, which encourages shallow surface roots to form. The best time to water is in the evening, since this minimizes evaporation and possibly damaging foliage in the sun.

Few of the common culinary herbs are rich feeders, but heavy cropping will increase nutritional requirements. An annual application of bulky organic matter, such as composted bark or mushroom compost, replaces nutrients, inhibits weeds, and improves soil texture. Apply mulches in spring after a shower of rain, but make sure that the ground has warmed up, since covering dry, cold soil will retard growth. Potting mixes have sufficient nutrients to support only a few weeks of vigorous growth, so feed container herbs regularly during the growing season with an all-purpose liquid fertilizer.

Controlling growth

Without routine attention, many herbs outgrow their allotted space or become rangy. To check the growth of invasive herbs such as periwinkles and mints, remove any runners as they develop, or lift the entire clump each spring and replant only with a small portion. Herbs that are grown for their fresh, young foliage may be cut back hard once or twice in the growing season to produce a supply of new leaves. It is a good idea to

Deadheading to Prevent Self-Seeding

Remove the seedheads of vigorous plants (here, angelica) before the seeds ripen to prevent seedlings from smothering small neighboring plants.

Retaining Variegation

Variegated plants (here, Teucrium x lucidrys 'Variegatum') sometimes produce shoots that revert to plain green. These growths tend to be more vigorous than the variegated shoots and need to be removed as soon as they emerge. If left, the whole plant will eventually lose its variegation and become entirely green.

cut back lemon balm (*Melissa officinalis*) and mints before flowering and again in late summer, but leave marjoram and chives until after flowering.

Prune deciduous shrubs, trees, and climbers when dormant to enhance their shape. Most evergreens require little pruning other than the removal of dead wood and trimming to shape, while boxwood needs clipping two or three times in the growing season if trained as a hedge or topiary. If you dislike the smell of the foliage, cut the hedge after rain or water it well after trimming. Most shrubby Mediterranean herbs benefit from hard pruning in spring to about 1in (2.5cm) or more of growth, followed by a trim with shears or scissors after flowering to remove dead flower stems. The exception is thyme, which dislikes hard pruning and should be only lightly trimmed after flowering. When pruning

Encouraging New Growth

Mediterranean herbs, such as lavender cotton (Santolina chamaecyparissus), *need to be pruned hard in spring. Cut back into old wood to stimulate fresh, bushy growth, and trim the plant again after flowering.*

Pruning Shrubby Herbs

1 *Using pruners or shears, remove all dry flower stalks (here, lavender) in late summer or early autumn. Lightly clip the plant to maintain a neat finish and compact shape.*

Clearing Debris

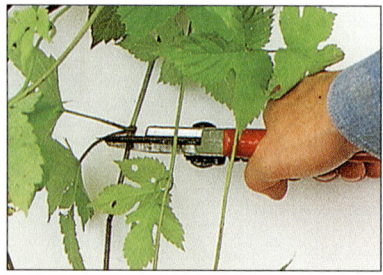

Commonly found on hops, a mass of dead stems can be difficult to manage when it becomes entangled with new growth in spring. Using pruners, remove all dead stems and other debris in winter.

2 *Encourage new growth by harder pruning early in the following spring. Cut back shoots by 1in (2.5cm) or more of the previous year's growth, but leave some green shoots on the plant.*

rue in spring, always wear gloves to protect against skin blistering, and take care not to cut far into the main stem as this may kill the plant. Cultivars of elder should be pruned hard in late winter, since they come into growth very early in the year. If left unpruned or only lightly pruned, the plant becomes woody and produces small, less colorful leaves.

A combination of pruning and training is needed throughout the growing season for hops and other vigorous climbers such as jasmine. Golden hop (*Humulus lupulus* 'Aureus') dies down completely in winter. Cut out the remaining tangle of twining stems before new growth begins in spring.

Repotting

Herbs grown in containers can quickly become root-bound and starved. The most common symptoms are yellowing foliage, weak growth, roots protruding from the base of the pot, or proneness to pests and diseases (see p. 150). To keep these herbs in good condition, pot them on into larger containers or replace them with young specimens. It is best to overhaul all containers in early spring, replacing or repotting plants as required.

Divide clump-forming herbs to obtain a small healthy piece for repotting, and cut back shrubby herbs to encourage compact new growth. Large specimens that cannot be repotted benefit from a top-dressing. Remove the top 2in (5cm) of soil mix and replace with a fresh layer of mix with a little slow-release fertilizer added. Boxwood and bay thrive for many years in the same container if they are top-dressed each spring.

Strawberry jars are best repotted annually, as they hold relatively little soil mix in relation to the number of plants. Some damage is inevitable when removing plants, so, wherever possible, take cuttings or divide while replanting. Invasive herbs grown in containers also need repotting annually. Discard most of the runners, replanting just a handful of the healthiest growths.

REPLANTING A STRAWBERRY JAR

1 *Lift the plants from the top, then dig out the soil mix. Remove plants carefully from the pockets. Tip out the rest of the soil mix, and replace drainage material.*

2 *Add fresh soil mix as far as the lowest pockets. Divide or replace old plants. Replant from inside each pocket, gently pulling the foliage through the hole.*

3 *Pack soil mix around the roots and fill to the next level of pockets. Firm well at each stage of planting, and water the completed jar thoroughly.*

Pests, Diseases, and Disorders

Herbs are prone to the same ailments as other garden plants, but they require careful treatment if grown for culinary or medicinal use. For this reason, organic cultivation is favored by many herb gardeners. Ventilation and hygiene are particularly important under glass. Keep fungal diseases at bay by regularly removing dead leaves and flowers, and use sticky traps to catch flying pests before temperatures are high enough to introduce biological controls. When spraying is necessary, use only safe contact insecticides recommended by suppliers of biological controls, and follow instructions carefully. Soak pots brought under glass with a biological solution to control any slugs and snails.

Common Pests and Diseases

Aphids
Control aphids with insecticidal soft soaps, or direct a strong, fine stream of water onto the infested parts to knock aphids off the plant.

Gray mold (*Botrytis*)
Soft leaves and flowers are prone to gray mold under glass. Allow ample space between plants and ventilate well. Remove dead material and discard infected plants.

Leaf miners
The larvae of various flies, moths, and beetles mine through leaves. To control, remove and destroy any affected leaves, and spray the plant with water.

Spider mites
This pest thrives in hot and dry conditions. Remove any webs on leaves, spray with water and insecticidal soap; or introduce Phytoseiulus, *a predatory mite.*

Rusts
Patches of rust appear in poor air circulation and high humidity. Give plants ample space and ventilation. Discard infected plants, and do not replant same species.

Whitefly
In low temperatures, increase air circulation, hang sticky traps, and spray with insecticidal soap. Under glass, introduce Encarsia, *a parasitic wasp.*

PROPAGATION

An interesting range of herbs can be propagated from produce bought in a grocery store. Pots of culinary herbs, such as parsley, basil, and dill, often hold numerous seedlings, which can be divided and grown on to form much larger clumps. Some seedlings inevitably are damaged, so remove any that wilt, but the majority will soon put out new roots and leaves. Fresh roots of ginger, turmeric (*Curcuma longa*), and galangal rapidly produce handsome, reedlike growths if planted in pots of moist soil mix and kept at 70°F (21°C) or more. Bulbs of garlic, divided into separate cloves, may be planted in the herb garden during autumn. Peppers contain viable seeds from which ornamental and useful plants can easily be grown, if placed in an environment with sufficient warmth and light. Likewise, grapevines and pomegranates can be raised from fruit seeds.

Raising herbs from seed

As a rule, it is best to buy seed for herbs that are difficult to obtain as container-grown plants, such as unusual cultivars of basil, or for herbs that are used in large quantities, such as parsley. Seed is usually the only means of propagation for annuals and biennials. It is best to sow most seeds in spring, although some germinate better as soon as they are ripe. Hardy annuals tend to be larger and flower earlier if sown in autumn, which is also the best time to sow biennials for flowering the following summer.

Seeds of tropical herbs often have little or no dormant period and must be sown immediately, while those from cold areas may need stratifying to trigger germination. In some cases, soaking or scarifying the seed accelerates germination. Parsley is notoriously slow unless soaked in warm water, while passionflower seed invariably germinates more readily if the seedcoat is nicked with a sharp knife, allowing it to absorb moisture.

Many herbs are easy to grow from seed, either indoors in containers or trays of seed soil mix, or outdoors in a bed that has been weeded thoroughly, leveled, and raked to a fine tilth. Always sow the seeds thinly, since overcrowded seedlings are more prone to disease. The seeds of herbs such as dill, parsley, and coriander are large enough to handle individually, while basils and thymes have tiny seeds that are easier to sow thinly if mixed with sand.

Annuals and biennials, such as chervil and dill, tend to bolt in response to root damage, so they are best sown *in situ* and thinned – the thinnings of edible herbs can be used in cooking. Herbs that are cropped for their young leaves should be sown at intervals of 3 to 4 weeks from early spring to early autumn to ensure a continuous supply. Early and late sowings may need to be covered with cloches. Basils frequently succumb to fungal diseases in cool, dull weather, especially when overcrowded. In cooler areas, sow them in late spring when ample warmth and light are available.

RAISING FRUIT FROM SEED

Grapes (above), *pomegranates, and lemons can all be grown successfully from seed, although they may not come true. Sow in seed soil mix in spring, and allow 3 to 4 weeks for germination.*

Sowing Parsley in Containers

1. *Soak seed in warm water for several hours, then dry. From a paper fold, tap seeds onto firmed seed soil mix and lightly cover with sieved mix.*

2. *When the seedlings are large enough to handle, carefully lift them out of the tray. Take care to hold them by the leaves rather than the stems.*

3. *Prick out seedlings individually into packs of firmed soil mix. When they are 2–2½in (5–6cm) tall, transplant them into outdoor beds. Do not harvest any leaves for several weeks until plants have become established.*

Seedlings that are to be transplanted should be thinned promptly and pricked out as soon as they are large enough to handle. Whether the seedlings are in individual pots or seed trays, they should be transferred before the roots are congested to avoid checking growth. Prior to moving young plants outdoors, harden them off in a cold greenhouse or cold frame so that they are not unduly stressed by the change in environment.

Saving seed

If you save seed from your own plants, bear in mind that certain herbs may cross-pollinate, yielding seedlings with features that differ from those of the mother plant. Most herb gardens host different varieties of marjoram, thyme, mint, and lavender, so the likelihood of hybridization is high. Closely related genera may also interbreed if they are grown together and flower at the same time. For example, fennel and dill plants are known to cross-breed, resulting in offspring of indeterminate flavor. More reliable results can be achieved by collecting home-grown seeds from borage, coriander, and caraway.

Planting Out in Open Ground

When seedlings are sufficiently advanced, they may be transplanted outdoors into prepared ground. Plant them out at the recommended spacing and depth. Firm the soil around the roots and water well.

With the exception of variegated rue (*Ruta graveolens* 'Variegata'), very few variegated plants come true from seed. Nevertheless, several colored-leaf variants, including red orache, golden marjoram, golden hop, and red plantain, are largely reliable. Flower-color variants are less dependable and produce mostly the same color as the species. Seeds saved from double-flowered cultivars of pot marigold (*Calendula officinalis*) usually yield a high proportion of offspring with single flowers, which increases throughout successive years.

Offsets
Most herbs with bulbs or corms increase naturally by producing offsets. These can be detached during the dormant period and planted separately to grow on. Pull the offsets gently from the parent plant or cut the basal plate at the point at which they are attached to the large bulb. The term "offsets" is also used to refer to the detachable plantlets that form at the tips of stolons and runners in wild strawberries (*Fragaria vesca*) and bugles, for example.

Division
Clumps of herbaceous perennials need to be divided every few years, or when they become too large and overcrowded. Choose a mild, damp day to lift the plant, either when it is dormant or at the beginning of spring before new growth emerges. Divide the plant into smaller pieces and, using a spade or knife, cut through any tough roots. Discard old plant material found at the center of the clump in favor of the more vigorous outer parts. Replant any divided pieces with a good root system and growth buds, and water them well to settle the soil around the roots.

Primulas need to be divided regularly to maintain their vigor, while peonies resent disturbance and may take several years to flower after division. Irises are best divided from two to three months after flowering. Check for any signs of disease or damage, especially where

SAVING SEED

Dry seedheads on absorbent paper, then shake out the seeds. Remove any debris and store them in labeled envelopes (not plastic bags) in a cool, dry place.

DIVIDING RHIZOMATOUS PLANTS

1 *Remove any loose soil. Use hands or a handfork to split each clump (here, iris) into manageable pieces. Discard any diseased or damaged material.*

2 *Detach young rhizomes from the clump and trim the ends and leaves. Dust the cut rhizome with fungicide, and shake off any excess powder.*

Dividing Perennial Herbs

1. Using a fork, gently lift out the plant that is to be divided, taking care not to damage the roots. Shake off any surplus soil from the clump.

2. Tease apart the clump, and select healthy pieces with several new shoots. Cut back old top-growth and replant the divisions. Firm in and water well.

Mound-layering

1. In spring, mound 3–5in (8–12cm) of sandy loam over the crown of the plant (here, thyme) to promote stem rooting. Keep the shoot tips visible.

2. In late summer, using a knife or pruners, remove rooted pieces from the parent clump. Pot up the rooted layers individually or plant them out.

plants have suffered from overcrowding. Remove one-half to two-thirds of the leaves to compensate for root loss. Replant the divisions so that the tops of the rhizomes are exposed above the surface of the soil and facing the sun.

Layering
Various deciduous and evergreen shrubs and climbers, such as jasmine, passionflower, and witch hazel, can be increased by layering, whereby a stem or shoot is induced to form roots while still attached to the parent plant. In spring, choose a strong, flexible shoot that bends easily to the ground. Make a small cut in the underside, and bury it in the soil so that the shoot tip still protrudes above the surface. Add grit or sand to the soil to improve the texture of heavy soils, and anchor the buried section with a large stone. In the following autumn or spring, provided that the layer has rooted, it can be severed from the parent plant and potted up separately.

Mound-layering
Shrubby herbs that tend to become woody and sparse with age can be increased by mound-layering in spring. If kept moist, the shoots will develop roots and, by late summer, they can be detached and potted up separately.

Cuttings

Propagation by cuttings is the quickest and most reliable method of increasing the majority of perennial and shrubby herbs, and produces a young plant that is identical to its parents. All cuttings should be made with a clean, sharp knife or pruners to reduce the risk of infecting the cutting. Insert them as soon as possible into open, well-drained seed soil mix, sand, or a mixture of peat and sand. Dip cut surfaces in hormone powder to encourage rooting, and keep hardy and marginally hardy species at 64–77°F (18–25°C) and tender plants at 77–90°F (25–32°C). Provide humidity for leafy cuttings, either by using a propagator or by enclosing the potted cuttings in a plastic bag, making sure that the leaves are not in direct contact with wet surfaces. Pinching out growing shoot tips often improves rooting.

Types of stem cutting

BASAL CUTTINGS are taken from new growth on perennial herbs at or just below ground level in spring. The lower leaves should be removed, since these will rot if inserted into soil mix.
GREENWOOD CUTTINGS are slightly firmer than softwood cuttings and suit shrubby or perennial herbs. They may be taken when the first flush of spring growth has slowed down. A "heel" or slip of tissue from the main stem is often taken with the cutting and should be trimmed, together with any bottom leaves, if the cutting is longer than 3–4in (8–10cm).
HARDWOOD CUTTINGS are taken from the mature wood of evergreen and deciduous trees and shrubs, such as willow and pomegranate, at the end of the growing season. Although hardwood cuttings tend to be slow to root, it is not difficult to keep them in good condition because they are unlikely to wilt.
SOFTWOOD CUTTINGS are taken in spring from immature, non-flowering growth of shrubby herbs. Softwood cuttings wilt readily and are best misted initially to keep them turgid. One exception is cuttings from scented geraniums, which root better and are less likely to rot if they are left to dry off for a day. Most gray-leaved and succulent herbs are also sensitive to excessive moisture and humidity. Softwood cuttings taken from herbs such as patchouli (*Pogostemon cablin*) and basils, root easily in water.
STEM-TIP CUTTINGS are taken from the tips of strong, non-flowering shoots and measure between 3 and 5in (8–13cm) long. They can be taken at any time in the growing season from herbaceous perennials such as geraniums. Remove the lower leaves, since these will rot if inserted into soil mix.
SEMI-RIPE CUTTINGS suit evergreen, shrubby herbs such as rosemaries, artemisias, and thymes, and are taken from mid-summer to early autumn. Cut just above a node from the current season's growth, choosing a section that is firm at the base and soft at the tip. Remove the tip and bottom leaves, and trim the cutting to 4–6in (10–15cm).

Root cuttings

When large numbers of cuttings are required, or when the parent plant is being discarded, root cuttings are especially useful. Variegated cultivars cannot be propagated by root cuttings; new plants will yield only green foliage.

TAKING ROOT CUTTINGS

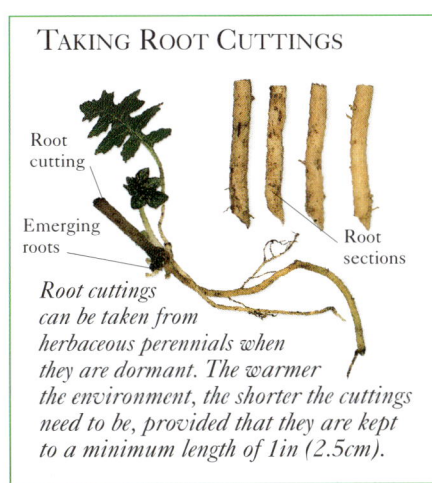

Root cutting

Emerging roots

Root sections

Root cuttings can be taken from herbaceous perennials when they are dormant. The warmer the environment, the shorter the cuttings need to be, provided that they are kept to a minimum length of 1in (2.5cm).

Harvesting and Storage

Herbs should be harvested on a fine, dry day, preferably after any morning dew has dried but before the plants are exposed to hot sunshine, which evaporates their essential oils. To prevent any confusion over a plant's identity and the transfer of fragrances between different crops, collect just one kind of herb at a time. Use sharp scissors or pruners to ensure a clean cut from the parent plant, and wear gloves to avoid any irritation to the skin. Try to maintain the plant's shape and vigor when harvesting by choosing straggly or invasive shoots, or older leaves as long as these are unblemished. Select material from only clean, healthy plants and check for any diseased or infested parts. Herb flowers are harvested when first open, or just 10 percent open in the case of spikes and clusters, while leaves and shoots may be picked at any time during the growing season, although they are usually most flavorsome before flowering. Roots may be lifted at any time, but are best harvested in autumn. Seeds may be collected by cutting off fully formed seedheads before they are

Drying Flowerheads

Remove stalks, then lay the cut flowerheads (here, pot marigolds) to dry on a tray lined with paper towels.

Where only the dried petals are required, detach them from the flower disk and discard any unused parts.

Dry lavender flowerheads on the stem by storing them upside down in a bag to catch any loose flowers.

Drying Leaves and Stems

1 *Thyme and other small-leaved herbs are best dried on the stem. Tie cleaned stems in small bunches, and hang them upside down in a warm, well-ventilated place.*

2 *Rub brittle leaves off the dried stems onto paper. Crumble pieces together if all parts are being used.*

3 *Transfer dried herbs to a storage jar with a tight seal and dark glass, to reduce light oxidation.*

completely ripe, since mature seedheads tend to scatter seed when the stem is cut. It is important to process herbs as soon as possible after harvesting and to avoid bruising or cutting them, which releases essential oils.

Storing herbs

With the exception of oil extraction, which requires special equipment and expertise, most of the techniques used for storing herbs are traditional and easily carried out at home. The most common method is air-drying, for which a simple drying rack can be made from a slatted shelf or mesh-covered wooden frame. It is best not to wash leaves and flowers since this makes them more difficult to dry. Wash roots thoroughly first and then peel, chop, or slice them to speed the drying process. Place a single layer of individual leaves, petals, flowerheads, or chopped roots on a rack covered with paper towels, or hang the foliage in small bunches. Keep the harvested herbs in a warm, dark, well-ventilated place. Once crisp, they can be packed into clean storage jars with airtight seals and used for infusions, potpourris, and culinary recipes. Marigold petals are often used as a substitute for saffron or to decorate salads, while lavender flowerheads are used to scent linen and potpourri.

Culinary uses for herbs

Soft-leaved herbs, such as basil, parsley, and chives, often retain their color and flavor better when frozen in food-grade plastic bags or boxes. There is no need to defrost frozen herbs before using them in cooking since they will crumble easily. Herb ice cubes are a good way of freezing flowers and sprigs for use in cold drinks or for adding directly to dishes. Stems of angelica and sliced ginger roots can be crystallized by steeping them in sugar syrup; for best results, follow a recommended recipe. Rose petals and violets may be crystallized using a different technique. First, paint them with egg white, then apply a coating of sugar before drying.

The flavors of many herbs, including tarragon, rosemary, and thyme, are traditionally preserved by steeping the herbs in oil or vinegar. Herb-flavored vinegars are very useful in the kitchen and look most attractive when the herbs are left inside the storage jar. Place lightly crushed sprigs into a bottle, adding warmed wine or cider (not malt) vinegar to cover, and leave for several weeks to allow the flavor to permeate. Herb-flavored oils are more difficult to make safely at home because there is a risk of bacterial contamination from the foliage.

FREEZING HERBS

Freezing is a convenient way of storing small quantities of herbs. Seal clean foliage in a plastic bag and label them. Place the bag in a freezer until needed.

MAKING HERB ICE CUBES

Choose a selection of fresh herbs, such as mint leaves and borage flowers, and place them in ice-cube trays. Fill each compartment with water, and freeze.

Glossary of Terms

Italicized words have their own entry.

ACIDIC [of soil] With a *pH* value of less than 7; see also *alkaline* and *neutral*.

ALKALINE [of soil] With a *pH* value of more than 7; some plants will not tolerate alkaline soils and must be grown in soil that is *neutral* or *acidic*.

ALTERNATE [of leaves] Borne singly at each node, on either side of a *stem*.

AXIL The spot between a leaf and *stem* where an axillary bud develops.

BLOOM 1. A flower or blossom. 2. A fine, waxy, whitish or bluish white coating found on *stems*, leaves, or fruits.

BRACT A modified leaf at the base of a *flower* or flower cluster. Bracts may resemble normal leaves or can be reduced and scalelike in appearance; they are often large and brightly colored.

BUD A rudimentary or condensed *shoot* containing embryonic leaves or *flowers*.

CALYX (pl. calyces) The outer part of a *flower*, usually small and green but sometimes showy and brightly colored, that encloses the *petals* in *bud* and is formed from the sepals.

CAPSULE A dry fruit that splits open when ripe to release its *seeds*.

COROLLA 1. Collective name for *petals*. 2. Inner *whorl* of perianth segments in some monocotyledons.

COTYLEDON A seed leaf; the first leaf or leaves to emerge from the seed after germination.

CROWN The part of the plant at or just below the soil surface from which new shoots are produced and to which they die back in autumn.

CUTTING A section of a plant that is removed and used for propagation (see page 155).

CULTIVAR (CV) A contraction of "cultivated variety"; a group (or one among such a group) consisting of cultivated plants that are clearly distinguished by one or more characteristics that are retained when propagation is performed.

DEADHEAD To remove spent *flowerheads* to promote further growth or flowering, prevent seeding, or improve appearance.

DECIDUOUS Losing its leaves annually at the end of the growing season.

DIEBACK Death of the tips of shoots due to cold or disease.

DISK FLORET, DISK FLOWER A small and often individually inconspicuous, usually tubular *flower*, often making the central portion of a composite *flowerhead*, such as a daisy.

DIVISION A method of propagation by which a clump is dug up and divided into several parts.

DORMANCY The state of temporary cessation of growth and slowing down of other activities in whole plants, usually during winter.

ENTIRE [of leaves] With untoothed margins.

EVERGREEN Retaining its leaves at the end of the growing season, but losing some older leaves during the year. **Semi-evergreen** plants retain some leaves, or lose older ones only when new growth is produced.

EYE The center of a *flower*, of particular note if different in color from the *petals*.

FLORET A single *flower* in a head of many flowers.

FLOWER The part of the plant containing the reproductive organs, usually surrounded by *sepals* and *petals*.

FLOWERHEAD A mass of small *flowers* or *florets* that, together, appear to form a single flower.

GENUS (pl. genera) A category in plant classification, consisting of a group of related *species*.

HABIT The characteristic growth or general appearance of a plant.

HARDEN OFF To acclimatize plants raised under cover to cooler outdoor conditions.

HARDY Able to withstand year-round climatic conditions without protection.

HERBACEOUS Dying down at the end of the growing season.

HYBRID The offspring of genetically different parents, usually produced accidentally or artificially in cultivation, but occasionally arising in the wild.

LAYERING A propagation method whereby a *stem* is induced to root by being pegged down in the soil while still attached to the parent plant.

LEAF MOLD Fibrous, flaky material derived from decomposed leaves, used as a soil improver.

LIME Compounds of calcium. The amount of lime in the soil determines whether it is *acidic*, *neutral*, or *alkaline*.

LINEAR [of leaves] Very narrow with parallel sides.

GLOSSARY • 159

Loam Well-structured, fertile soil that is moisture-retentive but free-draining.

Lobed Applied to leaves that are divided by clefts into usually rounded segments.

Mulch A layer of organic matter applied to the soil over or around a plant to conserve moisture, protect the *roots* from damage, reduce growth of weeds, and enrich the soil.

Naturalize To establish and grow as if in the wild.

Neutral [of soil] With a *pH* value of 7, the point at which soil is neither *acidic* nor *alkaline*.

Node Point on a stem from which leaves, leaf buds, and shoots arise.

Perennial Living for at least three seasons. A woody-based perennial dies down only partially, leaving a woody stem at the base.

Petal One portion of the usually showy and colored part of the *corolla*.

Petiole The stalk of a leaf.

pH The scale by which the acidity or alkalinity of soil is measured. See also *acidic*, *alkaline*, and *neutral*.

Prostrate With *stems* growing along the ground.

Ray flower The *petal*-like outer flowers of a composite flowerhead.

Recurved Applied to the *petals* of *flowers* and *florets* that curve backward.

Reflexed Applied to *petals* that are bent backward at an angle of more than 90°. Also referred to as fully reflexed.

Rhizome An underground, creeping *stem* that acts as a storage organ and bears leafy *shoots*.

Root The part of a plant, normally underground, that functions as an anchor and through which water and nutrients are absorbed.

Rosette A group of leaves that radiate from about the same point, often borne at ground level and arising from a very short *stem*.

Runner A horizontally spreading, usually slender *stem*, that forms *roots* at each *node*, often confused with *stolon*.

Scale A reduced or modified leaf.

Scorch To wither, burn, or cause marks on foliage through excessive light or heat.

Seed The ripened, fertilized ovule containing a dormant embryo capable of developing into an adult plant.

Seedhead Any usually dry structure of multiple fruits.

Seedling A young plant that has developed from a *seed*.

Self-seed To produce *seedlings* around the parent plant.

Sepal Part of a *calyx*, usually insignificant, but sometimes showy and *petal*-like.

Shoot The aerial part of a plant which bears leaves.

Simple [of leaves] Not divided into leaflets.

Single A flower with the normal number of *petals* or tepals for the species, arranged in a single *whorl*.

Solitary Flower borne singly rather than in an inflorescence.

Spathe One, or sometimes two, large *bracts* that surround a flower cluster or individual *bud*.

Species A category in plant classification, the rank below *genus*, containing closely related, very similar individual plants.

Spray A group of *flowers* or *flowerheads* on a single, branching stem.

Spur A hollow projection from a *petal*, which often produces nectar.

Stamen The male reproductive organ in a plant, consisting of the *anther* and usually its *filament* or *stalk*.

Stem The main axis of a plant, usually above ground and supporting leaves, *flowers*, and fruits. Sometimes referred to as a stalk.

Sterile Infertile, not bearing spores, pollen, or *seeds*.

Stigma The part of the female portion of the *flower*, borne at the tip of the *style*, that receives pollen.

Stolon A horizontally spreading or arching *stem*, usually above ground, which roots at its tip to produce a new plant.

Stratify To expose seeds to cold conditions to break dormancy and aid germination.

Style The part of the *flower* on which the *stigma* is borne.

Subshrub A plant that is woody at the base although the terminal shoots die back in winter.

Tooth A small, marginal, often pointed lobe on a *leaf*, *petal*, or *sepal*.

Tender Of a plant that is vulnerable to cold damage.

True [of seedlings] Retaining the distinctive characteristics of the parent when raised from *seed*.

Upright [of habit] With vertical or semi-vertical main branches.

Whorl The arrangement of 3 or more organs arising from one point.

INDEX

Each genus name is shown in bold type, followed by a brief description. Species, varieties and subspecies are given in *italics*; cultivars are in roman type with single quotes. Common names appear in parentheses.

A

Aaron's rod see
Verbascum thapsus
Absinth see
Artemisia absinthium

Achillea (Yarrow)
Fully hardy perennials grown for their foliage and daisylike flowerheads in summer.
millefolium (Milfoil) 68
f. *rosea* 73

Acinos (Calamint)
Fully to frost-hardy annuals and perennials with aromatic leaves and tubular flowers borne in summer.
arvensis (Basil thyme, Mother of thyme) 33

Acorus (Sweet flag)
Fully to frost-hardy perennials, marginals, and water plants grown for their foliage.
calamus (Calamus, Sweet flag) 106
'Variegatus' (Variegated sweet flag) 106

Aegopodium (Ground elder, goutweed)
Fully hardy perennials, many of which are invasive, with

Aegopodium continued
clusters of white flowers in summer.
podagraria 'Variegata' (Variegated goutweed) 103

Agastache
Fully to half-hardy perennials with aromatic leaves and long-lasting summer flowers.
anethiodora see
A. foeniculum
anisata see *A. foeniculum*
foeniculum (Anise hyssop) 87

Agnus castus see
Vitex agnus-castus

Ajuga (Bugle)
Fully hardy annuals and perennials grown for their spreading habit, attractive leaves, and usually blue flowers.
reptans 35
'Atropurpurea' 32
'Burgundy Glow' 27

Alcea (Hollyhock)
Fully hardy biennials and short-lived perennials grown for their tall spikes of colorful flowers.
rosea 42

Alchemilla (Lady's mantle)
Fully to frost-hardy perennials grown for their foliage and sprays of tiny, summer flowers.
vulgaris see *A. xanthoclora*
xanthoclora (Lion's foot) 134

Alder buckthorn see
Rhamnus frangula

Alexanders see
Smyrnium olusatrum
All heal see
Valeriana officinalis

Allium (Onion)
Fully to frost-hardy perennials, some of which are edible. Most bear dense clusters of small flowers in spring or summer.
sativum (Garlic) 86
schoenoprasum (Chives) 122 'Wallington White' 116
tuberosum (Chinese chives, Garlic chives) 65

Aloe
Frost-tender rosetted perennials with succulent foliage, tubular flowers, and papery or woody fruits.
arabica see *A. vera*
barbadensis see *A. vera*
indica see *A. vera*
vera (Barbados aloe) 106

Aloysia
Frost- to half-hardy shrubs with aromatic foliage and spikes or sprays of tiny, summer flowers.
citriodora see *triphylla*
triphylla (Lemon verbena) 41

Alpinia (Ginger lily)
Frost-tender perennials grown for their spikes of showy flowers produced in summer.
galanga (Galangal, Siamese ginger) 55

Althaea
Fully hardy annuals and perennials with spikes or sprays of small, 5-petaled

Althaea continued
flowers borne from summer
to autumn.
 officinalis (Marsh mallow)
 41
 rosea see *Alcea rosea*

Alum root see
 Geranium maculatum
American pennyroyal see
 Hedeoma pulegioides
American sanicle see
 Heuchera americana

Ammi
Fully hardy annuals and
biennials with fernlike
leaves and clusters of
lacelike flowers in summer.
 majus (Bullwort) 40

Anacyclus
Fully to frost-hardy
perennials bearing daisylike
flowerheads on short stems
in summer.
 pyrethrum (Pellitory,
  Pellitory of Spain) 25

Anethum (Dill)
Fully hardy annuals or
biennials with feathery
foliage and small, yellow
flowers in summer.
 graveolens 109
  'Mammoth' 109

Angelica
Fully hardy perennials and
biennials grown for their
architectural form.
 archangelica (Angelica) 56

Anise hyssop see
 Agastache foeniculum
Annual clary see *Salvia
 viridis*
Anthemis nobilis see
 Chamaemelum nobile

Anthriscus
Fully hardy annuals,
biennials, and perennials
with finely divided foliage
and tiny, white flowers
borne in summer.
 cerefolium (Common
  chervil) 132

Aphanes
Fully hardy annuals grown
for their clusters of tiny
flowers, which are produced
from spring to autumn.
 arvensis (Breakstone
  parsley, Parsley piert)
  37

Apothecary's rose see *Rosa
 gallica* var. *officinalis*

Arctium
Fully hardy biennials that
produce thistlelike flowers
and rough-coated fruits.
 lappa (Beggar's buttons,
  Burdock, Lappa) 46

**Arctostaphylos
(Bearberry)**
Fully hardy to frost-tender
trees and shrubs grown for
their tiny flowers and fruits.
 uva-ursi (Kinnikinnick) 27

**Armoracia
(Horseradish)**
Fully hardy perennials with
fleshy roots often used for
culinary purposes.
 rusticana 103
  'Variegata' (Variegated
   horseradish) 107

Arnica
Fully hardy perennials
grown for their large,
daisylike flowerheads
borne in summer.

Arnica continued
 montana (Arnica,
  Mountain tobacco) 136

**Artemisia
(Wormwood)**
Fully to half-hardy shrubs,
perennials, and annuals
grown for their silvery or
gray foliage, which are
often fragrant.
 abrotanum (Lad's love,
  Old man,
  Southernwood) 99
 absinthium (Absinth) 99
 arborescens (Tree
  wormwood) 98
 assoana see
  A. pedemontana
 'Brass Band' see
  A. 'Powis Castle'
 caucasica see *A.
  pedemontana*
 dracunculus (Estragon,
  French tarragon) 99
 kitadakensis 'Guizhou' see
  A. lactiflora Guizhou
  Group
 lactiflora (White mugwort)
  97
  Guizhou Group 97
 lanata see
  A. pedemontana
 ludoviciana (Cudweed,
  White sage, Western
  mugwort) 98
  'Valerie Finnis' 98
 pedemontana 98
 pontica (Roman
  wormwood, Small
  absinthe) 99
 'Powis Castle' 98
 vulgaris (Felon herb,
  Mugwort) 99

Arugula see
 Eruca vesicaria var. *sativa*
Asafoetida see
 Ferula assa-foetida

Asarum (Wild ginger)
Fully hardy perennials with pitcher-shaped flowers borne in late spring and summer.
 canadense 37

Asclepias (Milkweed, Silkweed)
Fully hardy to frost-tender perennials or subshrubs with spindle-shaped fruits.
 tuberosa (Butterfly weed) 114

Asperula odorata see *Galium odoratum*

Atriplex
Fully to half-hardy annuals, perennials, and shrubs grown for their silver or gray foliage.
 hortensis var *rubra* (Red orache) 87

— B —

Balm of Gilead see *Cedronella canariensis*
Basil see *Ocimum basilicum*
Basil thyme see *Acinos arvensis*
Batchelor's buttons see *Centaurea cyanus*
Bay see *Laurus nobilis*
Beggar's buttons see *Arctium lappa*
Betonica officinalis see *Stachys officinalis*
Bishopswort see *Stachys officinalis*
Bitterwort see *Gentiana lutea*
Black cohosh see *Cimicifuga racemosa*
Black snake root see *Cimicifuga racemosa*
Black lovage see *Smyrnium olusatrum*

Black mustard see *Brassica nigra*
Blackroot see *Veronicastrum virginicum*
Blessed thistle see *Cnicus benedictus*
Blue flag see *Iris versicolor*
Blue gum see *Eucalyptus globulus*
Boldo see *Peumus boldus*

Borago (Borage)
Fully hardy annuals and perennials grown for their attractive nodding clear blue flowers.
 officinalis 89

Bouncing Bet see *Saponaria officinalis*
Bourtree see *Sambucus nigra*
Bowman's root see *Gillenia trifoliata*
Boxwood see *Buxus*

Brassica
Fully hardy annuals, biennials, and perennials, most of which are cultivated as edible vegetables.
 nigra (Black mustard) 62

Breakstone parsley see *Aphanes arvensis*
Buckler-leaf sorrel see *Rumex scutatus*
Burdock see *Arctium lappa*
Butterfly weed see *Asclepias tuberosa*

Buxus (Boxwood)
Fully to frost-hardy evergreen shrubs and small trees grown for their dense foliage and habit.
 sempervirens (Common boxwood) 62
 'Suffruticosa' (Edging boxwood) 104

— C —

Calamus see *Acorus calamus*

Calamintha (Calamint)
Fully hardy, aromatic perennials that bear sprays of blue, pink, or white flowers.
 nepeta (Lesser calamint) 122
 subsp. *nepeta* 118

Calendula (Pot marigold)
Fully hardy annuals and frost-tender evergreen perennials grown for their summer flowers.
 officinalis 136

Capparis (Caper)
Frost-hardy shrubs and small trees that produce solitary, delicate flowers in summer.
 spinosa (Caper bush, Common caper) 68

Capsicum (Chili pepper)
Frost-tender annuals and perennials cultivated mostly for their colorful fruits.
 annuum var. *annuum*
  'Anaheim' 85
  'Chili Serrano' 84
  'Hungarian Wax' 85
  'Jalapeño' 85
  'Super Cayenne' 84
 baccatum 85
 frutescens 'Tabasco' 85

Cardamine (Bitter cress)
Fully hardy annuals (often invasive) and perennials that bear flower spikes in spring.
 pratensis (Cuckoo flower, Lady's smock) 119

Cardamine continued
'Flore Pleno' 118

Cardamom see
Elettaria cardamomum

Carica (Papaya)
Frost-tender trees and shrubs with characteristic unbranched trunks, grown for their ornamental shape and fruits.
papaya 58

Carthamus (Safflower)
Fully to half-hardy annuals and perennials with thistlelike flowerheads borne in summer.
tinctorius (False saffron) 114

Carum (Caraway)
Fully hardy biennials and perennials that bear small white flowers in mid-summer.
carvi 66

Castor bean see
Ricinis communis

Cedronella
Frost-tender perennial grown for its aromatic cedar-scented foliage.
canariensis (Balm of Gilead) 70
triphylla see *C. canariensis*

Centaurea (Knapweed)
Fully hardy annuals, biennials, perennials, and subshrubs with thistlelike flowerheads.
cyanus (Batchelor's buttons, Cornflower) 89

Chamaemelum (Chamomile)
Fully hardy annuals and perennials that provide aromatic groundcover.
nobile (Lawn chamomile, Roman chamomile) 25
'Flore Pleno' (Double chamomile) 25
'Treneague' 37

Chamomilla recutita see
Matricaria recutita
Chaste tree see
Vitex agnus-castus
Checkerberry see
Gaultheria procumbens
Cheese rennet see
Galium verum

Chelidonium
Fully hardy, short-lived perennial grown for its poppy-like summer flowers.
majus (Greater celandine, Swallow wort) 111
'Laciniatum Flore Pleno' 112

Chenopodium
Frost-hardy annuals, perennials, and subshrubs, many of which are aromatic.
bonus-henricus (Good King Henry) 104

Chinese chives see
Allium tuberosum
Chinese rhubarb see
Rheum palmatum
Cilantro see *Coriandrum sativum*

Cichorium (Chicory)
Fully to frost-hardy annuals and perennials, which have flowerheads that close by mid-day.
intybus 88

Cimicifuga (Bugbane)
Fully hardy perennials grown for their spikes of flowers from mid-summer to autumn.
racemosa (Black snake root, Black cohosh) 38

Citrus
Frost-tender trees and shrubs that produce scented white flowers and citrus fruits in late autumn.
limon (Lemon) 64

Clinopodium arvensis see
Acinos arvensis 33
Clove pink see
Dianthus caryophyllus

Cnicus
Fully hardy, thistlelike annual that bears solitary yellow flowers in summer.
benedictus (Blessed thistle, Holy thistle) 112

Convallaria (Lily of the valley)
Fully hardy perennials that produce fragrant, bell-shaped flowers in spring.
majalis 26
var. *rosea* (Pink lily of the valley) 26

Coriandrum (Cilantro, Coriander)
Fully hardy annuals grown for their aromatic foliage.
sativum 68

Corn poppy see
Papaver rhoeas
Cornflower see
Centaurea cyanus
Cowslip see *Primula veris*
Crimson damask see
Rosa gallica var. *officinalis*

Crithmum (Samphire)
Fully hardy perennial that produces clusters of yellow-green flowers in summer.
 maritimum (Sea fennel) 130

Crocus
Fully to frost-hardy perennials grown for their funnel-shaped flowers in spring or autumn.
 sativus (Saffron crocus) 122
 var. *cashmirianus* see *C. sativus*

Cuckoo flower see
 Cardamine pratensis
Cudweed see
 Artemisia ludoviciana
Culver's root see
 Veronicastrum virginicum

Cuminum (Cumin)
Half-hardy annuals that bear small, white to pale pink flowers in mid-summer.
 cyminum 115

Curcuma
Frost-tender perennials with cones of colorful bracts that often obscure the tiny flowers.
 domestica see *C. longa*
 longa (Turmeric) 105

Curly beefsteak plant see
 Perilla frutescens 'Crispa'
Curry leaf see *Murraya koenigii*
Curry plant see
 Helichrysum italicum

Cymbopogon
Frost-tender perennial grasses grown for their aromatic leaves.

Cymbopogon continued
 citratus (Lemon grass) 55

Cynara
Fully to frost-hardy perennials that produce tall, thistlelike flowerheads in summer.
 cardunculus Scolymus Group (Globe artichoke) 46
 scolymus see *C. cardunculus* Scolymus Group

D

Devil's dung see
 Ferula assa-foetida

Dianthus
Fully to half-hardy perennials, annuals, biennials, and sub-shrubs grown for their mass of usually scented flowers.
 caryophyllus (Clove pink, Wild carnation) 121

Dictamnus (Gas plant)
Fully hardy perennials with long, open spikes of flowers borne in summer.
 albus (Dittany) 65
 fraxinella see *D. albus*
 var. *purpureus* 70

Digitalis (Foxglove)
Fully to frost-hardy biennials and perennials grown for their tall spikes of flowers borne in summer.
 lanata (Woolly foxglove) 113
 purpurea (Common foxglove) 72

Dittany see *Dictamnus albus*

E

Ecballium (Squirting cucumber)
Half-hardy perennial grown for its touch-sensitive fruits.
 elaterium 23

Echinacea (Coneflower)
Fully hardy perennials that produce daisylike flowerheads with pronounced central disks.
 purpurea 87

Eglantine see
 Rosa eglanteria
Elecampane see *Inula helenium*

Elettaria
Frost-tender perennials with spikes of flowers borne on horizontal shoots in summer.
 cardamomum (Cardamom) 55

English ivy see *Hedera helix*

Eruca
Frost-hardy annuals and perennials grown for their salad leaves.
 vesicaria subsp. *sativa* (Arugula, Roquette, Rucola, Salad rocket) 67

Eryngium (Eryngo, Sea holly)
Fully to half-hardy annuals, biennials, and perennials with thistlelike flowers.
 maritimum 125

Eucalyptus (Gum tree)
Frost-hardy to frost-tender trees and shrubs grown for

Eucalyptus continued
their bark and aromatic
foliage.
  globulus (Blue gum,
    Tasmanian blue gum) 51

**Eupatorium
(Hemp agrimony)**
Fully hardy to frost-tender
sub-shrubs, shrubs and
perennials that produce
nectar-rich flowerheads.
  purpurem (Joe Pye weed)
    43

Eutrema wasabia see
  Wasabia japonica

---— F ——

False saffron see
  Carthamus tinctorius
Felon herb see
  Artemisia vulgaris
Fenugreek see *Trigonella
  foenum-graecum*

Ferula (Giant fennel)
Hardy perennials grown for
their bold, architectural form.
  assa-foetida (Asafoetida,
    Devil's dung) 56

Ficus (Fig)
Frost-hardy to frost-tender
trees, shrubs, and climbers
that produce edible fruits.
  carica (Common fig) 58

Field poppy see *Papaver
  rhoeas*

Filipendula
Fully hardy perennials that
bear plumes of fluffy flowers.
  ulmaria (Meadowsweet)
    66

Foeniculum (Fennel)
Fully hardy biennial or
perennial grown for its
foliage and summer flowers.
  vulgare 57
    'Purpureum' 56

**Fragaria
(Strawberry)**
Fully hardy perennials that
produce usually white
flowers and succulent fruits.
  vesca (Wild strawberry)
    116

---— G ——

Galangal see *Alpinia galanga*

Galega (Goat's rue)
Fully hardy perennials with
blue-tinged leaves and
spikes of mainly blue or
white pealike flowers borne
in summer.
  officinalis 41

**Galium
(Bedstraw)**
Fully to frost-hardy annuals
and perennials, often used
as groundcover.
  odoratum (Sweet woodruff)
    24
  verum (Cheese rennet,
    Lady's bedstraw) 134

Garlic see *Allium sativum*
Garlic chives see
  Allium tuberosum
Gas plant see
  Dictamnus albus

Gaultheria
Fully to half-hardy shrubs
grown for their foliage, urn-
shaped flowers, and fruits.

Eucalyptus continued
  procumbens (Checkerberry,
    Wintergreen) 27

Gentiana (Gentian)
Fully hardy annuals,
biennials, and perennials
grown for their trumpet-
shaped flowers in summer
and early autumn.
  lutea (Bitterwort, Great
    yellow gentian,) 60

**Geranium
(Cranesbill)**
Fully to half-hardy annuals,
biennials, and perennials
that bear attractive flat or
star-shaped flowers.
  maculatum (Alum root) 88

Gillenia
Fully hardy perennials with
bronze-green leaves and
loose sprays of flowers.
  trifoliata (Bowman's root,
    Indian physic) 66

**Ginkgo
(Maidenhair tree)**
Fully hardy tree grown for its
attractive fan-shaped leaves.
  biloba 52

**Glechoma
(Ground ivy)**
Fully hardy perennials grown
for their creeping habit and
handsome foliage.
  hederacea 33
    'Variegata' (Variegated
    ground ivy) 33

Globe artichoke see *Cynara
  cardunculus* Scolymus
  Group

Gloriosa
Frost-tender climbers grown

Gloriosa continued
for their scrambling habit
and colorful flowers.
  carsonii see *G. superba*
  minor see *G. superba*
  simplex see *G. superba*
  superba (Glory lily,
    Mozambique lily) 19

Glycyrrhiza (Licorice)
Fully hardy perennials that
produce spikes of pealike
flowers in late summer.
  glabra (Licorice,
    Sweetwood) 45
  glandulifera see *G. glabra*

Goat's rue see *Galega officinalis*
Golden bay see
  Laurus nobilis 'Aurea'
Goldenseal see
  Hydrastis canadensis
Good King Henry see
  Chenopodium bonus-henricus

Gratiola
Hardy perennials that bear
tubular flowers in summer.
  officinalis (Gratiole, Hedge
    hyssop) 115

Greater celandine see
  Chelidonium majus
Greek valerian see
  Polemonium caeruleum, P. reptans

Grindelia (Gum plant, Tarweed)
Frost- to half-hardy annuals,
perennials, and subshrubs
with daisylike flowerheads.
  camporum 112

Guelder rose see
  Viburnum opulus

H

Hamamelis (Witch hazel)
Fully hardy shrubs grown
for their autumn color and
fragrant, spiderlike flowers.
  virginiana (Common witch
    hazel) 64

Hedeoma
Fully hardy annuals and
perennials with fragrant
foliage.
  pulegioides (American
    pennyroyal) 132

Hedera (Ivy)
Fully to half-hardy climbers
used for covering walls and
fences, and as groundcover.
  helix (English ivy) 21

Hedge hyssop see
  Gratiola officinalis
Hedgehog rose see
  Rosa rugosa

Helichrysum
Fully hardy to frost-tender
perennials, annuals,
subshrubs, and shrubs whose
flowerheads are "everlasting"
when dried.
  angustifolium see *H. italicum*
  italicum (Curry plant) 109

Hen and chicks see
  Sempervivum tectorum
Herb of grace see
  Ruta graveolens

Heuchera
Fully to frost-hardy
perennials grown for their
attractive foliage and
summer flowers.

Heuchera continued
  americana (Alum root,
    American sanicle) 121

Hibiscus
Fully hardy to frost-tender
shrubs, trees, perennials, and
annuals that produce showy
flowers in summer.
  sabdariffa (Jamaica sorrel,
    Roselle) 60

Holy thistle see
  Cnicus benedictus
Hop tree see *Ptelea trifoliata*
Horseradish see
  Armoracia rusticana

Houttuynia
Fully hardy perennial grown
mainly for its unusual
orange-scented foliage.
  cordata 116

Humulus (Hops)
Fully to half-hardy
perennials grown for their
brightly colored foliage.
  lupulus 22
    'Aureus' (Golden hops)
      23

Hydrastis
Fully hardy perennials with
large palmate leaves, tiny
flowers, and inedible fruits.
  canadensis (Goldenseal,
    Yellowroot) 130

Hypericum (St John's wort)
Fully hardy to frost-tender
shrubs, trees, annuals, and
perennials that are usually
grown for their showy,
yellow flowers.
  perforatum (Perforate St
    John's wort) 111

Hyssopus (Hyssop)
Fully hardy perennials and shrubs with aromatic foliage and summer flowers.
officinalis 89
 f. *roseus* 72
 subsp. *aristatus* (Rock hyssop) 124

I

Indian physic see
 Gillenia trifoliata

Inula
Fully to frost-hardy perennials, annuals, and biennials with daisylike flowers.
helenium (Elecampane) 63

Iris
Fully hardy to frost-tender perennials grown for their distinctive flowers.
florentina see
 I. germanica 'Florentina'
germanica
 'Florentina' (Orris root) 69
 var. florentina see
 I. g. 'Florentina'
versicolor (Blue flag) 88

Isatis (Woad)
Fully hardy annuals, biennials, and perennials grown for their small summer flowers.
tinctoria 63

JK

Jamaica sorrel see
 Hibiscus sabdariffa
Japanese rose see *Rosa rugosa*

Jasminum (Jasmine)
Fully hardy to frost-tender shrubs and climbers with fragrant, star-shaped flowers.
officinale 18
 'Fiona Sunrise' 18
sambac 18
 'Grand Duke of Tuscany' 18

Joe Pye weed see
 Eupatorium purpureum

Juniperus (Juniper)
Fully to frost-hardy shrubs and trees with cones and berrylike fruits.
communis (Common juniper) 58

Knitbone see
 Symphytum officinale

L

Lad's love see
 Artemisia abrotanum
Lady's bedstraw see
 Galium verum
Lady's smock see
 Cardamine pratensis
Lappa see *Arctium lappa*

Laurus (Bay)
Frost-hardy trees and shrubs grown for their aromatic foliage.
nobilis (Bay, Laurel, Sweet bay) 61
 'Aurea' (Golden bay) 64

Lavandula (Lavender)
Fully to half-hardy shrubs with aromatic foliage and flowers.
x *allardii* (Giant lavender) 93

Lavandula continued
 angustifolia (Common lavender) 91
 'Folgate' 92
 'Hidcote' 92
 'Imperial Gem' 92
 'Munstead' 92
 'Nana Alba' 90
 'Rosea' 90
dentata (Fringed lavender) 91
x *intermedia* (Lavandin) 93
 Dutch Group 91
 'Grappenhall' 91
 Old English Group 93
 'Sawyers' 93
 'Seal' 92
 'Twickel Purple' 93
lanata (Woolly lavender) 93
pinnata 92
stoechas (French lavender) 91
 f. *leucantha* 90
 subsp. *pedunculata* (Spanish lavender) 91
viridis (Green lavender) 93

Lavender cotton see
 Santolina chamaecyparissus

Lawsonia (Henna tree)
Frost-tender shrub or tree bearing small fragrant flowers.
alba see *L. inermis*
inermis 40

Lemon see *Citrus limon*
Lemon balm see
 Melissa officinalis
Lemon grass see
 Cymbopogon citratus
Lemon verbena see
 Aloysia triphylla
Lentisc see *Pistacia lentiscus*

Leonurus
Fully hardy biennials and perennials grown for their deeply veined foliage.
cardiaca (Motherwort) 54

Levisticum (Lovage)
Fully hardy perennial that produces clusters of star-shaped flowers in mid-summer.
officinale 53

Licorice see *Glycyrrhiza glabra*

Lilium (Lily)
Frost-hardy bulbs grown for their often fragrant, colorful flowers borne in summer.
candidum (Madonna lily) 38

Lion's foot see *Alchemilla xanthoclora*

Lippia
Half-hardy and frost-tender shrubs and small trees grown for their aromatic foliage.
citriodora see *Aloysia triphylla*
graveolens (Mexican oregano) 40

—— M ——

Madonna lily see *Lilium candidum*

Mandragora (Mandrake)
Fully to frost-hardy perennials that produce fleshy fruits.
officinarum (Devil's apples) 134

Marrubium (Horehound)
Fully to half-hardy perennials grown for their woolly leaves.
vulgare (White horehound) 115

Marsh mallow see *Althaea officinalis*
Mastic tree see *Pistacia lentiscus*

Matricaria
Fully hardy annuals grown for their feathery foliage and daisy-like flowers during summer.
chamomilla see *M. recutita*
recutita (German chamomile, Scented mayweed) 117

Meadowsweet see *Filipendula ulmaria*

Melilotus (Sweet clover)
Fully hardy annuals, biennials, and perennials with honey-scented summer flowers.
arvensis see *M. officinalis*
officinalis (Melilot, Yellow sweet clover) 111

Melissa (Balm)
Fully hardy perennials grown for their lemon fragrance.
officinalis (Lemon balm) 102
'Aurea' (Golden lemon balm) 107

Mentha (Mint)
Fully to frost-hardy perennials grown for their aromatic foliage.
aquatica (Water mint) 75

Mentha continued
corsica see *M. requienii*
x *gracilis* (Gingermint, Red mint) 75
'Variegata' 76
incana see *M. longifolia* 76
longifolia (Horse mint) 76
Buddleia Mint Group 76
x *piperita* (Peppermint) 74
'Citrata' (Bergamot, lemon, or Eau-de Cologne mint) 75
pulegium (Pennyroyal) 75
'Cunningham Mint' (Creeping pennyroyal) 76
requienii (Corsican mint) 76
rotundifolia of gardens see *M. suaveolens*
x *smithiana* (Red raripila mint) 75
spicata (Spearmint) 76
'Crispa' (Curly spearmint) 75
'Moroccan' (Moroccan spearmint) 76
suaveolens (Apple mint, woolly mint) 74
'Variegata' (Pineapple mint) 74
sylvestris see *M. longifolia*
x *villosa* f. *alopecuroides* (Bowles' mint) 74
viridis see *M. spicata*

Menyanthes
Fully hardy perennials that bear white flowers in spring.
trifoliata (Bog bean) 25

Mexican marigold see *Tagetes lucida*
Mexican oregano see *Lippia graveolens*
Milfoil see *Achillea millefolium*
Milk thistle see *Silybum marianum*

Monarda (Bergamot)

Fully hardy annuals and perennials grown for their foliage and summer flowers.
'Aquarius' 78
'Balance' 78
'Beauty of Cobham' 79
'Bowman' see *M.* 'Sagittarius'
'Cambridge Scarlet' 78
'Croftway Pink' 78
didyma (Bee balm, Bergamot, Oswego tea) 79
'Fishes' 77
fistulosa (Wild bergamot) 78
'Libra' see *M.* 'Balance'
'Mahogany' 79
'Mohawk' 78
'Pisces' see *M.* 'Fishes'
'Prairie Night' see *M.* 'Prärienacht'
'Prärienacht' 79
punctata (Horsemint) 79
'Sagittarius' 79
'Scorpio' see *M.* 'Scorpion'
'Scorpion' 78

Mother of thyme see *Acinos arvensis*
Motherwort see *Leonurus cardiaca*
Mountain tobacco see *Arnica montana*
Mozambique lily see *Gloriosa superba*

Murraya

Frost-tender evergreen trees and shrubs with aromatic foliage and fragrant flowers.
koenigii (Curry leaf) 51

Myrrhis (Sweet Cicely)

Fully hardy perennial with delicate, fernlike foliage.
odorata 39

Myrtus (Myrtle)

Frost-hardy trees or shrubs grown for their solitary flowers and aromatic foliage.
communis 38
'Variegata' (Variegated myrtle) 51

――― N ―――

Nepeta

Fully to half-hardy perennials grown for their flowers.
cataria (Catnip) 68
glechoma see *Glechoma hederacea*
hederacea see *Glechoma hederacea*

Nigella

Fully hardy annuals with fern-like foliage and solitary flowers.
sativa (Black cumin, Nutmeg flower) 125

――― O ―――

Ocimum (Basil)

Half-hardy to frost-tender annuals and perennials grown for their aromatic foliage.
americanum (Hoary basil, Spice basil) 129
basilicum (Basil, Sweet basil) 126
'Cinnamon' 127
var. *citriodorum* (Lemon basil) 126
'Dark Opal' 128
'Genovese' (Perfume basil) 126
'Green Bouquet' 129
'Green Globe'

Origanum continued
'Green Ruffles' 128
'Horapha' 129
'Mexican' (Mexican basil) 127
'Purple Ruffles' 128
'Red Rubin' 127
'Spicy Globe' 129
campechianum (Peruvian basil, Duppy basil) 129
canum see *O. americanum*
'Glycyrrhiza' see *O. b.* 'Horapha'
'MengLuk' see *O. americanum*
micranthum see *O. campechianum*
var. *minimum* (Bush basil, Greek basil) 129
var. *purpurascens* (Purple basil) 127
sanctum see *O. tenuiflorum*
'Spice' see *O. americanum*
tenuiflorum (Holy basil, Sacred basil) 127
'Thai' see *O. b.* 'Horapha'

Oenothera (Evening primrose)

Fully to frost-hardy annuals, biennials, and perennials bearing flowers throughout the summer.
biennis 63

Old man see *Artemisia abrotanum*

Olea (Olive)

Frost- to half-hardy trees grown for their foliage and fruits.
europaea 59

Origanum (Marjoram)

Fully to frost-hardy sub-shrubs and perennials grown for their aromatic foliage.

170 • INDEX

Origanum continued
'Curly Gold' see *O. vulgare*
'Aureum Crispum'
dictamnus (Cretan dittany, Hop marjoram) 138
heracleoticum see *O. vulgare* subsp. *hirtum*
majorana (Sweet marjoram, Knotted marjoram) 137
x *majoricum* (Hardy marjoram, Italian oregano) 137
'Norton Gold' 139
onites (Greek oregano, Pot marjoram) 137
'Aureum' 139
vulgare (Wild marjoram) 138
'Acorn Bank' 139
var. *album* 137
'*Aureum*' (Golden marjoram) 139
'Aureum Crispum' 138
'Compactum' (Compact marjoram) 138
'County Cream' 139
'Gold Tip' 139
subsp. *hirtum* 138
'Nanum' 138
'Polyphant' 138
'Variegatum' see *O. v.* 'Gold Tip'

Orris root see *Iris germanica* 'Florentina'

PQ

Paeonia (Peony)
Fully to frost-hardy perennials and shrubs grown for their foliage and showy flowers.
officinalis (Common peony) 72

Paigle see *Primula veris*

Papaver (Poppy)
Fully to frost-hardy annuals, biennials, and perennials with short-lived flowers.
rhoeas (Corn poppy, Field poppy) 73
somniferum (Opium poppy) 71
'Paeony-flowered' 70

Papaya see *Carica papaya*
Parsley piert see *Aphanes arvensis*

Passiflora (Passionflower)
Fully hardy to frost-tender climbers grown for their unique flowers and edible fruits.
incarnata (Maypops) 20

Patchouli see *Pogostemon cablin*

Pelargonium (Geranium)
Frost-tender perennials, shrubs, and subshrubs with colorful, clustered flowers.
abrotanifolium 80
'Attar of Roses ' 83
capitatum (Wild rose geranium) 82
'Chocolate Peppermint' 83
citronellum 81
'Variegatum' 82
'Clorinda' 81
crispum (Lemon geranium) 81
'Fair Ellen' 81
'Filicifolium' 82
'Fragrans' (Nutmeg geranium) 80
'Fragrans Variegatum' 80
'Galway Star' 82
'Graveolens' (Rose geranium) 83

Pelargonium continued
'Lady Plymouth' 82
'Mabel Grey' 82
odoratissimum (Apple geranium) 80
'Old Spice' 83
'Prince of Orange' 81
quercifolium (Oak-leaved geranium) 82
Radula Group 81
'Rober's Lemon Rose' 81
'Royal Oak' 83
'Sweet Mimosa' 81
tomentosum (Peppermint geranium) 83

Pellitory see *Anacyclus pyrethrum*
Perforate St John's wort see *Hypericum perforatum*

Perilla
Frost-hardy annuals with bell-shaped flowers borne in late summer and autumn.
frutescens 'Crispa' (Curly beefsteak plant) 87
var. *nankinensis* see *P. frutescens* 'Crispa'

Persicaria
Fully to frost-hardy annuals and perennials that produce spikes of long-lasting flowers in summer.
bistorta (Bistort) 119

Petroselinum (Parsley)
Fully hardy biennials grown for their distinctive, triangular leaves with toothed leaflets.
crispum 133
'Afro' 133
'Italian' see *P. c.* var. *neapolitanum*
var. *neapolitanum* (French parsley, Italian parsley) 133

Peucedanum graveolens see
    Anethum graveolens

Peumus
Half-hardy shrub or small tree grown for its aromatic leaves, bark, and edible fruits.
    boldus (Boldo) 53

Phytolacca (Pokeweed)
Fully to half-hardy perennials, shrubs, and trees with attractive fruits and autumn foliage.
    americana (Pokeroot) 43
    decandra see *P. americana*

Pimpinella
Fully hardy annuals, biennials, and perennials bearing clusters of tiny star-shaped flowers.
    anisum (Anise) 116

Piper (Pepper)
Frost-tender shrubs, climbers, and small trees that produce fleshy, single-seeded fruits.
    nigrum 20

Pistacia (Pistachio)
Frost- to half-hardy trees and shrubs grown for their foliage, petal-less flowers, and peppercorn-like fruits.
    lentiscus (Lentisc, Mastic tree) 57

Plantago (Plantain)
Fully hardy to frost-tender shrubs, annuals, biennials, and perennials with leaf rosettes and tiny, summer flowers.
    major 'Atropurpurea' see
    P. m. 'Rubrifolia'

Plantago continued
    'Rubrifolia' (Red greater plantain) 124

Pogostemon
Tender perennials and subshrubs grown for their distinctive fragrance.
    cablin (Patchouli) 104
    patchouli see *P. cablin*

Pokeroot see
    Phytolacca americana

Polemonium (Jacob's ladder)
Fully hardy annuals and perennials bearing flowers in late spring or summer.
    caeruleum (Greek valerian) 88
    var. *album* see
        P. c. var. *lacteum*
    var. *lacteum* 65
    reptans (Abscess root) 125

Polygonum bistorta see
    Persicaria bistorta

Portulaca (Purslane)
Half-hardy to frost-tender annuals and perennials with showy, cup-shaped flowers.
    oleracea 131

Primula (Primrose)
Fully hardy to frost-tender perennials with colorful spring flowers.
    veris (Cowslip, Paigle) 134
    vulgaris 135

Prostanthera (Mint bush)
Half-hardy to frost-tender shrubs grown for the flowers and mint-scented foliage.
    rotundifolia (Round-leaved mint bush) 46

Prunella (Selfheal)
Fully hardy perennials grown for their tubular flowers borne in summer.
    vulgaris 34

Ptelea
Fully to frost-hardy trees and shrubs with aromatic foliage and winged fruits.
    trifoliata (Hop tree, Wafer ash) 57

Pulmonaria (Lungwort)
Fully hardy perennials that produce flowers from late winter to spring.
    officinalis (Jerusalem cowslip) 124

Punica (Pomegranate)
Frost-hardy shrubs and trees grown for their summer flowers and edible fruits.
    granatum 44

──── R ────

Ramanas rose see *Rosa rugosa*

Ranunculus (Buttercup)
Fully to half-hardy annuals, aquatics, and perennials grown for their flowers.
    ficaria (Lesser celandine, Pilewort) 135
    var. *flore pleno* 136

Rehmannia
Fully to half-hardy perennials with foxglove-like flowers.
    glutinosa (Chinese foxglove) 120

Rhamnus (Buckthorn)
Fully to frost-hardy shrubs and trees grown for their foliage and decorative fruits.
frangula (Alder buckthorn) 53

Rheum (Rhubarb)
Fully hardy perennials, often used architecturally.
palmatum (Chinese rhubarb) 54

Ricinus (Castor bean)
Half-hardy shrub grown for its large, glossy leaves.
communis 54
  'Carmencita' 47

Roman wormwood see *Artemisia pontica*
Roquette see *Eruca vesicaria* var. *sativa*

Rosa (Rose)
Fully hardy climbers and shrubs that produce usually fragrant flowers and fruits.
eglanteria (Eglantine, Sweet briar) 42
gallica var. *officinalis* (Apothecary's rose, Crimson damask) 73
rubiginosa see *R. eglanteria*
rugosa (Japanese rose, Ramanas rose) 43
officinalis see
  R. gallica var. *officinalis*
'Red Damask' see
  R. gallica var. *officinalis*

Roselle see
  Hibiscus sabdariffa

Rosmarinus (Rosemary)
Frost-hardy shrubs with white, pink, or blue flowers and aromatic foliage.

Rosmarinus continued
officinalis 50
  var. *albiflorus* 48
  'Aureovariegatus' see
    R. o. 'Aureus'
  'Aureus' 50
  'Benenden Blue' 50
  'Collingwood Ingram'
    see *R. o.* 'Benenden Blue'
  'Fastigiatus' see *R. o.*
    'Miss Jessop's Upright'
  'Gilded' see *R. o.*
    'Aureus'
  'Majorca Pink' 49
  'McConnell's Blue' 49
  'Miss Jessopp's Upright' 50
  'Primley Blue' 50
  'Roseus' 48
  'Severn Sea' 50
  'Tuscan Blue' 49
  Prostratus Group (Creeping rosemary) 49
  Sissinghurst Blue' 49

Round-leaved mint bush see *Prostanthera rotundifolia*
Rucola see *Eruca vesicaria* var. *sativa*
Rudbeckia purpurea see *Echinacea purpurea*

Rumex (Dock)
Fully to half-hardy annuals, biennials, and perennials with decorative foliage.
acetosa (Common sorrel) 104
scutatus (Buckler-leaf sorrel) 130
  'Silver Shield' 130

Ruta (Rue)
Fully hardy sub-shrubs and

Ruta continued
perennials bearing aromatic leaves and summer flowers.
graveolens (Herb of grace) 109
  'Variegata' (Variegated rue) 107

S

Saffron crocus see *Crocus sativus*
Salad rocket see
  Eruca vesicaria var. *sativa*

Salvia (Sage)
Fully hardy to frost-tender annuals, biennials, perennials, and shrubs grown for their flowers and aromatic foliage.
apiana (California white sage, bee sage) 96
coccinea (Texas sage) 94
  'Lady in Red' 95
dorisiama (Fruit-scented sage) 96
elegans 'Scarlet Pineapple' (Pineapple sage) 95
fruticosa (Greek sage) 95
hispanica see
  S. lavandulifolia 96
horminum see *S. viridis*
lavandulifolia (Narrow-leaved sage, Spanish sage) 96
officinalis (Common sage) 96
  'Albiflora' 94
  'Berggarten' 96
  'Icterina' 96
  'Kew Gold' 96
  'Tricolor' 94
  Purpurascens Group (Purple sage, Red sage) 95

Salvia continued
 rutilans see *S. elegans*
 'Scarlet Pineapple'
 sclarea (Clary sage) 95
  var. *turkestanica* 94
 triloba see *S. fruticosa*
 viridis (Annual clary) 95
 'Claryssa' 95

Sambucus (Elder)
Fully hardy perennials, shrubs, and trees that produce dense clusters of flowers in summer, followed by fruits.
 nigra (Bourtree) 39
 'Guincho Purple' (Bronze elder) 41

Sanguisorba (Burnet)
Fully hardy perennials with bottlebrush-like flowers.
 officinalis (Great burnet) 73

Santolina
Frost-hardy shrubs grown for their aromatic foliage and buttonlike summer flowers.
 chamaecyparissus (Lavender cotton) 108
 incana see
  S. chamaecyparissus
 'Lemon Queen' 135

Saponaria (Soapwort)
Fully hardy annuals and perennials that produce flat, pink flowers in summer.
 officinalis (Bouncing Bet) 70

Satureja (Savory)
Fully hardy annuals, perennials, and subshrubs with aromatic leaves and nectar-rich flowers.

Satureja continued
 hortensis (Summer savory) 118
 montana (Winter savory) 115
 repanda see *S. spicigera*
 reptans see *S. spicigera*
 spicigera (Creeping savory) 24
 thymbra (Thyme-leaved savory) 122

Scutellaria (Skullcap)
Fully hardy to frost-tender annuals and perennials grown for their attractive summer flowers.
 lateriflora (Mad dog skullcap, Virginia skullcap) 124

Sea fennel see
 Crithmum maritimum

Sempervivum (Houseleek)
Fully hardy perennials with open rosettes of fleshy, pointed leaves and star-shaped flowers borne in summer.
 tectorum (Common houseleek, Hen and chicks) 26

Sesamum (Sesame)
Half-hardy annuals and perennials that produce edible seeds.
 indicum 103

Siamese ginger see
 Alpinia galanga

Silybum
Fully hardy annuals and biennials grown for their attractive foliage and thistlelike flowers.

Silybum continued
 marianum (Milk thistle) 86

Sinapis nigra see *Brassica nigra*

Smyrnium
Fully hardy biennials or perennials bearing yellowish green flowers in summer.
 olusatrum (Alexanders, Black lovage) 110

Solidago (Goldenrod)
Fully hardy, vigorous perennials grown for their flowers produced in summer and autumn.
 virgaurea 111

Southernwood see
 Artemisia abrotanum

Stachys (Betony)
Fully hardy to frost-hardy perennials, shrubs, and sub-shrubs that flower in late spring or summer.
 betonica see *S. officinalis*
 officinalis (Bishopswort) 123

Swallow wort see
 Chelidonium majus
Sweet briar see *Rosa eglanteria*
Sweet flag see *Acorus calamus*
Sweet mace see *Tagetes lucida*
Sweet woodruff see
 Galium odoratum
Sweetwood see
 Glycyrrhiza glabra

Symphytum (Comfrey)
Fully hardy perennials often

INDEX • 173

Symphytum continued
used as groundcover plants.
officinale (Knitbone) 42
peregrinum of gardens see
S. × *uplandicum*
× *uplandicum* (Russian
comfrey) 46
'Variegatum' (Variegated
Russian comfrey) 86

T

**Tagetes
(Marigold)**
Half-hardy annuals with
often aromatic fern-like
leaves and bright orange
flowers in summer.
lucida (Sweet mace,
Mexican marigold) 114
patula (French marigold)
136

Tanacetum
Fully to half-hardy annuals,
subshrubs, and perennials
with daisylike flowerheads.
balsamita (Alecost,
costmary) 100
subsp. *balsametoides* 101
var. *tomentosum* see
T. b. subsp.
balsametoides
cinerariifolium (Dalmatian
pellitory, Pyrethrum)
100
parthenium (Feverfew)
101
'Aureum' 101
'Golden Moss' 101
'Plenum' 100
vulgare (Tansy) 101
var. *crispum* (Fern-leaved
tansy) 101

Tasmanian blue gum see
Eucalyptus globulus

**Teucrium
(Germander)**
Fully to frost-hardy shrubs,
subshrubs, and perennials
grown for their attractive
Teucrium continued
habit and aromatic foliage.
chamaedrys (Wall
germander) 119
× *lucidrys* 121

Thymus (Thyme)
Fully to half-hardy
shrubs, sub-shrubs, and
perennials grown for their
aromatic foliage and small,
tubular flowers.
azoricus see *T. caespititius*
caespititius (Azores thyme)
29
cilicicus (Cilician thyme)
30
× *citriodorus* (Lemon
thyme, lemon-scented
thyme) 31
'Anderson's Gold' see *T.*
× *c.* 'Bertram
Anderson'
'Archer's Gold' 31
'Aureus' (Golden lemon
thyme) 31
'Bertram Anderson' 29
'Fragrantissimus' 28
'Golden King' 29
'Silver Queen' 28
'Doone Valley' 31
herba-barona (Caraway
thyme) 30
mastichina (Mastic thyme,
Spanish wood
marjoram) 29
micans see *T. caespititius*
polytrichus (Creeping
thyme, Wild thyme) 31
subsp. *britannicus* 30
praecox see *T. polytrichus*
'Coccineus' see
T. serpyllum var.
coccineus

Thymus continued
subsp. *arcticus* see
T. polytrichus subsp.
britannicus
pseudolanuginosus
(Woolly thyme) 31
pulegioides (Broad-leaved
thyme, Large thyme)
30
serpyllum (Creeping or
wild thyme, Mother-of-
thyme) 29
var. *albus* 28
'Annie Hall' 29
var. *coccineus* 30
'Elfin' 30
'Goldstream' 31
'Minimus' 30
'Minor' 29
'Pink Chintz' 29
vulgaris (Common thyme,
garden thyme) 28
'Silver Posie' 30

Tilia (Linden)
Fully hardy trees with
fragrant flowers and a
stately habit
cordata (Small-leaved
linden) 62

Trigonella
Fully hardy annuals grown
for their foliage and seeds.
foenum-graecum
(Fenugreek) 103

**Tropaeolum
(Nasturtium)**
Fully hardy to frost-tender
annuals, perennials, and
climbers grown for their
colorful flowers.
majus (Garden
nasturtium, Indian
cress) 23
'Jewel of Africa' 23

Turmeric see *Curcuma longa*

V

Valeriana (Valerian)
Fully hardy perennials, shrubs, and subshrubs that produce small, saucer-shaped flowers in summer.
officinalis (All heal, Common valerian) 40

Verbascum (Mullein)
Fully to frost-hardy annuals, biennials, perennials, and sub-shrubs with short-lived flowers.
thapsus (Aaron's rod, Great mullein) 60

Verbena
Fully hardy to frost-tender biennials and perennials that bear dense spikes of flowers.
officinalis (Vervain) 86

Veronica virginica see *Veronicastrum virginicum*
Vervain see *Verbena officinalis*
Virginian pokeweed see *Phytolacca americana*

Veronicastrum
Fully hardy perennials that produce spikes of usually pale blue flowers in summer.
virginicum (Culver's root, Blackroot) 45

Viburnum
Fully to frost-hardy shrubs and trees grown for their autumn foliage, flowers, and fruit.
opulus (Guelder rose) 39

Vinca (Periwinkle)
Fully to frost-hardy subshrubs and perennials

Viburnum continued
grown for their foliage and star-shaped flowers.
major (Greater periwinkle) 34
'Variegata' 34
minor (Lesser periwinkle) 36
'Gertrude Jekyll' 24

Viola (Violet, Pansy)
Fully to half-hardy annuals and perennials that flower profusely in spring.
odorata (Sweet violet) 34
'Alba' (White sweet violet) 24
tricolor (Heartsease, Wild pansy) 135

Vitex
Frost-hardy to frost-tender trees and shrubs grown for their elegant foliage and tubular flowers borne in early autumn.
agnus-castus (Agnus castus, Chaste tree) 45

Vitis (Grape)
Fully hardy climbers grown for their habit and fruits.
vinifera 20
'Pinot Noir' (Burgundy grape) 20
'Spätburgunder' see *V. vinifera* 'Pinot Noir'

W

Wasabia
Fully hardy perennials that produce spikes of small, white flowers in summer.
japonica (Wasabi) 132

Water ash see *Ptelea trifoliata*
White sage see *Artemisia ludoviciana*
Wintergreen see *Gaultheria procumbens*
Woad see *Isatis tinctoria*
Woolly foxglove see *Digitalis lanata*

YZ

Yellow sweet clover see *Melilotus officinalis*
Yellowroot see *Hydrastis canadensis*

Zingiber (Ginger)
Tender perennials grown for their exotic foliage and aromatic rhizomes.
officinale 55

ACKNOWLEDGMENTS

Key: t=top; b=bottom; r=right; l=left; c=center; cra=center right above; cla=center left above; crb=center right below; clb=center left below

The publishers would like to thank the following for their kind permission to reproduce the photographs:

A-Z Botanical Collection 75br, 75tr; Peter Etchells 86tr; T. Foster 28cr; Ian Gowland 27r; Julia Hancock 55tl; Geoff Kidd 34tl, 34bl, 138br; Elsa M. Megson 91br; Glenis Moore 62br; J. Maurice Nimmo 79cr; Brunsden Rapkins 50tr, 92cr; Malcolm Richards 95bcl, 98b; D. C. Robinson 74br; Dan Sams 29tr, 31tcl, 68tr; Mike Vardy 92br, 93tl; Colin Whatmo 75cl; Gillian Beckett 30tcr; **Biofotos** Heather Angel 20tl, 101bl, 138tcl; **Deni Bown** 2, 5, 13bl, 13t, 18bl, 18tl, 19, 20br, 21, 22, 23br, 25bl, 25tr, 25tl, 27tl, 31tr, 33tl, 34br, 38r, 39tl, 39r, 40bl, 40tr, 41bl, 43r, 45bl, 46r, 48l, 48r, 50br, 51l, 54br, 54tr, 55bl, 56br, 57l, 58l, 59, 61, 62l, 63r, 63tl, 65tr, 65bl, 66tr, 66l, 67, 70b, 71, 72r, 72bl, 73tr, 76br, 80cr, 81tcl, 81tl, 82tr, 83cr, 83br, 86tl, 87bl, 87tl, 90l, 91bl, 93br, 94cl, 94br, 96tl, 96cr, 96bcl, 96br, 99b, 102, 105r, 105bl, 107tl, 108, 109tl, 111cl, 111br, 112bl, 113, 127b, 127cl, 127tl, 128b, 129cr, 129cl, 137cl, 138tr, 139br, 139tcr; **Pat Brindley** 80bl, 83tl, 92tr, 94cr, 95bl, 105tl, 126r, 129br, 139tl; Neil Campbell-Sharp 145tr; **Eric Crichton Photos** 11, 14, 15; **The Garden Picture Library** Bob Challinor 147t; John Glover 82bcl; Lamontagne 51tr; Howard Rice 78bcr; Gary Rogers 44; Steven Wooster 10; **Garden & Wildlife Matters** 78bl; **John Glover** 29bl, 30tl, 93bl, 146b; **Holt Studios International** Nigel Cattlin 20bl, 34tr; Bob Gibbons 99cr; Duncan Smith 75bl; **Andrew Lawson** 50cr, 50bl, 76tr, 89r; **Clive Nichols Garden Pictures** Barnsley House, Gloustershire 144bl; **Photo Flora** Andrew Gagg 31tl, 74bl, 104r, 111cr, 137bl; **Photos Horticultural** 18br, 24br, 24tr, 28cl, 28bl, 31br, 35, 49b, 75cr, 79tr, 81tcr, 92bl, 95tr, 97br, 98tr, 127cr, 128tr, 129tr; **Pictor International** 151; **Plant Pictures Worldwide** Daan Smit 18tr, 64bl, 68bl, 73bl, 77, 78tcr, 78tr, 129bl; **RHS Gardens, Wisley** 150 bc; **Harry Smith Collection** 20tr, 23tr, 49tl, 79br, 80br, 85tl, 91cl, 93bcr, 93tcr, 138tl, 139bl; **Steven Wooster** 12

In addition to the above, the publishers would also like to thank the staff of the Royal Horticultural Society Publications.

Abbreviations

C	centigrade	in	inch, inches
cm	centimeter	m	meter
cv.	cultivar	mm	millimeter
F	Fahrenheit	oz	ounce
f.	forma	sp.	species
ft	foot, feet	subsp.	subspecies
g	gram	var.	variant

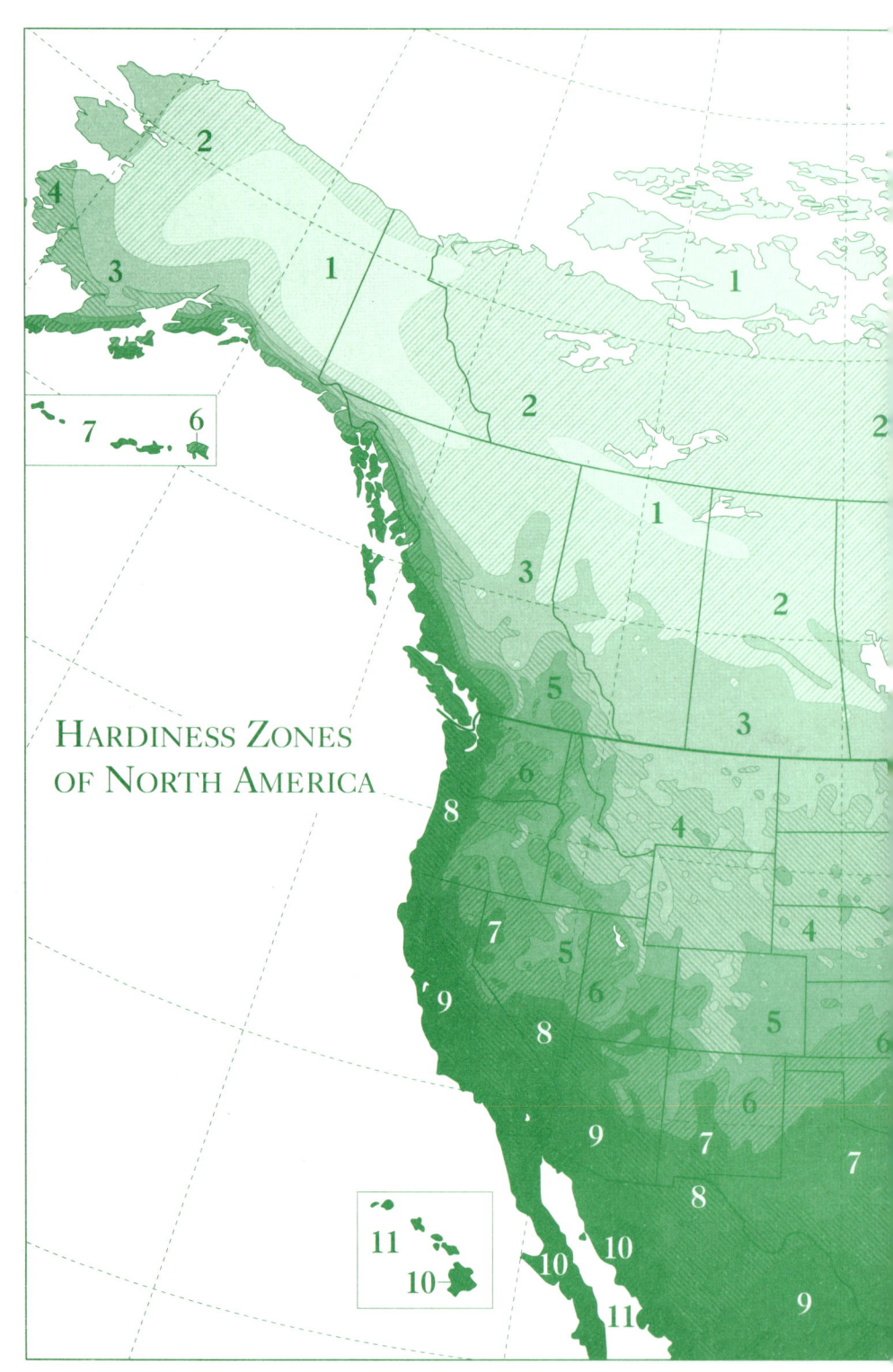